CONSOLIDATED
WISDOM

THE ULTIMATE BOOK OF QUOTATIONS FOR SUCCESS, HAPPINESS AND HEALTH

GENE S. JONES

Dreamquest Publishing

ɸ

Publisher's Cataloguing-in-Publication Data

Names:	Jones, Gene S., author.
Title:	Consolidated wisdom: The ultimate book of quotations for success, happiness and health / Gene S. Jones.
Description:	First edition.	Katonah, New York: Dreamquest Publishing, [2023]	Includes bibliographical references and index.
Identifiers:	ISBN: 9780998324029	LCCN: 2023920605
Subjects:	LCSH: Self-help techniques--Quotations.	Success--Quotations.	Technological innovations-- Quotations.	Arts--Quotations.	Leadership--Quotations.	History--Quotations.	Spirituality --Quotations.	Indians of North America--Quotations.	Education--Quotations.	Science-- Quotations.	Technology--Quotations.	Philosophy and science--Quotations.	Time-- Quotations.	Dreams--Quotations.	Nature--Quotations.	Feng shui--Quotations.	Wit and humor--Health aspects--Quotations.	Meditation--Quotations.	Inspiration--Quotations.	Wisdom--Quotations.	Self-realization--Quotations.	Business--Quotations.	LCGFT: Quotations.	BISAC: SELF-HELP / General.	BUSINESS & ECONOMICS / General.	REFERENCE / Quotations.
Classification:	LCC: PN6081 .J66 2023	DDC: 808.88/2--dc23

Cover art: Ric Faust
Book design: Clarity Designworks
Editing: Pendley's Pro Editing
Book coach: Simon Golden

db Dreamquest Publishing
A Division of Royal Production Services, Inc.
P.O. Box 623
Katonah, New York 10536
www.dreamquestpublishing.com

Published in the United States of America

Fads come and go,
mountains may crumble,
and even the sky may fall...
but wisdom will always be in style.

Great quotes provide a portal to an ability of transcendence of time by becoming friends with great minds past and present...we mingle with them as if they were still alive, demonstrating the immortality of great thoughts.
—Abraham Maslow (1908–1970)

CONTENTS

INTRODUCTION

The reading of all good books is like conversation
with the finest minds of past centuries.
—Rene Descartes (1596–1650)

Some people collect stamps, coins, or works of art. Others collect bottles of fine wine or automobiles. There's a vast assortment of items humans deem collectible. As a game show host for more than thirty years, I've been an avid collector of phrases, continuously searching for timeless wisdom to use in my game shows and guide decisions in every phase of my life. *Consolidated Wisdom*'s collection of phrases offers diverse blueprints for people of all ages, ethnicities, and nationalities to pursue maximum success and happiness. It's meant to serve as comfort food for the mind; a benevolent mentor filling the void left by the lack of wisdom detectable on a day-to-day basis in the modern world. This collection of insights, advice, and observations from approximately 5,000 years of recorded history demonstrates the marvelous ability of language to convey intelligence capable of inspiring great achievement. The pages of *Consolidated Wisdom* are a veritable museum of thoughts...a cross-cultural montage of anecdotes rising from the sands of time.

The primary objective of *Consolidated Wisdom* is to present a panoramic view of the evolution of human thinking throughout the global rise of civilizations with the ultimate goal of harnessing the insightful power of timeless wisdom, advice, and observation to create a better future for us all. Wisdom is the umbrella that covers every arena of human activity. It offers us protection while illuminating a better path forward. It explains us to ourselves while enhancing our ability to relate to each other. It provides guidance for businesses and governments as well as the populations they serve. Wisdom also fuels creativity and the arts. It enriches education while opening the door to deep spirituality. Wisdom is the way, and the key to living a happy and fulfilled life. It provides a plethora of blessings to the poor while simultaneously warning the wealthy about the perils inherent in opulence, fame, and greed. Everywhere we turn, wisdom is there waiting for us to open our eyes to see it, and to open our hearts to embrace each other.

The mind opens to a great phrase much like a bank vault welcoming a new deposit. A certain "click" occurs similar to the sound of giant combination locks the moment a correct combination is entered. When the mind absorbs a stimulating new phrase, the brain's filing system immediately goes to work connecting that phrase with previously ingested ones, so it is primed for recall at opportune moments. *Consolidated Wisdom* is not just a collection of phrases; it's also a collection of stories about the many fascinating people who coined those phrases. While embracing the many dimensions of wisdom, it's important to acknowledge the great minds of all millennia who contributed to humanity's immense storehouse of insights and ideas. In every moment, we stand on the shoulders of their greatness.

It's refreshing to discover that the wisdom of antiquity still applies to contemporary life. This becomes apparent as the musings of great minds from antiquity echo through the pages of *Consolidated Wisdom*, reminding us that every quote represents a vibrant life from a consequential period in history. Researching the lives and times of those quoted in this book weaves together numerous threads of history to illuminate the tapestry of human development. Such ancestral wisdom elevates us to stand on the shoulders of the brilliant icons of history. It allows us to peek over the heights of human intelligence to view our current conditions with greater clarity and devise better ways to proceed with integrity. Sir Isaac Newton embodied the spirit of embracing ancestral wisdom when he coined the famous phrase:

> ### If I have seen further than others, it is by standing upon the shoulders of giants.
> —*Sir Isaac Newton (1643–1727)*

An underlying theme of this book is the historical context of wisdom interwoven with the many individuals who have contemplated the human condition during the past 5,000 years. Each quote represents the tip of a vibrant metaphorical iceberg; an insight from someone's lifetime of experience. This begs us to investigate the lives of those who distilled such wonderful thoughts, and explore their personal sagas. It's equally important to bear in mind that each treasure from a great mind has a historical period attached to it. In other words, there's a story behind every quote, and an expansive story behind the creator of each quote, both of which beg for further investigation. To fully research those quoted in *Consolidated Wisdom* is to unearth innumerable dramas from the past 5,000 years. Such a noble quest for knowledge and understanding leads to the roots of our humanity, revealing universal truths to guide our journey into the future. As CBS News reporter John Dickerson eloquently stated:

> ### The way we prepare for the future is by understanding the past.

Every moment of life is a potential learning experience. The full tapestry of a human life can be seen as an ever-expanding jigsaw puzzle that continually adds new pieces. No two lives possess the exact same experiences, which explains the infinite variety of unique individuals populating our planet. Some puzzle parts are rather mundane, while others can be extremely enlightening. If our lives do not fall into repetitive ruts, the montage of our experiences blend together in some meaningful way, creating opportunities to acquire wisdom. The more diverse our experiences, the richer and more expansive our potential wisdom, which can be displayed by words, actions, or both. Ideally, wise words inspire enlightened actions. That's where *Consolidated Wisdom* enters, volunteering a treasure trove of ideas aimed at deciphering and mastering life's struggles. No single phrase can solve all of life's complex issues, but the combined perspectives offered by diverse great minds can help assemble thought processes capable of tackling any challenge life may throw our way. It's fascinating to realize that the great minds of hundreds and thousands of years ago were contemplating many of the same issues we currently confront. This reality points not only to universal truths, but also to universal weaknesses ingrained in the human psyche. Wisdom has a poignant ability to point out human frailties, inequities, and tendencies, while also recommending preferable methods and courses of action. An unfortunate shortcoming of wisdom is that it depends upon humans to follow the advice it offers. History documents the tragic fact that all too often, humans deviate drastically from advice offered by the wise.

So why bother presenting wisdom to the world if it's likely to be ignored? The answer is simple: A world totally devoid of wisdom would certainly be far worse than the one we inhabit at present. There's always a glimmer of hope that some enlightened guidance will be put to good use. Optimists offer the everlasting belief of humanity eventually embracing universal truths offered by wisdom traditions, thereby putting those concepts into practice at pivotal levels of society. Visions of societies steering themselves toward utopia initially depend upon the spread of wisdom from individual to individual, well before those insights can develop into trends powerful enough to influence governments and adjust the course of whole societies. This is the dynamic process *Consolidated Wisdom* attempts to stimulate by equipping readers with insights and ideas that hopefully become contagious enough to create a peaceful grassroots surge capable of uplifting the human condition.

Consolidated Wisdom seeks to fill in spaces between what you've learned from firsthand experiences and the cornucopia of teachings available to us via all media. In addition to our own experiences and the insights of others, wisdom can also be derived from attentive observation. Although wisdom lessons are more powerful when experienced firsthand, life is too short to provide us the opportunity to experience everything ourselves. It's helpful to remember that some wisdom teachings are capable of preventing catastrophes. Clearly, it's preferable to observe catastrophic events from a distance rather than risk unnecessary suffering.

Wisdom phrases can also pinpoint the enemies of wisdom, such as unquenchable thirst for wealth and power. It's unrealistic to expect those perilous passions to completely vanish from the palette of existence, but it's possible that those who seek wealth and power may someday proceed in a more compassionate manner. While politics will never become a lovefest, it need not always be practiced as a blood sport. Perhaps some politicians of the future will find success by being considerate and kind instead of attacking their opponents. If that tactic enjoys success, other politicians may embrace compassionate modes of behavior as preferable routes to power.

Researching this book revealed that the issues confronting humanity have remained surprisingly similar throughout the annals of history, a truth rendering ancient wisdom as useful today as it was hundreds, or even thousands, of years ago. While technology has been revolutionizing mankind's ability to build modern societies and explore outer space, fundamental human issues and daily challenges have hardly changed. This highlights the glaring need for humanity to evolve on spiritual and emotional levels to cope with the unstoppable expansion of technology. Otherwise, our destructive tendencies threaten humanity's existence as a species. Rather than viewing these challenges as a colossal battle between good and evil, it's more constructive to see the struggle as a matter of productive versus destructive behavior...of enlightened versus misguided thinking and actions. Throughout the thousands of years of recorded history, humanity has proven to be an imperfect species capable of spectacular greatness as well as immense folly. History has recorded profound brilliance from ancient times until the present, but unfortunately, humanity's tragic flaws have often overshadowed the wisdom of the ages. The following quote by British novelist Charles Dickens captures the essence of almost every era in human history, thereby rendering his famous phrase from *A Tale of Two Cities* just as applicable to today's world as it was in the 19th century when Dickens penned it.

It was the best of times, it was the worst of times.
It was the age of wisdom, it was the age of foolishness.
—Charles Dickens (1812–1870)

Humankind has mostly existed at some sort of crossroads throughout its existence. That's why Dickens' quote, although composed to describe the period leading up to the French Revolution and its ensuing Reign of Terror, can be aptly applied to most any era in recorded history. Every major player in the saga of human history created methods to rationalize their actions. The solution to our human dilemma is not an opinionated application of blame, but a consolidation of thought processes that produce productive behaviors leading to enhanced prosperity and well-being, hence the title *Consolidated Wisdom*. Consolidating wisdom is just the first step in a multi-layered process. The dissemination and usage of wisdom on a broad scale becomes the next step. If enough of us absorb and take to heart the wisdom of the ages, hopefully, the process will evolve to manifest a better future.

***The goal is to decipher the lessons of history
and move in a more sensible direction.***
—David J. Schwartz (1927–1987)

Within this desired outcome, infinite variables abound offering unlimited opportunities for everyone to contribute. Although such a monumental shift must begin on an individual level, if enough individuals embrace the concept of living with wisdom and grace, it has potential to seep into and influence the political landscape to bring about the most grandiose aspect of this book's vision:

To provide an influx of wisdom leading to enlightened leadership by governments and large corporations worldwide...to stop history from repeating its many follies and instead find solutions superior to warfare for resolving conflicts.

Clearly, this is a lofty goal whose final outcome depends on the microcosm being able to influence the macrocosm.

In addition to disseminating wisdom of the ages, *Consolidated Wisdom* offers tools to build your own personal wisdom tradition. The goal is to inspire curiosity, encourage meaningful discussion, illuminate historical perspectives, and provide useful advice across a broad spectrum of genres. In the spirit of Sir Isaac Newton, let us perch ourselves on the shoulders of the giants quoted in this book to help humanity rise toward its potential greatness. Wisdom is all around us...it's our challenge to locate it, absorb it, and put it to good use.

Using the earlier metaphor of collecting fine wines, you are invited to let this book become your metaphorical wine cellar as you seize an opportunity to absorb the power of brilliant minds and synthesize their ideas to augment your own unique greatness. Every shred of wisdom has value, but wisdom's true power is manifested when wisdom concepts are consolidated to form systems of thinking and improved codes of behavior...in other words, *better ways of living*. Collections are best when shared. This book was written to serve as a bubbling brook of wisdom, beckoning you to dive in and begin creating the life you've always dreamed of by formulating your own personal wisdom reservoir. Scouring all types of media during a 40-year expedition to unearth mankind's accumulated wisdom was a journey that enriched my life. I hope reading this collection of thoughts enriches yours.

May the wisdom of the ages bring you happiness and fulfillment!

HOW TO NAVIGATE THIS BOOK

Consolidated Wisdom is intended to serve as a resource for speeches, presentations, term papers, trivia contests, and life in general. Hopefully, the subject of wisdom will someday be valued enough to be included in school curricula. No matter how you use this book, it's my heartfelt desire that the wisdom you gain from reading *Consolidated Wisdom* greatly enhances your life. Each chapter refers to specific arenas of human activity, many of which overlap, such as *Creativity* with *The Arts, Business* with *Technology,* or *Sports* with *Play* and *Leadership.* The recommended way of reading this book is to begin by locating your favorite subject, and then be led to your next category by that chapter's *Wisdom Trails.*

Since many phrases relate to more than one category, this reality caused serious debate as to where such quotes should be located. For example, John Madden's quote about *play* being important for the *education* of children appears in *The Lessons of Sports* rather than *Play* or *Education* because John Madden was a Hall of Fame football coach. A desire to address such multi-pronged connections inspired creation of the *Wisdom Trails* feature at the end of each chapter.

Wisdom Trails highlight the expansive reach of many quotes across multiple categories. By following paths of *Wisdom Trails,* you can weave together threads of thought, navigating from category to category in a journey that parallels the intriguing interconnections between all aspects of life. Powerful statements about this phenomenon are found in two Chapter 17 quotes under the *Power of the Circle.* These quotes express a Native American reverence for the circle as representative of the interconnectedness of all existence. Because the contents of *Consolidated Wisdom* form a circle of interconnected thoughts and ideas, no matter what chapter you begin with, connections to other categories and chapters will lead you to traverse your own unique path...your personal wisdom journey. I recommended you let this web of interconnection become your guide while reading *Consolidated Wisdom.* In so doing, you will blaze your own personal wisdom trail. If you follow your trail to the end, the interconnection of all wisdom should lead you through every chapter, eventually returning you to where you started... fully demonstrating the power of the circle. There are an infinite number of possible combinations and paths, so it's important you know that whichever wisdom journey you choose, it's the correct one for you.

Like bacon & eggs or wine & cheese, great minds often offer similar wisdom concepts using their own unique voices. Consequently, there are many instances where great minds of different eras express similar thoughts. Such quotes are almost always mutually supportive as they expand on each other or focus on different aspects of a common theme. This occurrence inspired the creation of *Great Minds Think Alike* and *Great Minds Connect*.

Each *Great Minds Think Alike* features likeminded phrases grouped together in the same chapter from contributors of different eras and/or regions of the world, demonstrating the fact that people in all areas of the world have been dealing with similar challenges throughout recorded history. An alphabetical list of every *Great Minds Think Alike* subject appears in the *Great Minds Subject Index*. *Great Minds Connect* spotlights contributors in different chapters who have made mutually supporting statements, thereby illustrating how insightful wisdom phrases frequently extend beyond their originally intended genre.

Please note that the first quote by each contributor includes a biographical profile accompanied by the contributor's lifespan and birth year if publicly available; subsequent quotes only include their lifespans. Other features designed to make it easier to locate specific quotes and contributors are the *Alphabetical Index* and the *Wisdom Timeline*. Each person quoted in this book is listed in the *Alphabetical Index*, which locates all of a contributor's quotes throughout the book. Contributors are also listed in the *Wisdom Timeline*, which is organized chronologically by birth year. Please note that the *Recommended Reading* section is arranged in alphabetical order by contributors' names, not their book titles, and is composed primarily of books written after 1940. For the curious, a *Wisdom Demographics* page has been added to highlight the diversity of nations providing wisdom for this book.

All chapter titles are self-explanatory with the exception of Chapter 21: *Wisdom Meditations*. This very different chapter ventures into the exploratory realm of converting your favorite quotemasters into personal mentors by employing the process of *autobrainstorming*. Autobrainstorming is a protocol for internally discussing your challenges and problems with individuals you greatly respect, although you are essentially brainstorming with yourself. In this book, all meditation examples use contributors from one specific category, but you can always bring in heroes from your own life experience to be a part of the mix. Autobrainstorm meditations can serve as powerful transformative experiences that provide valuable insights and feedback on any problem or challenge.

For those interested in experimenting with this eclectic exercise, simply follow the instructions provided in Chapter 21. Once you become comfortable with the autobrainstorm technique, you will discover it can be applied to challenges in any arena of your life.

CHAPTER 1

WISDOM, HISTORY & THE FUTURE

When the wisdomkeepers speak, all should listen.
—*Lucius Annaeus Seneca (4 BC–65 AD)*
Stoic philosopher, statesman, and dramatist of ancient Rome

It is easier to be wise for others than for ourselves.
—*Francois de la Rochefoucauld (1613–1680)*
Influential French nobleman and author of numerous memoirs & maxims

Each one of us has all the wisdom and knowledge we need within us. It is available to us through our intuitive mind, which is our connection with universal intelligence.
—*Shakti Gawain (1948–2018)*
Birth name: Carol Louisa Gawain
New Age and personal self-help author whose books have sold millions of copies.
This quote aligns with the philosophy of Socrates, who utilized extensive questioning to draw out his students' innate knowledge.

Happy are those who find wisdom...she is more precious than jewels, and nothing you desire can compare with her. Her ways are ways of pleasantness, and all her paths are peace.
—*King Solomon (990–931 BC)*
Wealthy and powerful king of Israel who built the first temple of Jerusalem and is hailed in the Bible as being supremely wise

By three methods we learn wisdom:
First, by reflection, which is noblest;
Second, by imitation, which is easiest;
third by experience, which is the bitterest.
—*Confucius (551–479 BC)*
Legendary Chinese teacher, politician, and philosopher

Besides the noble art of getting things done, there is the noble art of leaving things undone. The wisdom of life consists in the elimination of nonessentials.
—*Lin Yutang (1895–1976)*
Chinese philosopher, inventor, and translator of classic Chinese texts, from *The Importance of Living*

The art of being wise is the art of knowing what to overlook.
—*William James (1842–1910)*
American philosopher, psychologist, educator, and author

*The capacity to embrace paradox, to perceive the
validity of opposites, is a major key to wisdom.*
—*M. Scott Peck (1936–2005)*
Psychiatrist and author best known for his book
The Road Less Travelled; this quote is from *Abounding Grace*

*The more tranquil a man becomes, the greater his success and power
for good. Calmness of mind is a beautiful jewel of wisdom.*
—*James Allen (1864–1912)*
British philosophical writer and pioneer of the self-help movement
known for inspirational books and poetry

*A state of mind called immovable wisdom...means having complete
fluidity around an unmoving center so your mind is clear and ready
to direct its attention wherever it may be needed.*
—*Takuan Sōhō (1573–1645)*
Japanese monk of the Rinzai sect of Zen Buddhism, from *The Unfettered Mind*

*If you follow the root of your affliction down to its end
this will open up the message it is offering, and you will be
given the opportunity to become initiated to genuine wisdom.*
—*Rick Jarow (1952-2024)*
College professor, author, and spiritual teacher, from *The Ultimate Anti Career Guide*

GREAT MINDS THINK ALIKE: *Common Sense*

*Common sense from an uncommon degree
is what the world calls wisdom.*
—*Samuel Taylor Coleridge (1772–1834)*
British poet, philosopher, and theologian who wrote the epic poem
The Rime of the Ancient Mariner, containing the famous phrase
Water, water everywhere, but not a drop to drink.

Common sense is not so common.
—*Voltaire (1694–1778)*
Birth name: Francois-Marie Arouet
Prolific French writer, playwright, historian, and philosopher

For Plato and his teacher Socrates, the process
of questioning is the key to deepening wisdom.
—*Michael J. Gelb (1952)*
Motivational speaker and author of self-help books, from *Discover Your Genius*

Kindness is just as important as wisdom. The recognition
of this truth is the beginning of wisdom. The wise person
stays calm and unruffled by circumstance.
—*Lillian Too (1946)*
Malaysian feng shui expert, corporate executive, author
and television personality, from her book *Chinese Wisdom*

Patience is the better part of wisdom.
Decide when to act and when to be still.
—*Dan Millman (1946)*
Author of the *Peaceful Warrior* book series, self-help lecturer, and workshop facilitator

Integrating thoughts into concepts that are lived daily is the path of
wisdom. The gifts of authentic wisdom require a marriage to occur
within each individual. The head and the heart have to be used in
equal measure if we are to attain wisdom.
—*Jamie Sams (1951)*
Native American author and spiritual teacher, from *Dancing the Dream*

Honesty is the first chapter in the book of wisdom.
—*Thomas Jefferson (1743–1826)*
Third president of the United States who also served as U.S. secretary of state
and was instrumental in the crafting of the *Declaration of Independence*

Every house, no matter how humble, can be a house of wisdom. Every
age, no matter how dark its shadow, holds the potential for a golden
age...and the message these great voices share is always the same:
"Learn from us."
—*James Weiss*
American storyteller, author, and recording artist,
from his book *Swordsmen, Saints, and Scholars*

GREAT MINDS THINK ALIKE: *Know Yourself*

Knowing yourself is the beginning of all wisdom.
—Aristotle (384–322 BC)
Seminal figure in the development of Western philosophy
who also tutored Alexander the Great

Knowing others is wisdom.
Knowing yourself is enlightenment.
—Lao Tzu (571–unknown BC)
Legendary ancient Chinese philosopher and writer
believed to be the founder of Taoism

The beginning of wisdom is found in doubting.
—Peter Abelard (1079–1142)
French scholar, philosopher, teacher, musician, and poet
(A longer version of this quote appears on page 115)

You can tell whether a man is clever by his answers.
You can tell a man is wise by his questions.
—Naguib Mahfouz (1911–2006)
Prolific Egyptian writer of novels, short stories, stage plays, and screenplays
who won the 1988 Nobel Prize for Literature

What, in the name of heaven, is more to be desired
than wisdom? What is more to be prized? What is
better for a man, what more worthy of his nature?
—Marcus Tullius Cicero (106–43 BC)
Roman lawyer, politician, philosopher, scholar, orator, and writer
brutally beheaded by order of arch-enemy Mark Antony

Losing an illusion makes you wiser than finding a truth.
—Ludwig Borne (1786–1837)
German writer and political philosopher

He that walketh with wise men shall be wise.
—King James Bible
Proverbs 13:20

Wisdom and compassion are inseparable...
wisdom is not worth acquiring unless each moment
it is applied in acts of compassion.
—Christmas Humphreys (1901–1983)
English barrister who prosecuted controversial high profile cases
and founded the London Buddhist Society, from *Zen Wisdom*

It takes a wise man to recognize a wise man.
—Xenophanes (c.570–475 BC)
Major Greek poet and pre-Socratic philosopher

Wise people, even if all laws were abolished,
would still lead the same life.
—Aristophanes (446–386 BC)
Ancient Greek playwright

I am the wisest man alive, for I know one thing,
and that is that I know nothing.
—Socrates (470–399 BC)
Ancient Greek philosopher who was one of the founding fathers of
Western philosophy and mentor of Plato, as quoted by Ronald Gross in
Socrates Way. Another Socrates quote on the subject of wisdom is
May I regard wisdom as the only wealth.

A wise man can learn more from a foolish question
than a fool can learn from a wise answer.
—Bruce Lee (1940–1973)
Birth name: Lee Ju-fan
Chinese-American martial artist and philosopher
who became an iconic movie star

The heart of the fool is in his mouth,
but the mouth of the wise man is in his heart.
—Benjamin Franklin (1706–1790)
One of America's founding fathers who was also an author, printer,
political theorist, politician, Freemason, postmaster, scientist, inventor,
humorist, civic activist, statesman, and diplomat

Virtue is the habit of acting according to wisdom.
—Gottfried Wilhelm Leibniz (1646–1716)
German philosopher, mathematician, author and scientist instrumental in the
development of calculus and the calculator. Leibniz was the first to realize that the trigrams
of the *I Ching* could serve as a source for binary arithmetic, currently known as binary code.

It is truly in solitude that wisdom can bloom, uncompromised
by the difficulties associated with all forms of attachment.
—Luc Ferry (1951)
French philosopher, author, and politician paraphrasing Buddhist wisdom,
from *A Brief History of Thought*

If I have seen further than others,
it is by standing upon the shoulders of giants.
—Sir Isaac Newton (1643–1727)
English mathematician, physicist, astronomer, theologian, and author
recognized as one of the most influential scientists of all time

There is nothing new except what has been forgotten.
—Marie Antoinette (1755–1793)
Controversial Austrian-born final Queen of France prior to the French Revolution;
she and her husband, Louis XVI, were executed by the Revolutionary Tribunal

The superior man acquaints himself with many sayings
of antiquity and many deeds of the past, in order to
strengthen his character.
—Fu Hsi, aka Fu Xi (29th-27th century BC)
Mythical Chinese emperor credited with creating the *I Ching*, Tai Chi, and
the trigrams of the Bagua. It's estimated he reigned somewhere between 2952 and 2737
BC, although numerous other estimates vary by as much as a few centuries.

We do not know the whole of man's history;
there were probably many civilizations before
the Sumerian or the Egyptian; we have just begun to dig!
—Will Durant (1885–1981) & Ariel Durant (1898–1981)
American historians and philosophers from their co-written book *The Lessons of History*

An entire episode in the story of mankind might have been forgotten. Our species could have been afflicted with some terrible amnesia. What is pre-history...if not a time forgotten...a time for which we have no records...if not an epoch of impenetrable obscurity through which our ancestors passed, but about which we have no conscious remembrance.

—*Graham Hancock (1950)*

British writer, researcher, and journalist well known for his theories regarding the origins of ancient civilizations and myths, from *Fingerprints of the Gods*

History never looks like history when you are living through it. It always looks confusing and messy, and always feels uncomfortable.

—*John W. Gardner (1912–2002)*

Secretary of Health, Education, and Welfare under Lyndon Johnson who founded *Common Cause* and became known as the "father of campaign finance reform"

GREAT MINDS THINK ALIKE: *Warped History*

History as usually written is quite different from history as usually lived.

—*Will Durant (1885–1981) & Ariel Durant (1898–1981)*

from their co-written book *The Lessons of History*

History is a distorted record because it's always written by the victors.

—*Erich Fromm (1900-1980)*

German psychologist, philosopher, and author. This quote highlights a significant educational issue, as the stories of history vary greatly depending on the perspective of the historian. For example, the events of 19th century American history would appear very different to a Native American. Such discrepancies exist in every era of history in every region of the world.

What is history, but a fable agreed upon?

—*Napoleon Bonaparte (1769–1821)*

Italian-born French military officer who rose to power during the French Revolution and was emperor of France 1804–1814, during which time he sold the Louisiana Territory to the United States; he is considered one of the greatest military minds in history

A people without the knowledge of their past history, origin and culture is like a tree without roots.

—*Marcus Garvey (1887–1940)*

African American social activist, writer, and public speaker

GREAT MINDS THINK ALIKE: *Learning from History*

Those who cannot remember the past are condemned to repeat it.
—George Santayana (1863–1952)
Spanish-born American philosopher, essayist, poet, and novelist
from his 1905 book *Life of Reason*

***We learn nothing from history except that
we learn nothing from history.***
—Marcus Tullius Cicero (106–43 BC)

***That men do not learn very much from the lessons of history
is the most important lesson of history.***
—Aldous Huxley (1894–1963)
British writer and philosopher most famous for his novel *Brave New World*. The above
quote is from *Collected Essays*. It's interesting to witness great minds 2,000 years apart
arrive at the same conclusion about history. In essence, Cicero and Huxley explain
why history keeps repeating itself.

***The society that loses its grip on the past is in danger, for it produces
men who know nothing but the present and who are not aware that
life had been, and could be, different from what it is.***
—Aristotle (384–322 BC)

***History teaches that men and nations behave wisely
only after they have exhausted all other alternatives.***
—Abba Eban (1915–2002)
South African-born Israeli diplomat, politician, and linguistic scholar who was raised and
educated in England, where he served in the British army during WWII before moving to
Israel, as quoted in *The Week* magazine

***History is the best vehicle for understanding
who we are and where we are going.***
—Doris Kearns Goodwin (1943)
Biographer, historian, and political commentator, from *Leadership in Turbulent Times*

***Intuition is really a sudden immersion of the soul into the
universal current of life where the histories of all people are
connected...no matter what he does, every person on Earth
plays a central role in the history of the world.***
—Paulo Coelho (1947)
Portuguese-born Brazilian lyricist and author, from *The Alchemist*

Well-behaved women seldom make history.
—Laurel Thatcher Ulrich (1938)
Pulitzer Prize-winning American historian who specializes in the study
of how women have shaped history

History is not the past. It is the present.
We carry our history with us. We are our history.
—*James Baldwin (1924-1987)*
African American playwright, author, and social change activist quoted on December 10, 1986 at National Press Club; this quote also appears in the 2016 film *I Am Not Your Negro*

It makes no sense to sugarcoat history...
history is mankind's great teacher.
—*Jean-Claude van Rijckeghem (1963)*
Belgian novelist, journalist, and film producer in an interview with Danielle Ballantyne about his book *Ironhead or Once a Young Lady*

A democratic ideal of liberty of thought cannot dispense with the
study of history if it is to approach the present without prejudices ...
History promises us that by progressively reclaiming and mastering
our past, by practicing this collective and heightened form of auto-
reflection, we shall come to a better understanding of our present,
and orient ourselves more effectively towards our future.
—*Luc Ferry (1951)*
From *A Brief History of Thought*

The best way to predict the future is to invent it.
—*Alan Curtis Kay (1940)*
Computer scientist who pioneered work on object-oriented programming and windowing graphical user interface design. A very similar version of this quote is attributed to Peter Drucker...and controversially, to Abraham Lincoln:
The best way to predict the future is to create it.

GREAT MINDS THINK ALIKE: *Yesterday, Today & Tomorrow*
Today is the tomorrow we worried about yesterday.
—*Grant Schreiber (1967)*
South African publisher, author and managing editor of the leadership magazine
Real Leaders

The present is saturated with the past
and pregnant with the future.
—*Gottfried Leibniz (1646–1716)*

The past, the present, and the future are really one: they are today.
—*Harriet Beecher Stowe (1811–1896)*
American abolitionist and author of more than 30 books,
most famous for *Uncle Tom's Cabin*

Every thought we think, and every word we speak
is creating our future.
—*Louise Hay (1926–2017)*
American motivational author and founder of Hay House, from a YouTube video interview

Yesterday I was clever, so I wanted to change the world.
Today I am wise, so I am changing myself.
—*Rumi (1207–1273)*
Afghan poet, Islamic scholar, theologian, and Sufi mystic born into
what was then part of the Persian empire

GREAT MINDS THINK ALIKE: *Past and Future*

To know the future, see the past. Look back to look forward.
—*I Ching (compiled 1000–500 BC)*
Also known as *The Book of Changes*, it was originally compiled
in China during the period 1000-500 BC

If you want the future to be different from the past,
study the past.
—*Baruch Spinoza (1632–1677)*
Iconic Dutch philosopher

The way we prepare for the future is by understanding the past.
—*John Dickerson (1968)*
American television journalist and reporter on CBS News January 6, 2022

If the future doesn't include being out there among
the stars and being a multi-planet species,
I find that incredibly depressing.
—*Elon Musk (1971)*
Eclectic South African technology entrepreneur, engineer, and aerospace designer
with a degree in physics, co-founder of PayPal, founder of Tesla, Space X,
and The Boring Company, and now owner of X (formerly Twitter)

Who controls the past controls the future:
who controls the present controls the past.
—*George Orwell (1903–1950)*
Birth name: Eric Arthur Blair
English novelist best known for his classic science fiction novel *1984*.
This profound quote alludes to the fact that those in power often change the
narratives of history to support their ambitions and tilt public opinion in their favor.

GREATMINDS THINK ALIKE: *Understanding Time*

If you try to get your hands on time, it's always slipping through your fingers. People are sure time is there, but they can't get hold of it. My feeling is that they can't get hold of it because it isn't there at all.
—*Julian Barbour (1937)*
British physicist from his book *The End of Time*. *Great Minds Connect* with
Yoko Ono and Lucretius on page 280

What we call time is actually quantified eternity.
—*Deepak Chopra (1946)*
Indian-born American author, teacher, public speaker, and prominent
alternative medicine advocate for quantum healing. *Great Minds Connect*
with Yoko Ono and Lucretius on page 280

The truest, most lasting forms of progress are often those that are built upon an understanding of the past.
—*Christopher Ryan (1962)*
American author from his book *Civilized To Death*

When modernity clashes with tradition, nobody emerges unscathed.
—*Suyin Haynes*
British editor in chief of *gal-dem* magazine and *Time* senior reporter
covering gender, culture, and underrepresented communities

To make no mistakes is not in the power of man; but from their errors and mistakes, the wise and good learn wisdom for the future.
—*Plutarch (46–120 AD)*
Greek priest at Delphi, historian, essayist, and biographer who became
a Roman citizen and detailed the lives of Alexander the Great, Julius Caesar,
and other famous Greeks and Romans, from his famous work *Plutarch's Lives*

Each time history repeats itself, the price goes up...The future of everything we have accomplished since our intelligence evolved will depend on the wisdom of our actions over the next few years... now is our last chance to get the future right.
—*Ronald Wright (1948)*
Canadian author with an honorary doctorate in archaeology who has written nonfiction
books about history and travel as well as fiction, from *A Short History of Progress*

Our Elders give us grounding. They give us a perspective that comes only with age and wisdom...Only when we know our true lineage can we place ourselves in historic time, and recognize where we are and where we belong. The knowledge and wisdom of ancient ways has simply been slumbering in our souls, awaiting a time to be reawakened. The Elders believe that time is now.
—*Anne Wilson Schaef (1934–2020)*
American clinical psychologist, author, and spiritual seeker who spent many years living with indigenous tribes around the world in *Native Wisdom For White Minds*

Knowledge is of the past; wisdom is of the future.
—*Vernon Cooper*
Revered healer of the Lumbee tribe of North Carolina

Futuring is an example of what I call "applied history", or the use of historical knowledge and methods to solve problems in the present...history provides indications of the future.
—*Stephen M. Millett (1947)*
American futurist, forecaster, strategic planner, and author, from his 2011 *The Futurist* magazine article

Science is organized knowledge. Wisdom is organized life.
—*Emanuel Kant (1724–1804)*
German philosopher considered one of the most influential thinkers of the Enlightenment period

Being in the company of the wise is considered one of the most powerful steps you can take to enhance happiness in life.
—*Marci Shimoff (1958)*
Renowned transformational and happiness expert, motivational speaker, and best-selling author, from *Happy For No Reason*

Even death is not to be feared by one who has lived wisely.
—*Buddha (563–483 BC)*
Birth name: Siddhartha Gautama
Son of an Indian king, he renounced his family privileges to wander through the forest for years before emerging to become the founder of Buddhism

CONSOLIDATING CHAPTER 1
Wisdom, History & the Future

Chapter 1 is where the voices of antiquity rise up from the sands of time, offering to lead us into the future. It attempts to capture the essence and evolution of wisdom, tracing wisdom's roots to the beginning of recorded history. By looking back in time and forward toward the future, we gain an expansive view that establishes a foundation for further exploration. In so doing, Chapter 1 reminds us wisdom never becomes obsolete.

The history of the world can be traced through the lens of wisdom, with each pearl of wisdom emerging from the conditions of its times. Chapter 1 was designed to serve as a canopy for all following chapters. Its contents encapsulate universal principles and truths that apply to many aspects of life. In so doing, it serves as a supremely connective category, as do the chapters *Observing Human Nature* and *Practical Advice*.

Chapter 1 begins *Consolidated Wisdom's* journey by excavating and exploring wisdom's historical roots. One of the most intriguing quotes is by Fu Hsi, not so much because of what he said, but because of when he said it. Fu Hsi's reference to "the wisdom of antiquity" is eyebrow-raising because Fu Hsi lived approximately 5,000 years ago. This means Fu Hsi was praising wisdom passed down to him from ancient cultures active before the beginning of recorded history, a stunning reference to the existence of prehistoric wisdom. To curious minds, this opens up a whole world of questions demanding further inquiry into the possibility that advanced prehistoric civilizations existed and then mysteriously vanished without a trace...a possibility broached by Graham Hancock's provocative quote as he joins Will and Ariel Durant to hint at the likelihood prehistory is humanity's greatest unsolved mystery.

Chapter 1 also highlights the lineage connecting Socrates to Alexander the Great through Plato and Aristotle. Over the course of approximately 120 years, Socrates was Plato's teacher, Plato was Aristotle's mentor, and Aristotle served as Alexander the Great's tutor. Such a lineage gives rise to the notion that although details constantly change with each era of history, the issues and challenges of human relations have remained remarkably similar. The more one investigates history, the clearer it becomes that the development of wisdom parallels the ascension of the human race.

This fundamental connection between history and wisdom provides an appropriate launching pad for Chapter 1, as it feels necessary to begin by acknowledging the platform contemporary life rests upon. Anyone born in an industrialized nation during the 20th or 21st century has been born into a long legacy of human history...specifically, societies with highly developed languages, technologies, and social structures. While it's easy to take all these pre-conditions of birth for granted, they represent thousands of years of struggles, innovation, and sweat. Mixed in with struggling and sweat is a lot of thinking...thinking that created language, invented the wheel, and built spectacular architecture and industrial societies, all while constantly bickering and waging brutally destructive wars.

Many lessons were learned along the way, as those who contemplated human strivings in every era often extracted and then shared valuable lessons. Like extracting nectar from a flower, human intelligence has deciphered sublime wisdom from both the beautiful and ugly states of existence. It's the goal of this book to present a tasty sampling of those nectars by linking the best of our past to our present, thereby paving the way for a better future. To illustrate the magnitude of developments preceding all our births, allow yourself to picture human existence in its most primitive state during prehistoric times, living in nature with no shelter, no language, and no tools.

In a nutshell, here is a brief list of major innovations since those primitive beginnings that we have all been born into; the platform of modern existence:

- *Humans gather in groups for hunting, safety and efficiency.* This created a need to communicate more effectively...hence, the evolution of language. Imagine a world with early humans communicating without the benefit of words. Every word of every contemporary language has evolved a prehistoric origin where one of our ancient ancestors needed to communicate something. It's a marvel early humans figured out how to assign meaning to various sounds, the precursors to modern language.
- *Humans figure out how to create fire* to ward off predators, warm their bodies, and cook food. This was the birth of *biomimicry*, a longstanding process of human innovation derived from observing nature. Biomimicry has been an essential process in the creation of tools and methods throughout human history. A current example of biomimicry are the designs of modern aircraft based on observing the flight of birds.
- *Humans begin sharpening stones and wood to use as tools, weapons, and to communicate by drawing symbols and pictures on the ground, cave walls, papyrus, and clay tablets*, leading to creation of alphabets and eventually, the written word. Not surprisingly, the word *paper* is derived from the word papyrus.
- *Humans invent the wheel*, revolutionizing the ability to transport people and equipment.
- *Humans domesticate animals*, creating new allies in the animal kingdom.
- *Humans develop agriculture*, leading to the establishment of dwellings. This gives rise to civilizations and the concept of governance.
- *Humans develop architecture* and build permanent villages and cities.
- *Humans build boats and ships* to explore the oceans and foreign lands.

- *Humans develop commerce* based on barter, and later, based on coins and currency.
- *Humans assign value to specific metals, stones, and other materials.*
- *Humans build machines*, beginning the Industrial Age.
- *Humans sophisticate engines*, facilitating the construction of railroads and large motorized vehicles and vessels.
- *Humans develop long-distance communication*, namely, the telegraph and telephone.
- *Humans develop fossil fuels*, as kerosene lamps provide artificial light. An unwanted byproduct of kerosene was gasoline until it was realized that gasoline is the more valuable fuel. Humans proceeded to sophisticate the combustion engine and realize the value of gasoline, which led to the development of the automobile, trucks, and tractors to replace the horse.
- *Humans harness electricity and create light bulbs*, facilitating electric power for municipal lighting and a plethora of other now-commonplace items such as the refrigerator, radio, television, and computer.
- *Humans invent motion pictures, the phonograph, radio, and television.*
- *Humans invent the airplane, and then rockets.*
- *Humans split the atom to build bombs and nuclear power plants.*
- *Humans create the modern computer, cell phone, smart devices, and the ubiquitous internet.*

Throughout the evolution of all these blockbuster achievements, our species continually created various forms of art, composed music, made medical advances, and fought among itself for a variety of reasons, both rational and irrational. While ancient architectural sites are still available for us to ponder, the ongoing growth of wisdom has been far less apparent to the naked eye. Much like the unearthing of underground artifacts, it takes determined digging to quarry wisdom from the annals of history. A different challenge exists in modern societies, as the internet presents torrents of quotes that threaten to exhaust our capacity to absorb them. The challenge of compiling great wisdom has become more a matter of sorting than digging, a process that resembles prospecting for gold in the 19th century.

This conjures up a vision of grimy prospectors sifting through mounds of excavated rubble in search of precious gold nuggets, similar to the decades-long compilation of phrases for this book...a prolonged project of digging and sorting, plus the reading of a mountain's worth of books on every subject imaginable. The research effort eventually expanded beyond wisdom phrases into an enthralling journey spanning the history of the world as viewed by its most exceptional inhabitants from multiple millennia. Unearthing stories about people quoted in this book became a consciousness-expanding experience featuring a panoramic history of the human psyche at its finest.

An extremely important aspect of history is its profound connection to the future. More than simply an anecdote, history actually determines the future by providing a foundation for present activities. This serves as a stern warning for anyone who believes we can ignore history, as doing so has always been a treacherous miscalculation. When gazing back into the past, it's vital we understand every year of history was the future for all preceding years. This means that to a great degree, history is a relative term. For instance, the rise of the Roman Empire is ancient history to our contemporary culture, but was the future in relation to earlier Sumerian, Egyptian, and Greek empires. Likewise, the Renaissance was the future for the Roman Empire, and the American Civil War was the future in relation to the American Revolution. These statements are not absurd simplicities. Rather, they point to the fact that each era in history evolves from previous ones. Therefore, every event and major decision made during any period in history has repercussions hundreds or even thousands of years later.

The other conceptual irony of history is how predictable it is that certain trends repeat themselves, even though details vary due to changing technologies and prevailing environmental conditions. The problem of history repeating itself is due to an unchanging constant:

Humans are fundamentally the same as they were thousands of years ago, especially on an emotional level.

This explains why wisdom from the distant past is still relevant to our modern existence, a truth rendering wisdom eternal and always valuable.

It's the great challenge of each generation to seek out, listen to, and heed the wisdom of its predecessors...and then act accordingly. By incorporating ancestral lessons into contemporary societies, wisdom traditions have the power to stabilize whole civilizations. Essentially, trails of ancestral wisdom trace human development from early civilizations through the middle ages, and then deposit us at future's front door. Hopefully, this journey leaves us all standing on firmer ground.

Chapter 1 also contains quotes about being wise vs. being foolish. These phrases are more about benefits of wisdom than the pitfalls of foolery.

They present a particularly vexing question: *Is it possible for humans to be wise and foolish at the same time?* The answer appears to be a resounding *YES!* Humanity is eternally and incurably imperfect, especially when situations become emotionally charged. People often forget or override their innate wisdom and make bad decisions due to other factors. Additionally, many individuals are very wise in one arena of life, yet foolish in others...for example: Successful business executives with failed family lives, someone who is repeatedly a "fool for love," or those who are too preoccupied with business to pay attention to their own needs.

Chapter 1's discussion of history and the future inevitably leads us to contemplate the nature of time itself, and requires a question about whether time actually exists in the rest of the universe. There is a strong argument contending the universe simply exists moment to moment, with each moment serving as its own unique slice of eternity. For practical reasons, humans decided to break up eternity into manageable segments based on observably reliable cycles of nature. Curiosity about this subject demands further inquiry, posing questions such as: *Can there be multiple eternities?* Continued investigation into the nature of time inevitably encounters a phenomenon known as the *Einstein Cross,* which will be discussed in Chapter 2.

WISDOM TRAILS: *Interconnected Categories*

Observing Human Nature, Happiness, Success, Spirituality, Compassion, Doubt, Creativity, Government, War, Nature, Education, Native American Wisdom, Science, Fear

Trails to Other Chapters

- Francois de la Rochefoucauld detects a flaw in human nature regarding wisdom. *(Observing Human Nature)*
- King Solomon connects wisdom to *Happiness.*
- James Allen connects wisdom with *Success* and *Spirituality.*
- Michael Gelb recommends the process of questioning as a path to wisdom and Naguib Mahfouz uses questions of others to evaluate their wisdom. *(Creativity)*
- Lillian Too, Rick Jarow, Christmas Humphreys, Ben Franklin, and Jamie Sams connect wisdom with *Compassion.*
- Peter Abelard connects wisdom with *Doubt.*
- Aristophanes's quote about laws connects wisdom with *Government.*
- In two different quotes, Luc Ferry connects wisdom with *Spirituality* and history with *Government.*
- Eric Fromm and George Orwell connect the recording of history to *War.*
- Abba Eban connects history, wisdom, and *Government.*
- Jean-Claude van Rijckeghem hails history as a great teacher. *(Education)*
- Marci Shimoff believes the company of wise people is a source of *Happiness.*
- Anne Wilson Schaef discusses the value of elders. *(Native American Wisdom)*
- Emanuel Kant's differentiates between wisdom and *Science.*
- Buddha tells us those who have lived wisely need not *Fear* death.

CHAPTER 2

SCIENCE & TECHNOLOGY

The great thing about science is that it is true,
even if you don't believe in it.
—Neil deGrasse Tyson (1958)
American astrophysicist, author, and director of the Hayden Planetarium in NYC

Curiosity is what science is all about:
the quest to reveal the unknown.
—Ahmed Zewail (1946–2016)
The "father of femtochemistry" who became the first Egyptian to win a Nobel Prize for
science when he won the Nobel Prize for Chemistry in 1999

It is not knowing, but the love of learning,
that characterizes the scientific man.
—Charles Sanders Peirce (1839–1914)
American philosopher and scientist who is considered the "father of pragmatism"

The main difference between scientists and engineers is that engineers
want to make things and scientists want to understand them.
—Alan Curtis Kay (1940)

Science cannot solve the ultimate mystery of nature.
That is because we ourselves are part of nature and therefore
part of the mystery we are trying to solve.
—Max Planck (1858–1947)
Nobel Prize-winning German physicist who originated modern quantum theory.
This quote makes the important point that nature is not something other than us.

The great tragedy of science is the slaying of
a beautiful hypothesis by an ugly fact.
—Thomas Huxley (1825–1895)
British biologist and anthropologist specializing in comparative anatomy

Nothing exists except atoms and empty space.
Everything else is opinion.
—Democritus (c.460–c.370 BC)
Pre-Socratic Greek philosopher who formulated the first atomic theory of the universe,
and is considered by many to be the "father of modern science"

There must be no barriers to freedom of inquiry...there is no place for dogma in science. The scientist must be free to ask any question, to doubt any assertion, to seek for any evidence, to correct any errors.
—J. Robert Oppenheimer (1904–1967)
American physicist who was director of the Manhattan Project and became known as the father of the atomic bomb; his life and work are depicted in the 2023 film *Oppenheimer*

GREAT MINDS THINK ALIKE: *The Language of Mathematics*

Mathematics is the alphabet with which God has written the universe.
—Galileo Galilei (1564–1642)
Italian astronomer, physicist, and engineer known as the "father of observational astronomy" and considered one of the founders of the scientific method

Mathematics expresses values that reflect the cosmos, including orderliness, balance, harmony, logic and abstract beauty.
—Deepak Chopra (1946)

Math is the language of the universe. So the more equations you know, the more you can converse with the cosmos.
—Neil deGrasse Tyson (1958)
From his Nov 21, 2011 Twitter post

Technology has always been a net job creator, so why do so many feel that robots are about to take our jobs?
—Rana Foroohar (1970)
Global business columnist and associate editor at the *Financial Times* and CNN's global economic analyst, as quoted in *Time* magazine

Man and machine are intertwined. We rely on creative minds to envision a future we want to inhabit, and create a blueprint for centuries to come. As we make our machines more intelligent and more human, we must also continually reexamine our own humanity.
—Ramona Pringle
Canadian digital journalist, television host, actress, producer, and professor named after punk rock group *The Ramones*

Technologies build on themselves in an exponential manner. Essentially, we always use the latest technology to create the next.
—Ray Kurzweil (1948)
Inventor, author, and futurist, from *How to Create a Mind*

It is indeed possible to inherit knowledge, which is stored in the form of nucleic acid codes within cells.
—M. Scott Peck (1936–2005)
From *The Road Less Traveled: A New Psychology of Love, Traditional Values and Spiritual Growth*

Being able to talk to people over long distances, to transmit images, flying, accessing vast amounts of data. These are all things that would have been considered magic a few hundred years ago.
—Elon Musk (1971)
As quoted in *Forbes Magazine* March 28, 2014 issue

Perhaps science fiction is really just pre-reality, and the artists the creators of a prototype of the future. Science fiction film is less about tomorrow than it is about today. The wake-up call is clear: To create a future we want to be a part of, we need to reexamine our way of living now.
—Ramona Pringle
From her article in *The Futurist* magazine July-August 2013 issue

Science fiction is a tool for imagining possible futures and technologies. It inspires us to strive for a better tomorrow.
—The Futurist magazine
This concept has led to the creation of Project Hieroglyph that encourages the conversion of science fiction stories and art designs into reality

Science fiction has become science fact.
—CBS News radio announcer April 10, 2019

Every point in the cosmos can be considered its center.
—Dorothy Maclean (1920–2020)
Canadian writer and educator specializing in spiritual subjects

The end of outer space is the beginning of time.
—Neil deGrasse Tyson (1958)

It's very hard to take yourself too seriously
when you look at the world from outer space.
—*Thomas K. Mattingly II (1936)*
Apollo 16 astronaut and retired rear admiral U.S. Navy

Where is everybody? Humans could theoretically colonize the galaxy
in a million years or so, and if they could, astronauts from older
civilizations could do the same. So why haven't they come to Earth?
—*Enrico Fermi (1901–1954)*
Italian physicist who created the world's first nuclear reactor and was instrumental in
building America's first atomic bomb during WWII. In his Fermi Paradox, he acknowledges
the lack of evidence of extraterrestrial life despite the high probability of its existence.
The Fermi Paradox insists that the sheer size of the universe favors the probability of
extraterrestrial life even though we have not yet discovered any evidence of it.

Time bends, proving that events in deep space appear to us at
multiple times depending on the different paths the light travels.
—*The Einstein Cross*
The Einstein Cross describes gravitational lensing: a large galaxy or group of galaxies that
bends or "lenses" light from a distant source as it travels toward an observer. The effect
was predicted by Albert Einstein's general theory of relativity, and first observed in 1979.

Studying whether there's life on Mars or studying how the universe
began, there's something magical about pushing back the frontiers of
knowledge. That's something that is almost part of being human, and
I'm certain that will continue.
—*Sally Ride (1951–2012)*
Physicist and astronaut who was the first American woman launched into space

Long ages ago, serious and intelligent people devised a system
for veiling the technical terminology of an advanced
astronomical science behind the everyday language of myth.
—*Graham Hancock (1950)*
From *Fingerprints of the Gods*. Hancock raises the provocative question as to whether
mythological stories are historical accounts of actual events and real people.

GREAT MINDS THINK ALIKE: *The Butterfly Effect*

If you cut a blade of grass, you shake the universe.
—*Ancient proverb*

Does the Flap of a Butterfly's Wings in Brazil set off a Tornado in Texas?
—*Edward Lorenz (1917–2008)*

This example of the Butterfly Effect was the title of a speech given by Lorenz, who is often referred to as the "father of chaos theory." Lorenz, an American meteorologist and mathematician, established a theoretical basis for weather and climate prediction. The Butterfly Effect has captured the imagination of numerous science fiction writers and screenwriters...most notably by Jeff Goldblum's character in the original *Jurassic Park* movie. The Butterfly Effect appears to have its roots in the ancient proverb that uses blades of grass as a metaphor to express the interconnection of all things.

Great Minds Connect with Mudrooroo on page 278

Information without human understanding is like an answer without its question...meaningless.
—*Archibald MacLeish (1892–1982)*
Pulitzer Prize-winning American poet and playwright
who also served as Librarian of Congress

GREAT MINDS THINK ALIKE: *Computers & Data*

Data is useless until we know what it means.
—*David R. Hawkins MD (1927–2012)*
Nationally renowned psychiatrist, physician, researcher, spiritual teacher,
and lecturer from *Power vs. Force*.

Remember that computers have no common sense.
—*Ray Dalio (1949)*
American billionaire hedge fund manager, philanthropist, and founder of Bridgewater Associates, the world's largest hedge fund, from his book *Principles: Life and Work*. These two quotes highlight the fact that data derives its meaning from humans, and computers still need human thought processes.

The notion that science and spirituality are somehow mutually exclusive does a disservice to both.
—*Carl Sagan (1934–1996)*
American professor of astronomy, astrophysicist, astrobiologist, author, and television personality who popularized the concept of space travel and searching the universe for extraterrestrial life

*While our brains have not changed appreciably
in the past five thousand years, the world around
us has changed to an extraordinary degree.*
—*14th Dalai Lama (1935)*
Birth name: Lhamo Thondup; religious name: Tenzin Gyatso
Born in Tibet, he was enthroned in 1940 and won the 1989 Nobel Peace Prize; currently
headquartered in India, he has served as Dalai Lama in exile since 1959

*The real problem of humanity is the following: We have Paleolithic
emotions, medieval institutions, and godlike technology.*
—*Edward Osborne (E.O.) Wilson (1929–2021)*
American biologist, entomologist, and writer best known for his work with ants

*In an electric information environment, minority groups can no
longer be contained—ignored. Too many people know too much
about each other. Our new environment compels commitment and
participation. We have become irrevocably involved with, and
responsible for, each other...the older, traditional ideas of private,
isolated thoughts and actions...are very seriously threatened by new
methods of instantaneous electric information retrieval.*
—*Marshall McLuhan (1911–1980)*
Canadian philosopher from his 1967 book *The Medium is the Massage*

GREAT MINDS THINK ALIKE: *Secrets of the Universe*

*If you want to find the secrets of the universe,
think in terms of energy, frequency and vibration.*
—*Nikola Tesla (1856–1943)*
Serbian-born visionary American electrical engineer, inventor, and futurist
best known as the
"father of alternating current."

*The secrets of the universe are imprinted
on the cells of each of our bodies.*
—*Dan Millman (1946)*

*Stone Age. Bronze Age. Iron Age.
We define entire epics of humanity by the technology they use.*
—*Reed Hastings (1960)*
Co-founder and CEO of Netflix, from *No Rules Rules*

GREAT MINDS THINK ALIKE: *The I Ching and Binary Code*

The I Ching's system of binary code is not only a representation of the duality of nature, but also a reminder that everything is connected and in a state of constant change. This idea is echoed in modern computer science, where binary code is the fundamental building block of all digital systems.
—*John D. Barrow (1952–2020)*
British mathematician, physicist, and author from *The Book of Nothing: Vacuums, Voids, and Latest Ideas About the Origins of the Universe*

The parallelism between the I Ching and the creation of binary code is not only a remarkable coincidence but also a testament to the timeless wisdom of ancient civilizations. The duality expressed in the I Ching's binary system continues to influence modern thought and technology, and serves as a reminder of the interconnectedness of all things.
—*Alessandro Mordini*
Italian research scientist in his February 4, 2023 medium.com. article; the binary nature of the I Ching was first realized by Gottfried Leibniz in the 17th century

Our scientific power has outrun our spiritual power. We have guided missiles and misguided men.
—*Martin Luther King Jr. (1929–1968)*
African American Baptist minister and civil rights leader who advanced the cause of civil rights through nonviolent civil disobedience

The success of the planet as a whole depends on scientific discoveries, each of which hands us a new bag of problems.
—*Maxine Singer (1931)*
American molecular biologist and science administrator best known for her work in helping to solve the genetic code and her role in debates over ethics and government policy on recombinant DNA techniques. This quote alludes to the fact that even though you know more, learning what you didn't know often unveils more of what you don't know.

We cannot solve the significant problems we face today on the same level we were on when we created them.
—*Albert Einstein (1879–1955)*
Nobel Prize winning German theoretical physicist who created the Theory of Relativity and the world's most famous equation, $E=mc^2$

GREAT MINDS THINK ALIKE: *The Price of Progress*

The saddest aspect of life right now is that science gathers knowledge faster than society gathers wisdom.

—*Isaac Asimov (1920–1992)*

American professor of biochemistry and prolific author of both science and science fiction from *The Week* magazine December 4, 2020. This quote elucidates humanity's great challenge of the technological age.

I fear that machines are ahead of morals by some centuries.

—*Harry S. Truman (1884–1972)*

Truman made this comment after witnessing the ruins of Berlin, Germany, after WWII. The Missouri senator served as FDR's vice president and inherited the presidency only 80 days into his term of office when Roosevelt died. Truman then won reelection in one of the greatest upsets in presidential history. Interestingly, Truman foresaw the great challenge of technology before it reached a critical stage.

Most of the dangers civilization claims to protect us from are in fact created or amplified by civilization itself. When you're going in the wrong direction, progress is the last thing that you need. The progress that defines our age often seems closer to the progression of a disease than to its cure.

—*Christopher Ryan (1962)*

American author from his book *Civilized to Death: The Price of Progress. Great Minds Connect* with William Ophuls on page 236. Ryan and Ophuls share the belief that civilization is moving in an unhealthy and unsustainable direction.

Human intelligence at its core foundation is universal intelligence, and at that level, you and I and everyone and everything in the universe are one. We are united at our core, and that truth, that ultimate truth of the unity of life is the most precious and crucially important understanding to emerge in the scientific age. This is the same reality that has been celebrated in all the spiritual traditions of the world, but now this same truth is open to objective verification through the empirical approach of modern physics.

—*John Hagelin, PhD (1954)*

American quantum physicist, educator, author, and unified field expert from *The Passion Test*. Hagelin equates the unified field theory of physics with the unified field of consciousness in transcendental meditation as practiced by Maharishi Mahesh Yogi. The above quote appears in *The Passion Test*. Hagelin added:

The observer, the process of observation, and the observed are all unified.

GREAT MINDS THINK ALIKE: *The Law of Evolutionary Potential*

The Law of Evolutionary Potential is a simple one:
The more specialized and adapted a form in a given evolutionary
stage, the smaller its potential for passing to the next stage. Specific
evolutionary progress is inversely related to general evolutionary
potential...Although compelled to follow after advanced countries,
a backward country does not take things in the same order. The
privilege of historic backwardness permits, or rather compels,
skipping a whole series of intermediate states.

From *Evolution and Culture* courtesy of University of Michigan Press (1960)

The study of man and civilization is not only a matter of scientific
interest, but at once passes into the practical business of life. We have
in it the means of understanding our own lives and our place in the
world more clearly than any former generation. The knowledge of
man's course of life, from the remote past to the present, will not only
help us to forecast the future, but may guide us in our duty of leaving
the world better than we found it.

–Edward Burnett Tylor (1832–1917)

British anthropologist, author and lecturer known as the found of cultural anthropology (the
study of the evolution of cultures), from his 1881 published work *Anthropology*. This quote
is courtesy the University of Michigan Press publication *Evolution and Culture* (1960).

Science is a technique whereby non-creative people
can create and discover.

–Abraham Maslow (1908–1970)

American psychology professor and founder of humanistic psychology,
from *The Farther Reaches of Human Nature*

Disconnecting from our technology to reconnect
with ourselves is absolutely essential for wisdom.

–Arianna Huffington (1950)

Greek businesswoman, columnist, author, and co-founder of the *Huffington Post*

By exploring nature for new ideas, you uncover insights you would
have otherwise missed by staying in the lab.

–Jeffrey Karp (1973)

A Canadian biomedical engineer and professor of medicine at Harvard Medical School
and Harvard Stem Cell Institute, Karp also runs a laboratory at Brigham and Women's
Hospital that uses nature's blueprints to create breakthrough medical technologies

CONSOLIDATING CHAPTER 2
Science & Technology

Science and technology are merged into one chapter because in essence, technology is a subdivision of science that seeps its way into all arenas of contemporary life. In this regard, technology becomes an example of "the tail wagging the dog." Quotes in Chapter 2 salute the value of curiosity in the pursuit of scientific progress, encourage blending technology with nature, offer an intergalactic perspective for viewing human existence, and challenge our species to evolve spiritually to match the relentless rise of technology.

All caveats regarding the challenges of technology serve as a fervent plea to apply wisdom to scientific methods by simultaneously expanding human consciousness. This now appears to be the greatest challenge modern societies face: *A struggle to harness technology and prevent it from overrunning all other realms of human existence*; a struggle stranding humanity between the beauty of nature and the power of technology with a desperate need to establish balance between the two. Without such balance, technology threatens to annihilate nature and lead our species to catastrophe. Ironically, while we have developed machinery capable of destroying nature, we have also created numerous nature-supporting technologies.

There are fundamentally four domains of human life: local, regional, national, and global. For the first time in history, these domains overlap, as the ubiquity of social media has created an ability to simultaneously exist regionally, nationally, and globally while living locally. This blurs the lines between the four realms of life, a reality that injects psychological confusion into the minds of many. As a source of both empowerment and vulnerability, social media has transformed modern existence. Loneliness is an undesirable side effect, especially for those who attempt to live globally without proper support on the local level. Such an existence can be deceptively hollow, as technology often creates phantom relationships as email, texts, and social media posts replace direct human interactions such as the telephone and in-person conversations. Relationships that exist solely in the ether can rupture and disappear in an instant, as many of them never truly exist. While spiritual teachers tell us we are all connected, many contemporary connections are artificial and/or hurtful, leaving those involved vulnerable to emotional damage. To be fair, the same internet that causes these problems also empowers us to travel globally without leaving home, enabling us to gather and exchange immense amounts of valuable information.

In this chapter, physicist Max Planck identifies humans as a part of nature. Since nature is not an entity other than us, no matter how much technology we create, the simple fact remains that humanity is part of, and dependent on, nature for survival. David R. Hawkins reminds us data and information need to be interpreted to have meaning, while Ray Kurzweil focuses on the cumulative effect of technological progress. Aldous Huxley hints at the disruptive aspect of science throughout history, as science invalidated many fallacious ancient theories about nature and the structure of the universe. Thus, science periodically incurred the wrath of religious institutions. In early civilizations, ancient philosophers and religious leaders served as quasi scientists, with their theories accepted as fact until most of those theories were threatened and eventually disproved by new scientific methods and devices, most notably the telescope.

Ramona Pringle notes the predictive aspect of science fiction as it imagines future scientific activity, thereby providing specific roadmaps for technological progress. However, rising technology equates to constantly accelerating change, which always encounters resistance. As previously mentioned, the solution is not necessarily a development of more advanced technologies, but cultivation of human mental capacities to match expanding and evolving technologies. Marshall McLuhan, Harry Truman, and the 14th Dalai Lama address the dark side of technology: the creation of powerful tools capable of wrecking our environment much faster than we can repair it.

On a more cheerful note, Thomas Mattingly changes the whole perspective of life on Earth by looking down at our planet from outer space. Opening our minds to the existence of intergalactic worlds changes the way our brains process daily existence. This is exemplified by Neil deGrasse Tyson's eye-opening statement about the borders of outer space representing the beginning of time. Another revelatory statement is Maxine Singer admitting each scientific discovery, no matter how magnificent, also creates a whole new set of problems. This leads to the paradoxical truth about how learning what you didn't know often unveils a whole new world of what you still don't know. It seems each time science opens a door to new knowledge, it simultaneously reveals how much we still have to learn. Exemplifying this conundrum, Graham Hancock presents a nagging question about whether the myths of antiquity are fabricated stories or vibrant depictions of actual history.

An extremely provocative entry in Chapter 2 refers to the intergalactic phenomenon known as the Einstein Cross that explains why the Hubble Space Telescope frequently observes the same star exploding at numerous different times and positions in the sky. Albert Einstein realized gravity causes matter and energy to "warp" the geometry of space the way a heavy body sags a mattress. His deciphering this phenomenon explains the bending of time due to gravity's effect on the movement of light. As they traverse the universe, light rays from supernovas are bent by the powerful gravity of intervening galaxies. As a result, visual images take different routes to arrive at Earth because those intervening forces of gravity reroute them. Events that occurred many thousands, millions, or even billions of years ago are just becoming visible to us now because of the time it takes for their images to reach Earth. Depending on the route the light from each supernova explosion takes, the Einstein Cross explains why we see that explosion over and over again at different times as well as from different locations in the sky.

By demonstrating the bending of time, the Einstein Cross renders time a *relative*, rather than *exact* measurement. When early humans first attempted to measure the speed objects move and when events occurred, it necessitated the creation of time as a way of calculating those movements and events. Speed cannot be measured without distance, and all speed is relative if multiple objects are in motion. Distance is not dependent on time, but time is dependent on distance traveled...hence, the relativity of time, speed, and distance calculations. Many believe this actually proves time is an artificial creation, a measurement of distance covered within artificially created intervals for the purpose of providing structure to human existence. For example: *How far can you run while someone stomps their foot five times?*

The answer depends on the speed of the foot stomping, since your top running speed will be constant. The basis for telling time has also been variable throughout the millennia, as demonstrated by different ways indigenous people told time without the use of clocks. Native Americans told time by positions of the sun and moon. Each day began at sunrise and ended at sunset. If someone asked when you would arrive during daytime, the answer was described by the sun's position in the sky. Longer amounts of time were described by phases of the moon, such as long journeys that took "many moons."

Chapter 2 directly and significantly intersects with Chapter 1 by indicating our approach to science and technology will determine the future of our species. Also, if science fiction is truly a harbinger of our destiny, mankind will someday press on to reach the edges of the universe. In so doing, theoretically, we will arrive at the beginning of time. The Einstein Cross informs us that somewhere in the universe, all our ancient history may still be viewable. This offers an incredible possibility of viewing prehistoric events to discover the origins of ancient mythologies and solve the mysteries of our prehistoric past. All we have to do is figure out how to travel faster than the speed of light!

WISDOM TRAILS: *Interconnected Categories*
Curiosity, Love, Education, Nature, Creativity, Innovation, Spirituality, Harmony, Business, Native American Wisdom, History, Nature, The Future

Trails to Other Chapters
- Ahmed Zewail connects science and *Curiosity*.
- Charles Sanders Peirce declares that a love of learning characterizes the scientific mind. *(Love, Education)*
- Max Planck discusses the connection science has with *Nature*.

- J. Robert Oppenheimer insists scientists must be free to question everything. *(Creativity, Innovation)*
- Galileo Galilei calls mathematics the language of God. *(Spirituality)*
- Rana Foroohar views technology as a job creator. *(Work, Business)*
- Ramona Pringle connects technology with *Human Nature* and *The Future*.
- Graham Hancock connects technology with the *History* of myth.
- *The Futurist* magazine highlights science fiction's role in providing visions for the creation of future technologies. *(The Future)*
- Carl Sagan connects science with *Spirituality*.
- The 14th Dalai Lama, E.O. Wilson, Marshall McLuhan, Isaac Asimov, and Harry Truman all discuss the struggle between technology and *Human Nature*.
- Reed Hastings states that eras of *History* are defined by the technology used.
- *The I Ching and Binary Code* mention the interconnectedness of all things and wisdom of ancient civilizations. *(Spirituality, Native American Wisdom, History)*
- Isaac Asimov and Martin Luther King Jr. observe how science has outpaced the development of human wisdom. *(Wisdom, Spirituality)*
- Maxine Singer believes scientific discoveries will determine the success or failure of our species. *(The Future)*
- Albert Einstein's classic quote on problem solving illuminates the need for *Creativity* and *Innovation*.
- John Hagelin establishes a profound connection between science and ancestral traditions. *(Spirituality)*
- Abraham Maslow finds a quirky connection between science and *Creativity*.
- *The Law of Evolutionary Potential* applies to *History, Government,* and *The Future*.
- Jeffrey Karp gains insights from studying nature that lead to scientific progress. *(Nature, Innovation, The Future)*

CHAPTER 3

DREAMS, MIRACLES & LUCK

Tell me, what is it you plan to do
with your one wild and precious life?
—*Mary Oliver (1935–2019)*
Pulitzer Prize-winning American poet from her poem *Summer Day*

It's the possibility of having a dream come true
that makes life interesting.
—*Paulo Coelho (1947)*
From *The Alchemist*

You're never too old...or too young, to reach
your dreams. All it takes is one step at a time.
—*Dylan Dreyer (1981)*
American television meteorologist and host on the NBC show *Journey:*
Climbing Mount Kilimanjaro, S2E11.
Great Minds Connect with *Great Minds Think Alike: One Step at a Time* on page 144

The biggest adventure you can ever take
is to live the life of your dreams.
—*Oprah Winfrey (1954)*
Iconic African American television talk show host, actress, television producer,
media executive, and philanthropist

How do you go from where you are to where you wanna be?
I think you have to have an enthusiasm for life. You have to
have a dream, a goal...and you have to be willing to work for it.
—*Jim Valvano (1946–1993)*
The transcendent basketball coach of North Carolina State University who was
immortalized by his inspirational ESPN speech shortly before his death. In that speech,
Valvano announced the V Foundation, a charity created to find a cure for cancer.

As you move toward a dream, the dream moves toward you.
—*Julia Cameron (1948)*
As quoted in *Spirituality & Health Magazine*

GREAT MINDS THINK ALIKE: *Big Dreams*

To accomplish big things, I am convinced
you must first dream big dreams.
—Conrad Hilton (1887–1979)
American businessman who founded the Hilton Hotel chain,
from his autobiography *Be My Guest*

You have to have the courage to dream great dreams. If you dream
small dreams, you may succeed in building something small...if you
want to achieve widespread impact, and lasting value, be bold.
—Howard Schultz (1953)
Founder of Starbucks, from his book *Pour Your Heart Into It*

You can't change the world if you don't dream big.
—Adam L. Penenberg (1962)
American investigative journalist, journalism professor, editor and author

Every great dream begins with a dreamer. Always remember,
you have within you the strength, the patience, and the passion
to reach for the stars to change the world.
—Harriet Tubman (1822–1913)
Birth name: Araminta Ross
American abolitionist and political activist who was born a slave, escaped, and then
dedicated herself to rescuing others from slavery, utilizing the Underground Railroad
that originated in the early 19th century.

Great dreams contain inexhaustible truths, and orient us toward our
futures. The more we put ourselves into a great dream, the more we
get back. Great dreams are wells that never run dry.
—Michael Grosso (1937)
American author, from *Soulmaker*

Sometimes a dream almost whispers...it never shouts. So you have to,
every day of your life, be ready to hear what whispers in your ear.
—Steven Spielberg (1946)
Academy Award-winning American filmmaker and co-founder of DreamWorks Pictures
Great Minds Connect with Raymond Inmon on page 165

All our dreams can come true
if we have the courage to pursue them.
—Walt Disney (1901–1966)
Iconic animator, film, and television producer who created Disneyland and Disney World

*The future belongs to those who believe
in the beauty of their dreams.*
—*Eleanor Roosevelt (1884–1962)*
Activist, diplomat, and first lady of the United States from 1932 until 1945

*Taoists believe that any dream remembered
with great coherence has a hidden message.*
—*Lillian Too (1946)*
From *Chinese Wisdom*

*The world of reality has its limits;
the world of imagination is boundless.*
—*Jean-Jacques Rousseau (1712–1778)*
Swiss-born philosopher and writer who moved to Paris in 1742; his political philosophy
had a strong influence on the politics of Europe and the French Revolution

*Dreams are often most profound when they seem the most crazy.
The interpretation of dreams is the royal road to a knowledge
of the unconscious activities of the mind.*
—*Sigmund Freud (1856–1939)*
Austrian neurologist who founded psychoanalysis

Sometimes fantasies are paths to reality.
—*Walter Isaacson (1952)*
American historian, journalist, and author best known for his biographies
of famous people

The best way to make your dreams come true is to wake up.
—*Paul Valéry (1871–1945)*
French poet, essayist, and philosopher nominated
for the Nobel Prize for Literature twelve times

*Without leaps of imagination, or dreaming, we lose the excitement
of possibilities. Dreaming, after all, is a form of planning.*
—*Gloria Steinem (1934)*
Feminist, journalist, political activist, and co-founder of *Ms.* magazine

Humanity needs dreamers for whom the disinterested development of an enterprise is so captivating that it becomes impossible for them to devote their care to their own material profit.
—Marie Curie (1867–1934)
Nobel Prize-winning Polish-born French physicist famous for her work
with radium and polonium; best known as Madame Curie

*Dreams do come true. Without that possibility,
nature would not incite us to have them.*
—John Updike (1939–2002)
Pulitzer Prize-winning novelist, poet, and short story writer

Throw your dreams into space like a kite and you do not know what it will bring back...a new life, new friend, new love, a new country.
—Anais Nin (1903–1977)
Birth name: Angela Anais Juana Antolina Rosa Edelmira Nin y Culmell
Essayist, novelist, and short story writer born to Cuban parents in France
who became famous in America

*Every second you spend thinking about someone else's dreams,
you take time away from your own.*
—Robin Sharma (1964)
Ugandan-born Canadian litigation lawyer-turned-author of spiritual books and founder
of Sharma Leadership International, from *The Monk Who Sold His Ferrari*

Build your own dreams, or someone else will hire you to build theirs.
—Farrah Gray (1984)
American businessman, author, and motivational speaker
who began his entrepreneurial career at the age of six

*If you don't talk about your dreams with others,
you still don't believe in them yourself.*
—Gonzalo Arzuaga (1971)
Argentinian fund manager, motivational speaker, and author

Never limit yourself because of others' limited imagination,
and never limit others because of your limited imagination.
—*Dr. Mae Jemison (1956)*
American engineer, physician, astronaut, and the first African American woman
to travel into outer space

GREAT MINDS THINK ALIKE: *Write It Down!*

As you identify your dream, write it down. Don't let it slip away.
After you write it down, turn it into a goal.
—*Jim Tressel (1952)*
American college football coach and university administrator,
from *The Winners Manual For The Game of Life*

The secret of turning desires into reality is to write them down.
—*Catherine Ponder (1927)*
American minister and author known for her numerous affirmations
and books on prosperity, from *Open Your Mind to Prosperity*

A goal is a dream with a deadline.
—*Napoleon Hill (1883–1970)*
Self-help author, from his classic book *Think and Grow Rich*

Attention is energy. What we imagine begins to happen.
—*Doe Lang, PhD*
American writer and president of the image consulting firm Charismedia

You are never too old to set another goal or to dream a new dream.
—*C.S. Lewis (1898–1963)*
Prolific Irish scholar and fiction writer

It's not true that people stop pursuing dreams because they grow old.
They grow old because they stop pursuing their dreams.
—*Gabriel Marquez (1927–2014)*
Colombian novelist, screenwriter, and journalist

Those who lose dreaming are lost.
—*Australian Aboriginal proverb*

Don't be pushed by your problems. Be led by your dreams.
—Ralph Waldo Emerson (1803–1882)
American essayist, lecturer, philosopher, poet, and leader
of the mid-19th century transcendentalist movement

Dreams are used in many spiritual traditions as a guideline for self-improvement and growth. When we heal ourselves, others are healed. When we nurture our dreams, we give birth to the dreams of humankind. When we honor our bodies, our health and our emotional needs, we make space for our dreams to come into being.
—Jamie Sams (1951)
From her book *Dancing the Dream*

When you're putting people on the moon, you're inspiring all of us to achieve the maximum of human potential, which is how our greatest problems will eventually be solved. Give yourself permission to dream.
—Randy Pausch (1960–2008)
American professor of computer science and expert on artificial intelligence famous for his presentation that went viral on YouTube, and book *The Last Lecture,* shortly before death from pancreatic cancer

Once upon a time, I dreamt I was a butterfly, fluttering hither and thither. Suddenly I awakened, and there I lay, myself again. Now I do not know whether I was then a man dreaming I was a butterfly, or whether I am now a butterfly dreaming I am a man.
—Zhuang Zhou (369–286 BC)
aka Zhuangzi or Chuang Tzu
Influential Chinese philosopher who wrote one of the foundational texts of Taoism

Sometimes dreams are wiser than waking.
—Black Elk (1863–1950)
aka Hehaka Sapa
Oglala Lakota Sioux holy man and visionary who made this statement in reference to one of his ancestors who dreamt that a foreign race of people would someday arrive and destroy the Lakota culture. This quote appears in the book *Black Elk Speaks*, and aligns with the Cheyenne proverb
Pay heed to the voices in your dreams.

You can talk yourself out of your dreams,
or you can talk yourself into your dreams.
—*Joel Osteen (1963)*
American pastor, televangelist, and best-selling author

What lies before us and what lies behind us are small matters
compared to what lies within us. When we bring what is within out
into the world, miracles happen.
—*Henry David Thoreau (1817–1862)*
Legendary American author, essayist, poet, philosopher, and environmentalist

You can often measure a person by the size of his dreams.
—*Robert H. Schuller (1926–2015)*
American televangelist, motivational speaker, and author, from a broadcast
of his weekly *Hour of Power* show that ran from 1970 until 2010

GREAT MINDS THINK ALIKE: *Impossible Is Possible*

In order to see the boundaries of the probabilities,
you need to try impossible.
–*Mehmed I/Mehmed the Conqueror I (1432–1481)*
His 53-day siege of Constantinople concluded with the fall of the Eastern Roman Empire
and the rise of the Ottoman Empire

Nothing is impossible; there are ways that lead to everything.
It is often merely for an excuse that we say things are impossible.
–*Francois de la Rochefoucauld (1613–1680)*

What once we deemed impossible becomes not only possible,
but probable when we live our vision through actions.
—*Gerald A. Michaelson (1929—2004)*
American Fortune 500 executive, writer, consultant, and speaker who was an expert
on the strategic concepts of Sun Tzu, from his book *Sun Tzu for Success*
Great Minds Connect with Napoleon Hill on page 286

Impossible situations can become possible miracles.
—*Robert H. Schuller (1926–2015)*

Impossible is just a big word thrown around by small men who find
it easier to live in the world they've been given than to explore the
power they have to change it. Impossible is not a fact. It's an opinion.
Impossible is not a declaration. It's a dare. Impossible is potential.
—*Muhammad Ali (1942–2016)*

The moment you're ready to quit is usually
the moment right before the miracle happens.
—*Tony Robbins (1960)*
Life coach, author, motivational speaker, and philanthropist

Miracles happen to those who believe in them.
—*Bernard Berenson (1865–1959)*
Birth name: Bernhard Valvrojenski
Lithuanian-born American art historian and renowned scholar of Renaissance art who wrote
numerous books and essays on the subject, from *Forbes* magazine December 26, 2005

Anything might happen, and I believe I can invest my life with
meaning. Such uncertainty is a blessing in disguise. Since everything
and anything are always possible, the miraculous is always nearby
and wonders shall never, ever cease.
—*Robert Fulghum (1937)*
Unitarian Universalist minister and author, from his book
Maybe (Maybe Not): Second Thoughts from a Secret Life

To be alive, to be able to see, to walk, to have houses,
music, paintings— it's all a miracle. I have adopted
a technique of living life from miracle to miracle.
—*Arthur Rubinstein (1887–1982)*
Renowned Polish American classical pianist

No luck, or anything else worthwhile will come your way unless you
take some form of action...action always beats inaction. What you
focus on expands...focus on opportunities, not obstacles.
—*T. Harv Eker (1954)*
Billionaire Canadian businessman, author, and motivational speaker,
from *Secrets of the Millionaire Mind*

Being in the right place at the right time is all about
being in the right state of mind.
—*Richard Wiseman (1966)*
British psychology professor and author, from his book *The Luck Factor*

When you are inspired by some great purpose, some extraordinary project, all your thoughts break their bonds; your mind transcends limitations; your consciousness expands in every direction, and you find yourself in a great, new and wonderful world.
—Patanjali (2nd century BC)
Sage of India who compiled and/or authored the Yoga Sutras; although there is no definitive record, scholars estimate he lived in the 2nd century BC

GREAT MINDS THINK ALIKE: *Luck Is a Skill*

Luck is a talent.
I've stopped believing in coincidence. You can manifest all types of luck depending on your outlook and actions.
—Raina Kumra (1977)
CEO of Juggernaut

Luck or fate has absolutely nothing to do with success or failure. What we call 'luck' is, in fact, a direct result of the correct or incorrect application of natural laws anyone can use effectively if he knows how.
—Joe Karbo (1925–1980)
American commercial copywriter, television personality, and author of *The Lazy Man's Way To Riches* who tragically died from a heart attack during a television interview

The harder I work, the luckier I get.
—Samuel Goldwyn (1879–1974)
Iconic Polish-born American movie producer who was one of the founding fathers of the Hollywood studio system. Various forms of this quote have been attributed to numerous sources, including Thomas Jefferson.

Luck is a dividend of sweat. The more you sweat, the luckier you get... The two most important requirements for major success are: first, being in the right place at the right time, and second, doing something about it.
—Ray Kroc (1902–1984)
After starting his career as a milkshake mixer salesman, Kroc became a visionary American businessman who revolutionized the fast food industry by building McDonald's into a global corporation. Kroc also owned the San Diego Padres baseball team. Kroc's book, *Grinding It Out*, led to a movie about his life titled *The Founder*.

A meeting "by chance" is not actually by chance, but by design. Every event is the Universe communicating.
—Wu Wei
A Taoist concept that arose from Confucianism, from *I Ching Wisdom Volumes I and II*

GREAT MINDS THINK ALIKE: *Prepare for Luck*

Luck is where preparation meets opportunity.
—Lucius Annaeus Seneca (4 BC–65 AD)

Chance favors the prepared mind.
—Louis Pasteur (1822–1895)
The French biologist and chemist known as the "father of microbiology" developed pasteurization as well as the first vaccinations for rabies and anthrax

Luck happens to those who greatly increase the chances of its occurrence.
—Horatio Alger (1832–1899)
American novelist famous for writing the *Ragged Dick* series of books

You make your own luck by being prepared.
—Tom Selleck (1945)
As police commissioner Frank Reagan during the April 9, 2021 episode of CBS' *Blue Bloods*. *Great Minds Connect* with *Great Minds Think Alike: Preparation* on page 168

There are only two ways to live life. One is as though nothing is a miracle. The other is as though everything is a miracle.
—Albert Einstein (1879–1955)

The miracle is this: The more we share, the more we have.
—Leonard Nimoy (1931–2015)
American actor who played the role of Spock on *Star Trek* in a Twitter post just before he died

Behold the turtle. He makes progress only when he sticks his neck out.
—James B. Conant (1893–1978)
American chemist, president of Harvard University, and ambassador to West Germany who disclaimed he created this phrase by crediting it to atomic scientists who worked on the Manhattan Project

The real fast track path to getting everything, anything, and more than everything you want is putting others ahead of what you want, and focusing on their needs, their wants, their desires, and fulfilling them.
—Jay Abraham (1949)
American business executive, executive coach, author, and speaker, as quoted in *The Passion Test*

GREAT MINDS THINK ALIKE: *Be Bold*

Fortune and love favor the brave.
—Ovid (43 BC–17 AD)
Full name: Publius Ovidius Naso
Major Roman poet during the reign of Augustus who authored *The Metamorphoses* and was banished from Rome in 8 AD

Fortune favors the bold.
—Virgil (70–19 BC)
Roman poet who authored the epic poem *The Aeneid.*

Act boldly and unseen forces will come to your aid.
—Dorothea Brande (1893–1948)
Prominent writer, editor, and New York literary figure

The moment one commits oneself, Providence moves too. All sorts of things occur to help that would never otherwise have occurred. A whole stream of events raises one's favor in all manner of unforeseen incidents, meetings and material assistance no man could dream would come his way. Whatever you can do or dream you can do, begin it. Boldness has genius, power and magic in it.
—Johann Wolfgang von Goethe (1749–1832)
German statesman, poet, novelist, playwright, philosopher, diplomat, and civil servant *Great Minds Connect* with Arnold Palmer on page 198

Go confidently in the direction of your dreams! Live the life you've imagined.
—Henry David Thoreau (1817–1862)

GREAT MINDS THINK ALIKE: *Optimism & Pessimism*

I have never seen a monument erected to a pessimist.
—Paul Harvey (1918–2009)
Iconic radio broadcaster; *The Paul Harvey News* was carried by 1,200 radio stations and reached 24 million people weekly

Perpetual optimism is a force multiplier.
—Colin Powell (1937–2021)
African American four-star general and chairman of the Joint Chiefs of Staff, from his autobiography *My American Journey*

Generosity is a source of good luck. Making others feel lucky will increase your good luck.
—Twyla Tharp (1941)
American dancer, choreographer, and author, from *The Creative Habit*

<u>GREAT MINDS THINK ALIKE:</u> *Bad Luck Can Be Good Luck*

*You never know what worse luck
your bad luck has saved you from.*
—*Cormac McCarthy (1933)*
American novelist, playwright, and screenwriter. His novel
No Country For Old Men was adapted into a movie.

*Remember that not getting what you want
is sometimes a wonderful stroke of luck.*
—*14th Dalai Lama (1935)*

*All fortune is good fortune; for it either rewards, disciplines,
amends, or punishes, and so is either useful or just.*
—*Boethius (477–524)*
Birth name: Anicius Manlius Severinus Boethius
Roman senator and philosopher, from his classic book *The Consolation of Philosophy*

*Every single thing you can see which was created by man, was an
idea in someone's mind at one time. If you want to create the life of
your dreams, it begins by writing your dreams down and getting as
clear as possible about them.*
—*Chris Attwood*
American business executive, author, and leader of transformational seminars,
from *The Passion Test,* co-authored with his wife, Janet Attwood

CONSOLIDATING CHAPTER 3
Dreams, Miracles & Luck

This chapter tackles the grand topics of dreams, miracles, and luck, providing advice on how to manifest seemingly impossible miracles by boldly acting on big life dreams. To accomplish anything significant in life, we need to start with some sort of dream, vision, or goal, with goals being defined by Napoleon Hill as dreams with deadlines. Phrases in Chapter 3 concur that everyone should dream often, dream big, write down their dreams, act boldly to pursue those dreams, and when faced with an impossibility, systematically break them down into small achievable increments. This spotlights one of the true miracles of life: the impossible becomes possible once you figure out how to divide it into manageable pieces. Accordingly, this chapter assures us:

If you can imagine it, you can do it.
Luck is a talent, so put in the work to create your own good luck.

When perceived in this manner, luck becomes a learnable skill linked to our powers of observation. For example: To find the $100 bill lying on the sidewalk, you must look down to see it. The real question is: How many $100 bills have you walked past without noticing? In other words:

How many opportunities have you missed in your lifetime?

Chapter 3 urges you to maintain faith while becoming more aware of, and then seizing, your opportunities, a lifestyle adjustment destined to improve your luck. The inspiring message is that everyone can improve their luck and eventually manifest their dreams. Numerous contributors concur that pursuing passionate dreams is an essential component of a fulfilled life. When contemplating the relationship between dreaming, boldness, and luck, it's impossible to miss their connection to fear and courage. This is an important intersection, since overcoming fear is a major component of acting boldly, which in turn facilitates the pursuit of dreams.

The concept of dreaming big comes with a sidebar that big dreams often evolve out of a series of smaller ones, so do not feel you've failed if your dreams start small. Incremental dreams have the potential to combine into something much larger. The universal advice is to act on visions and dreams to see how far they can take you. If you continue to work on moving dreams forward by refocusing and refining them, good things will happen. Have faith that a pile of small dreams will add up to something very special.

Before making any definitive statements on how to improve your luck, it's important to acknowledge some questions arising from the suggestion of luck being a learnable skill; an inquiry that presents substantial challenges. Three questions are:

1. Is luck a skill, divine intervention, or merely coincidence?

2. Are people who end up "in the right place at the right time" lucky or have they consciously placed themselves in a position to receive good fortune?
3. If luck is a skill, how does one cultivate it?

The wisdom in Chapter 3 readily answers the above questions, although each of us must evaluate all answers individually. Paul Harvey's quote "I have never seen a monument erected to a pessimist" implies that those who are optimistic are more apt to find success. Other quotes in this chapter strongly promote the belief that external forces rise to support those who actively pursue their dreams. This is a major tenet of the Law of Attraction, a maxim that infers it's necessary to make our desires known if we want them to find support. In turn, our odds of encountering good luck along the way will be greatly improved. This does not mean everyone will meet with equal success. There are many variables and exceptions to every theory, otherwise, success rates for those who make a grand effort would be 100%.

Wisdom quotes about success (Chapter 7) remind us the road to success often includes numerous setbacks and failures, which puts a premium on self-discipline and perseverance. Regardless, Chapter 3 concludes it *is* possible to cultivate your own luck; quotes in this chapter describe the relationship between courage and luck as the difference between acting boldly versus being timid or complacent. From Goethe to Arnold Palmer (in Chapter 12) and many in between, history's great minds agree that proceeding boldly increases your potential for success. Conversely, fear decreases the odds of synchronistic and serendipitous outcomes. For those not familiar with these two terms, *synchronicity* can be perceived as the occurrence of fortunate opportunities. *Serendipity* is the beneficial outcome resulting from identifying and taking advantage of synchronistic opportunities. When viewed this way, luck becomes a skill...the ability to recognize, act on, and harvest opportunity. Opportunity must be recognized and exploited to create superior outcomes, as opposed to blaming bad luck when opportunities are missed.

One of the heroes of Chapter 3 is Walt Disney who urges us to have the courage to pursue our dreams. Dylan Dryer tells us we are never too young or old to reach our dreams, and Gabriel Marquez believes working on our dreams keeps us young. For those who hope to change the world, Adam Penenberg advises "dream big!" and Harriet Tubman agrees, telling us we all have the ability to dream big and change the world. Farrah Gray warns if we don't work to manifest our own dreams, we'll probably end up working to support someone else's, and Jim Tressel reminds us to write down our dreams so they don't slip out of our consciousness prematurely. Tony Robbins notes that perseverance is necessary for anyone wishing to achieve a miracle...in other words, *don't quit too soon!* Robbins' advice is supported by Mehmed the Great, Francois de la Rochefoucauld, and Gerald Michaelson, who all agree nothing is impossible for those who never stop trying, while Bernard Berenson adds the element of faith into the mix by stating miracles happen to those who believe in them.

In discussing the many dimensions of luck, all contributors agree we can influence our luck by taking action. Samuel Goldwyn bluntly proclaims the harder he worked, the luckier he became. Along the same line of thinking, Cormac McCarthy whimsically points out that bad luck sometimes saves us from even worse luck, a thought supported by the 14th Dalai Lama's perceptive comment that sometimes not getting what we think we want is actually good for us. Boethius concludes the discussion of luck with his unique perspective that all luck is good luck because of the valuable lessons we can learn from our misfortunes.

As an all-encompassing category, dreams inspire creativity, the arts, business, sports and politics...which, in turn, affect the future, success, war, philosophy, spirituality, and even health. It's also important to note that dreams are a central component of Native American spirituality and rites of passage.

WISDOM TRAILS: *Interconnected Categories*

Courage, Spirituality, Business, Work, Nature, Love, Friendship, Native American Wisdom, Science, Technology, Politics, Sports, The Arts, Success, War, Love, Creativity, Innovation

Trails to Other Chapters

- Howard Schultz and Walt Disney connect dreams with *Courage.*
- Lillian Too and Jamie Sams discuss the *Spiritual* nature of dreams.
- Madame Curie says dreamers are necessary to develop a *Business.*
- Gloria Steinem says dreams are a form of *Business* planning.
- John Updike connects dreams with *Nature.*
- Anais Nin tells us dreams can be helpful in finding *Love* and *Friendship.*
- Black Elk provides a *Native American Wisdom* view of dreams.
- *Impossible Is Possible* directly applies to *Science, Sports, Technology, Business,* and *Politics.*
- Tony Robbins points out the need for perseverance to achieve *Miracles.*
- Arthur Rubinstein praises *The Arts* as creators of miracles. This directly applies to *Success, Work, Business,* and *Sports.*
- Lucius Annaeus Seneca believes good luck comes from preparation; this connects with *Success, Sports, The Arts, Business, Politics,* and *War.*
- *Be Bold's* advice connects with *Business, Success, Sports, The Arts, Work, War, Politics,* and *Love.*
- Chris Attwood provides *Practical Advice* on building the life of your dreams.
- Jay Abraham offers strong advice about fulfilling the dreams of others to create your own *Success.*

CHAPTER 4

LOVE, FRIENDSHIP & COMPASSION

Love is born into every human being. It calls back the halves of our original nature together; it tries to make one out of two and heal the wound of human nature. At the touch of love, everyone becomes a poet.
—Plato (429–347 BC)

Love is the only sane and satisfactory answer to the problem of human existence.
—Erich Fromm (1900–1980)

Tis better to have loved and lost than never to have loved at all.
– Alfred Lord Tennyson (1809–1892)
Poet laureate of Great Britain and Ireland who was greatly admired by Queen Victoria

Art and love are man's greatest gifts to himself.
—David R. Hawkins, MD (1927–2012)

The one thing we can never get enough of is love.
And the one thing we never give enough is love.
—Henry Miller (1891–1980)
American writer who developed a new literary style of semi-autobiographical novel blending character study, social criticism, stream of consciousness, sex, and mysticism. From *Ions Noetic Sciences Review* September 2001

Since love grows within you, so beauty grows.
For love is the beauty of the soul.
—Saint Augustine/Augustine of Hippo (354–430)
Birth name: Aurelias Augustinus Hipponensis
Roman philosopher and theologian who lived in Numidia, now known as Algeria

We are shaped and fashioned by what we love.
—Johann Wolfgang von Goethe (1749–1832)

The perfection of love is that it is not perfect.
–Taylor Swift (1989)
Iconic American singer/songwriter who has become one of the most popular recording and touring artists of all time

Real love is a permanently self-enlarging experience.
—M. Scott Peck (1936–2005)
From *Abounding Grace*

To learn to love is not easy. It requires discipline in one's whole life. It requires concentration, aloneness, thought, knowledge of oneself, listening, living in the present, patience. Above all, to love must be your supreme concern.
—Joseph Jaworski (1934)
Transformational leadership expert who founded the Global Leadership Initiative and the American Leadership Forum, from *Synchronicity: The Inner Path of Leadership*

*We are all born for love...
it is the principle of existence and its only end.*
—Benjamin Disraeli (1804–1881)
British statesman and twice-appointed prime minister of the United Kingdom

*We are in love with love because love is our salvation.
For a committed heart, everything is possible.
Let the beauty of what you love be what you do.
Love is the bridge between you and everything.*
—Rumi (1207-1273)
From *Rumi's Little Book of Love*

*Love is where we learn the really big lessons
of attachment and loss.*
—Stephen Nachmanovitch (1950)
Improvisation expert, violinist, educator, and author,
from his book on creativity, *Free Play*

*Love is a fire. But whether it is going to warm your hearth
or burn down your house, you can never tell.*
—Joan Crawford (1904–1977)
Birth Name: Lucille Fay LeSueur
American film star and title character of the movie *Mommy Dearest*

Love doesn't need reason. It speaks
from the irrational wisdom of the heart.
—*Deepak Chopra (1946)*

You know you're in love when you can't fall asleep
because reality is finally better than your dreams.
—*Dr. Seuss (1904–1991)*
Birth name: Theodor Seuss Geisel
American children's author, political cartoonist, illustrator,
poet, animator, screenwriter, and filmmaker

The more you give love away, the more you get.
—*Warren Buffett (1930)*
American business magnate, investor, speaker, philanthropist, and chairman and CEO
of Berkshire Hathaway, from *The Snowball: Warren Buffett & the Business of Life*

The simple act of being completely present
to another person is truly an act of love.
—*Sharon Salzberg (1952)*
American author and teacher of Buddhist meditation, from her book *Lovingkindness*

The first duty of love is to listen.
—*Paul Tillich (1886–1965)*
German American theologian, teacher, and author who has been described
as a Christian existential philosopher

Love all, trust few, do wrong to none.
—*William Shakespeare (1564–1616)*
The most famous playwright in history

Never be too busy for the people you love.
–*Dave Willis (1970)*
American actor, writer, producer, and musician

To love and be loved is life itself, without which we are naught.
—Abi Morgan (1968)
From her screenplay *The Invisible Woman* that depicts the clandestine affair
between Charles Dickens and a much younger actress named Ellen Ternan

Love is divine only and difficult always.
If you think it is easy, you are a fool.
—Toni Morrison (1931–2019)
Birth name: Chloe Ardelia Wofford
Nobel Prize and Pulitzer Prize-winning American novelist,
book editor, and college professor, from her book *Paradise*

GREAT MINDS THINK ALIKE: *Ever-Present Love*

What we once enjoyed and deeply loved we can never lose,
for all that we love deeply becomes a part of us.
—Helen Keller (1880–1968)
American author, political activist, lecturer, and the first deaf and blind person to earn
a Bachelor of Arts degree; her life story was the subject of the movie *The Miracle Worker*

Anyone you have ever touched in true love, that love is still present.
—Ram Dass (1931–2019)
Birth name: Richard Alpert
Clinical psychologist, spiritual teacher, and author, from *Compassion in Action*.
Great Minds Connect with Jamie Sams on page 267

Our partners are flowers. If we take care of them well, they will grow
beautifully. If we take care of them poorly, they will wither.
To help a flower grow well, we must understand its nature.
How much water does its need? How much sunshine?
—Thich Nhat Hanh (1926–2022)
Vietnamese Buddhist monk and peace activist,
from *Touching Peace: Practicing the Art of Mindful Living*

Whenever there is a touch of color, a note of a song,
grace in a form, this is a call to our love.
—Rabindranath Tagore (1861–1941)
Nobel Prize-winning Indian poet, philosopher, composer, and painter as quoted
in *Wisdom: 365 Thoughts from Indian Masters*

Love never keeps a man from pursuing his personal legend.
If he abandons that pursuit, it is because it wasn't true love...
the love that speaks the language of the world.
—Paulo Coelho (1947)
From *The Alchemist*

If you judge people, you have no time to love them.
—Mother Teresa (1910–1997)
Nobel Peace Prize-winning Albanian nun and missionary who also said:
It's not how much we give, but how much love we put into giving.

We can only learn to love by loving.
—Iris Murdoch (1919–1999)
British novelist and philosopher from the cover of her blank journal notebook

If she loves you now, what else matters?...the two of you may never
be perfect together, but if she can make you laugh, cause you to think
twice, and admit to being human and making mistakes, hold onto her
and give her the most you can...don't hurt her, don't change her,
don't analyze her and don't expect more than she can give.
—Bob Marley (1945–1981)
Jamaican singer, songwriter, and pioneer of reggae music

There is always some madness in love, but
there is also always some reason in that madness.
—Friedrich Nietzsche (1844–1900)
German philosopher, cultural critic, composer, poet, Latin & Greek scholar, and
philologist (a student of the structure and historical development of languages)

Age does not protect you from love, but
love, to some extent protects you from age.
—Jeanne Moreau (1928–2017)
French actress, singer, screenwriter, and director; this quote has also been attributed to
Anais Nin (1903–1977)

Love does not consist in gazing at each other,
but in looking together in the same direction.
—*Antoine de Saint-Exupery (1900–1944)*
French aviator and author killed during a WWII mission

Everything you are holding on to through fear is blocking you
from having more love in your life.
—*Karen Kingston*
World-renowned British feng shui expert who now lives in Australia

God breaks the heart again and again and again until it stays open.
—*Hazrat Inayat Kahn (1882–1927)*
Professor of musicology, singer, poet, philosopher, and pioneer of the spread of Sufism in
the West; Kahn was born in India, traveled extensively throughout Europe, and spent two
years touring the United States before spending his final years back in India

If anything appears to be complicated, it isn't love.
It is something else.
—*Marlo Morgan (1937)*
American author known for her controversial books about Aboriginal Australians,
from her novel *Mutant Message From Forever*

Our choice is to be in love or in fear. To choose to be in love means to
have a mountain inside of you, to have the heart of the world inside
you, to feel another's suffering inside your own body. You understand
this pain is your own because you are not separate from anyone
or anything else.
—*China Galland (1944)*
American author and professor from *The Sun* magazine April, 2012.

The first time you marry for love, the second for money,
and the third for companionship.
—*Jacqueline Kennedy Onassis (1929–1994)*
First lady during John F. Kennedy's presidency, fashion icon, and book editor;
interestingly, she only married twice

<u>GREAT MINDS THINK ALIKE:</u> *Hatred vs. Love*

Hatred will never cease by hatred. Hatred can only cease by love.
—*Buddha (563–483 BC)*

Darkness cannot drive out darkness. Only light can do that.
Hate cannot drive out hate. Only love can do that.
—*Martin Luther King Jr. (1929–1968)*

If we choose to dampen our anger, we also dampen our capacity
to love, because love and anger are two sides of the same coin.
—*Harville Hendrix, PhD (1935)*
American author of self-help relationship books, from *Getting the Love You Want*

All hatred of others is a reflection of self-hatred.
All love of others is a reflection of self-love.
—*Alan Cohen (1950)*
American author of numerous inspirational books
and daily online inspirational messages

If you close or armor your heart, you have become
a crippled instrument for the healing of the universe.
—*Ram Dass (1931)*
From his book *Compassion in Action*

No one is born hating another person because of the color of his skin,
his background or religion. People learn to hate, and if they can learn
to hate, they can be taught to love, for love comes more naturally to
the human heart.
—*Nelson Mandela (1918–2013)*
South African anti-apartheid revolutionary, political leader, and philanthropist who served
as South Africa's president from 1994 to 1999 after years of imprisonment,
from his autobiography *Long Walk To Freedom*

If we could read the secret history of our enemies, we would find in
each man's life, sorrow and suffering enough to disarm all hostility.
—*Henry Wadsworth Longfellow (1807–1882)*
Educator and one of America's foremost poets

Remember that everyone you meet is afraid of something,
loves something, and has lost something.
—*H. Jackson Brown, Jr. (1940)*
American author whose books have been translated into 35 languages

GREAT MINDS THINK ALIKE: *Self-Love*

Before we can give love to others,
we have to fill ourselves with love first.
—Elaine St. James (1943)
American businesswoman turned self-help author, from her book *Inner Simplicity*

Love yourself and everything else falls into line. You really have to
love yourself to get anything done in this world.
—Lucille Ball (1911–1989)
Iconic American actress, comedienne, and producer

Loving kindness is the canal through which compassion flows.
—Rinpoche
from *Ancient Wisdom*

To be compassionate is to sense from within what
it must be like to experience someone else's experience.
—Sharon Salzberg (1952)
From *Lovingkindness*

Tolerance and compassion are active, not passive states,
born of the capacity to listen, to observe and to respect others.
—Indira Gandhi (1917–1984)
The first female prime minister of India

Compassion is the basis of all truthful relationships.
It means being present with love for ourselves and all life including
animals, fish, birds, and trees. It is bringing our deepest truth into
our actions, no matter how much the world seems to resist, because
that is ultimately what we have to give this world.
—Ram Dass (1931)
From *Compassion in Action*

I expect to pass through life but once. If therefore, there can be any
kindness I can show, or any good thing I can do to any fellow being,
let me do it now, and not defer or neglect it, as I shall not pass
this way again.
—William Penn (1644–1718)
Quaker leader who founded the state of Pennsylvania

A single act of kindness throws out roots in all directions, and those roots spring up to make new trees. The greatest work that kindness does to others is that it makes them kind themselves.
—Amelia Earhart (1897–1937)
Passionate American adventurer and the first female aviator to fly solo across the Atlantic Ocean; Earhart disappeared during a trans Pacific flight and was never found

Your own soul is nourished when you are kind. It is destroyed when you are cruel.
—King Solomon (990–931 BC)

Always be a little kinder than necessary.
—James M. Barrie (1860–1937)
Scottish playwright and author who lived his adult life in London and is best known for writing *Peter Pan*

GREAT MINDS THINK ALIKE: *The Benefits of Kindness*

It is one of the most beautiful compensations of life that no man can sincerely help another without also helping himself.
—Ralph Waldo Emerson (1803–1882)

Simple kindness to oneself and all that lives, is the most powerful transformational force of all. Compassion is the doorway to grace. Without compassion, little of any significance is ever accomplished.
—David R. Hawkins MD (1927–2012)
From *Power vs. Force*

Kindness boosts happiness and optimism, bolsters your self-esteem, supports your immune system, improves the health of your heart, and promotes healthy aging.
—Dr. Josh Axe (1981)
American doctor of natural medicine, chiropractor, clinical nutritionist, and author, from *Ancient Remedies*

You cannot do a kindness too soon, for you never know how soon it will be too late.
—Henry David Thoreau (1817–1862)

Be kind whenever possible. It is always possible. My religion is kindness. Compassion is a marvel of human nature, a precious inner resource, the foundation of our well-being and the harmony of our societies.
—*14th Dalai Lama (1935)*
From *Beyond Religion: Ethics for a Whole World*

Breathe in the sorrows of the world, and breathe out compassion
—*Buddha (563–483 BC)*

Not forgiving is like drinking rat poison, and then waiting for the rat to die.
—*Anne Lamott (1954)*
American novelist, political activist, and public speaker, as quoted in *The Week* magazine December 17, 2021; her life story is featured in the documentary *Bird By Bird with Annie*

Wisdom has an embodied moral element; out of your own moments of suffering comes a compassionate regard for the frailty of others.
—*David Brooks (1961)*
American commentator, reporter, writer, and editor in his April 15, 2021
New York Times article

I learned compassion from being discriminated against. Everything bad that's ever happened to me has taught me compassion.
—*Ellen DeGeneres (1958)*
American comedian, television talk show host, actress, author, and producer

Compassion has no limit. Kindness has no enemy.
—*Yogi Tea teabag*
Courtesy of the East West Tea Company

Compassion, caring, teaching, loving, and sharing your gifts, talents, and abilities are the gateways to power.
—*Jamie Sams (1951)*
From *Dancing the Dream*

What wisdom can you find greater than kindness?
—Jean-Jacques Rousseau (1712–1778)

Only he who is smitten with the arrows of love
know its power. Nothing is impossible for pure love.
—Mohandas (Mahatma) Gandhi (1869–1948)
Legendary lawyer and civil rights activist who led the nonviolent revolution that
freed India from British rule. Gandhi was paraphrasing a hymn from his native land in
his autobiography *The Story of My Experiments with Truth*. Gandhi is widely known as
Mahatma, which means "great soul." *Great Minds Connect*
with Napoleon Hill on page 286

GREAT MINDS THINK ALIKE: *Friendship & Happiness*

Of all the things which wisdom provides to make us
entirely happy, much the greatest is the possession of friendship.
—Epicurus (341–270 BC)

Greek philosopher who founded Epicureanism
No one is more important than people. In other words, friendship is
the most important thing—not career or housework, or one's fatigue.
It needs to be tended and nurtured.
—Julia Child (1912–2004)
American cooking teacher, chef, author, television personality, from *My Life in France*

Interpersonal relationships of an intimate kind are the chief,
if not the only, sources of human happiness.
—Anthony Storr (1920–2001)
English Jungian psychiatrist, author, and teacher, from *A Return to the Self*

You can make more friends in two months by becoming interested in
other people than you can in two years by trying to get other people
interested in you.
—Dale Carnegie (1888–1965)
American writer, lecturer, and developer of courses on self-improvement,
salesmanship, corporate training, public speaking, and interpersonal skills,
from *How To Win Friends & Influence People*

The only way to have a friend is to be one.
—Ralph Waldo Emerson (1803–1882)

Anything will give up its secrets if you love it enough
—George Washington Carver (1864–1943)
Once called the "Black Leonardo" by *Time* Magazine, this African American agricultural scientist and inventor developed 285 uses for the peanut

For the first time in my life I saw the truth as it is set into song by so many poets, proclaimed as the final wisdom by so many thinkers —the truth that Love is the ultimate and highest goal to which man can aspire...The salvation of humanity is through love.
—Viktor Frankl (1905–1997)
Austrian neurologist, psychiatrist, author, and philosopher who survived the German concentration camps of WWII, from his book *Man's Search for Meaning*

To forgive is the highest, most beautiful form of love. In return, you will receive untold peace and happiness.
—Robert Muller (1923–2010)
Born in Belgium and raised in France, Muller served at the United Nations for 40 years, eventually rising to the rank of Assistant Secretary General. Muller was also an internationally acclaimed speaker and prolific author honored for his dedication to education and world peace. *Great Minds Connect* with Maya Angelou on page 317

Judge not too much and love more.
—Julia Huxley (1862–1908)
Aldous Huxley's mother and prominent British scholar who founded a girls' school in England wrote this advice in a note to Aldous as she was dying

The divine essence itself is love and wisdom. Our love is our life itself. What our love is like determines how we live, and therefore everything we are as human beings. If love is not married to wisdom, it cannot accomplish anything.
—Emanuel Swedenborg (1688–1772)
Prominent Swedish scientist, inventor, theologian, and philosopher

Love conquers all.
—Virgil (70–19 BC)
Birth Name: Publius Vergilius Maro
Roman poet who revolutionized Roman poetry...the Latin version of this famous phrase, as uttered by Gallus in Virgil's *Eclogue X*, line 69 is *Omnia vincit amor; et nos cedamus amori.* This translates as *Love conquers all; let us too, yield to love.*

CONSOLIDATING CHAPTER 4
Love, Friendship and Compassion

Chapter 4's kaleidoscopic view of love and friendship is a profound reminder of the importance of nurturing these elements to enrich our daily lives. It's apparent that all those quoted in this chapter view love as the greatest human attribute. Love is something everyone craves, even when we won't admit it. It's also something not enough of us give freely. These numerous phrases show why love and compassion are the most desirable components of all human activity. It becomes clear that love's scope reaches far beyond romance, serving as a major ingredient of overall happiness and success in business as well as work, since it's vital to build careers we love.

Chapter 4 suggests that the more love we give, the more love we will receive, we should never be too busy for the ones we love, and if we judge people, we cannot love them properly. Joseph Jaworski launches the discussion, urging us to adopt love as our primary concern above all else. Karen Kingston and China Galland warn us not to let fear block the flow of love, and Lucille Ball astutely points out we must love ourselves to fully love others, highlighting the importance of self-love. While love headlines the title of this chapter, friendship voices its role as a vital part of all meaningful relationships, with compassion and kindness serving as conduits through which love flows. This positions friendship, compassion, and kindness at the center of all wisdom traditions. The ultimate takeaway inherent in advice from this chapter is: *Find a way to love everyone and everything in your life, even your opponents and enemies.*

Some notable quotes in Chapter 4 are Goethe telling us we are shaped by what we love, an opinion echoed by M. Scott Peck who views love as a life-expanding experience. David Willis addresses a contemporary issue by advising us to never be too busy for the ones we love, Toni Morrison admits love can be both divine and difficult, and Ram Dass makes the intriguing claim that anyone we have loved still resides somewhere inside us. This implies true love lasts forever in some way, even after love relationships end. Rabindranath Tagore finds love in every aspect of nature, while Thich Nhat Hahn compares nurturing a lover to that of nurturing a flower. Antoine de Saint-Exupery believes love relationships blossom when partners share the same view of the world, Julia Child adds friendship as a critical component of successful love relationships, and Alan Cohen finds an element of self-loathing in all extreme hatred. Ram Dass returns to urge us not to close or armor our hearts, adding that people who armor their hearts not only hurt themselves but also damage the universe. This statement informs us that the Butterfly Effect (see page 40) also applies to negative behavior.

Martin Luther King Jr. and Buddha agree love is the antidote for hatred, which relates to Mahatma Gandhi's description of compassion as an active state of listening to and respecting others...before Gandhi adds his profound observation that if people can be taught to hate, they can also be taught to love. Multiple contributors, including the 14th Dalai Lama, praise the virtues of kindness. As the world's foremost authority on and spokesman for compassion, the Dali Lama declares kindness to be his religion. Jean-Jacques Rousseau agrees, declaring kindness to be the greatest form of wisdom. This leads to Dr. Josh Axe's medical opinion that being kind contributes to better health, and Ralph Waldo Emerson stating every act of kindness benefits the giver as well as the recipient. David R. Hawkins takes these thoughts a step further by declaring kindness to be the most powerful transformational force of existence. A Yogi teabag chimes in, claiming kindness has no enemies, while Jamie Sams views the Native American approach to love and compassion as a gateway to power, and Sharon Salzman defines compassion as an internal sensitivity to other people's life experiences. Chapter 4 concludes with George Washington Carver's provocative claim that anything will give up its secrets if you love it enough.

WISDOM TRAILS: *Interconnected Categories*
Observing Human Nature, Dreams, Nature, Spirituality, The Arts, Fear, History, Work, Sports, Practical Advice, Nature, Happiness, Education, Peace, Social Justice, Health

Trails to Other Chapters
- Plato believes love can heal the "wound" of *Human Nature*.
- David R. Hawkins declares love and *The Arts* to be man's greatest gifts.
- Benjamin Disraeli believes love is the only purpose of existence. (*Observing Human Nature*)
- Dr. Seuss connects love with *Dreams*.
- Thich Nhat Hanh uses a *Nature* metaphor to help explain how to love.
- Karen Kingston warns against allowing *Fear* to prevent love from entering your life.
- China Galland says choosing love is a triumph over *Fear*.
- Ram Dass extends the realm of loving to all of *Nature*.
- Henry Wadsworth Longfellow encourages us to learn the *History* of those we interact with in order to gain compassion.
- *The Benefits of Kindness* concludes that kindness is a source of *Happiness*.
- The 14th Dalai Lama announces that his religion is kindness *(Spirituality)* and that kindness is good for our *Health*.
- David R. Brooks links *Wisdom* and *Spirituality* with compassion.

- Epicurus, Julia Child, and Anthony Storr agree on the powerful connection between friendship and *Happiness*. Furthermore, Julia Child believes friendship is more important than one's *Work*, and Dr. Josh Axe points out kindness not only contributes to *Happiness*, but also boosts the immune system. (*Health)*
- Alfred Lord Tennyson, Joseph Jaworski, Dave Willis, Bob Marley, Mother Teresa, Iris Murdoch, Lucille Ball, and William Shakespeare all provide *Practical Advice* on love.
- Buddha, H. Jackson Brown, and James M. Barrie all offer *Practical Advice* on compassion.
- Ellen DeGeneres informs us she learned compassion from being discriminated against. (*Social Justice*)
- Jamie Sams hails compassion, caring, and loving as gateways to power, which applies to *Leadership*.
- Amelia Earhart finds *Spirituality* in kindness.
- St. Augustine views love as beauty of the soul. (*Spirituality*)
- Robert Muller and Maya Angelou connect forgiveness with *Peace* and *Happiness*.

CHAPTER 5

OBSERVING HUMAN NATURE

Every human has a reservoir of untapped potential.
—Colin O'Brady (1985)
American professional endurance athlete, motivational speaker,
Adventurer, and four-time triathlon world record holder

People at birth are inherently good.
—Chloé Zhao (1982)
Chinese filmmaker in her acceptance speech for best director
at the 2021 Academy Awards ceremony

Some of us learn from other people's mistakes,
and the rest of us have to be the other people.
—Zig Ziglar (1926–2012)
Author, salesman, sales trainer, and motivational speaker

The greatest tragedy of mankind comes from the inability of people
to have thoughtful disagreements to find out what is true.
—Ray Dalio (1949)
From *Principles: Life and Work*

All the faults of humanity are more pardonable
than the means employed to conceal them.
—Francois de la Rochefoucauld (1613–1680)

Things forbidden have a secret charm.
—Tacitus (56–120)
Senator and historian of the Roman Empire

We are all angels with only one wing.
We can only fly while embracing each other.
—Luciano De Crescenzo (1928)
Italian writer, film actor, director, and engineer

I have never met a man so ignorant
that I couldn't learn something from him.
—*Galileo Galilei (1564–1642)*

The reasonable man adapts himself to the world. The unreasonable
one persists in trying to adapt the world to himself. Therefore,
all progress depends on the unreasonable man.
—*George Bernard Shaw (1856–1950)*
Irish playwright, critic, polemicist, and political activist, from *Man and Superman*

The imperfections of man, his frailties, his faults, are just as
important as his virtues. You can't separate them. They are wedded.
—*Henry Miller (1891–1980)*
From *Ions Noetic Sciences Review* September 2001

Six mistakes mankind keeps making century after century: Believing
that personal gain is made by crushing others; Worrying about
things that cannot be changed or corrected; Insisting that a thing is
impossible because we cannot accomplish it; Refusing to set aside
trivial preferences; Neglecting development and refinement of the
mind; Attempting to compel others to believe and live as we do.
—*Marcus Tullius Cicero (106–43 BC)*
This analysis of human nature from more than 2,000 years ago
is just as relevant today as it was in Cicero's Rome

Good character is not formed in a week or a month.
It is created little by little, day by day. Protracted
and patient effort is needed to develop good character.
—*Heraclitus (535-475 BC)*
Greek pre-Socratic philosopher from Ephesus, at that time part of the Persian Empire,
now part of Turkey

You cannot hope to build a better world without improving
the individuals. To that end, each of us must work for our
own improvement.
—*Marie Curie (1867–1934)*

The deepest principle in human nature
is the craving to be appreciated.
—*William James (1842–1910)*

The deepest urge in human nature is the desire to be important.
—*Dale Carnegie (1888–1965)*
From *How To Win Friends & Influence People*

Most of the trouble in the world is
caused by people wanting to be important.
—*T.S. Eliot (1888–1965)*
British Nobel Prize-winning poet laureate, essayist, and playwright

Tact is the knack of making a point without making an enemy.
—*Sir Isaac Newton (1643–1727)*

When you walk with purpose, you collide with destiny.
—*Bertice Berry (1960)*
American sociologist, author, lecturer, and educator

The really great make you believe that you too, can become great.
—*Mark Twain (1835–1910)*
Birth name: Samuel L. Clemens
American writer, humorist, lecturer, and steamboat captain

When people are free to do as they please,
they usually imitate each other.
—*Eric Hoffer (1902–1983)*
American moral and social philosopher awarded
the Presidential Medal of Freedom in 1983

The most exquisite pleasure is giving pleasure to others.
—Jean de La Bruyere (1646–1696)
French philosopher

*Few men during their lifetime come anywhere near
exhausting the resources dwelling within them.
There are deep wells of strength that are never used.*
—Admiral Richard E. Byrd (1888–1957)
American naval officer and polar explorer famous for
his pioneering expeditions to Antarctica

It is not the mountain we conquer, but ourselves.
—George Mallory (1886–1924)
British mountaineer who died during his third attempt to reach the summit of Mt. Everest
and whose body was not found until 1999; this quote is often mistakenly attributed to
Sir Edmund Hilary

The journey is the thing.
—Homer (unknown, c. 1250–850 BC)
Legendary Greek poet who authored *The Odyssey* and *The Iliad*
lived and died before the Greeks recorded dates on calendars.
Great Minds Connect with Mihaly Csikszentmihalyi on page 318

*Only those who will risk going too far
can possibly find out how far one can go.*
—T.S. Eliot (1888–1965)
From *Four Quartets*

Nobody will believe in you unless you believe in yourself.
—Liberace (1919–1987)
Birth name: Wladziu Valentino Liberace
First professional name: Walter Busterkeys
Celebrity pianist, singer, and television personality known for his ostentatious costumes

Indeed, the condition of human nature is just this; man towers above the rest of creation so long as he realizes his own nature, and when he forgets it, he sinks lower than the beasts.
—Boethius (477–524)
From *The Consolation of Philosophy*

Truth is ever to be found in simplicity, and not in the multiplicity and confusion of things.
—Sir Isaac Newton (1643–1727)
Great Minds Connect with Lao Tzu on page 320, *Great Minds Think Alike: Simplicity* on page 166, and *Occam's Razor* on page 320

If you find a path with no obstacles, it probably doesn't lead anywhere.
—Frank A. Clark (1860–1935)
American lawyer, politician, and congressman

No pleasure lasts if unseasoned by variety.
—Publilius Syrus (85–40 BC)
This phrase is the precursor to the popular maxim
"Variety is the spice of life." A Syrian-born writer who was enslaved and taken to Italy during the reign of Julius Caesar, Syrus coined the iconic phrase
"A rolling stone gathers no moss"

It's hard to break something that bends.
—Bethany C. Meyers (1990)
American fitness and lifestyle trainer and LGBTQ activist

More is lost by indecision than wrong decision. Indecision is the thief of opportunity.
—Marcus Tullius Cicero (106–43 BC)

No persons are more frequently wrong than those who never admit they are wrong.
—François de la Rochefoucauld (1613–1680)

If you never change your mind, why have one?
—Edward de Bono (1933–2021)
Maltese physician, psychologist, philosopher, inventor, and
author of 85 books who originated the phrase "lateral thinking"

GREAT MINDS THINK ALIKE: *Change*

You cannot change what you do not acknowledge.
—Dr. Phil McGraw (1950)
American relationship and life strategy expert, television talk show host, and author.
The above quote is known as Life Law #4

Change is a process. More gradual implementation allows deeper shifts to occur and lays foundations of new lifelong habits.
—Dr. Nicola McFadzean
Naturopathic doctor specializing in treatment of Lyme disease

Progress is impossible without change, and those who cannot change their minds cannot change anything.
—George Bernard Shaw (1856–1950)

The foolish and the dead alone never change their opinions.
—James Russell Lowell (1819–1892)
American romantic poet, editor, and diplomat who also had a law degree.
Great Minds Connect with Georg Christoph Lichtenberg on page 111

Open your arms to change but don't let go of your values.
—14th Dalai Lama

Our sensitivity diminishes in proportion to the total amount of stimulation. If there are two candles lit in a room, we easily notice the difference in brightness when a third candle is lit. But if there are fifty candles burning, we are unlikely to notice the difference made by a fifty-first.
—Stephen Nachmanovitch (1950)
From his book *Free Play*

The weak can never forgive. Forgiveness is an attribute of the strong.
—Mohandas (Mahatma) Gandhi (1869–1948)

The road uphill and the road downhill are one and the same.
—Heraclitus (535–475 BC)

Hatred is the coward's revenge for being intimidated.
—George Bernard Shaw (1856–1950)

Rudeness is the weak man's imitation of strength.
—Eric Hoffer (1902–1983)

Weapons themselves can tempt a man to fight.
—Homer (unknown, c. 1250–850 BC)

GREAT MINDS THINK ALIKE: *Indifference*

The worst sin towards our fellow-creatures is not to hate them but to be indifferent to them. That is the essence of inhumanity.
—George Bernard Shaw (1856-1950)

The opposite of love is not hate, it's indifference.
The opposite of art is not ugliness, it's indifference.
The opposite of faith is not heresy, it's indifference.
And the opposite of life is not death, it's indifference.
—Elie Wiesel (1928–2016)
Romanian-born Holocaust survivor who became an American writer, professor, political activist, and winner of the Nobel Peace Prize, as quoted in the September 27, 1986 issue of *U.S. News and World Report*

There is only one thing in the world worse than being talked about, and that is not being talked about.
—Oscar Wilde (1854–1900)
Irish poet and playwright

People who love to eat are always the best people.
—Julia Child (1912–2004)
From *My Life in France*

People hear better with their eyes closed.
—Kay Gardner (1940–2002)
American musician, composer, producer, and author known for using music as a healing modality

On Earth, things are either green & growing, or ripe & rotting.
When you think you have all the answers, you are ripe & rotting.
—*Sun Tzu (544–496 BC)*
From his military masterpiece *The Art of War*

Life consists not in holding good cards,
but in playing well those you do hold.
—*Josh Billings (1818–1885)*
Birth name: Henry Wheeler Shaw
A 19th-century American humorist and lecturer often compared to Mark Twain

Neglect mending a small fault and it will soon be
a large one. A small leak will sink a great ship.
—*Benjamin Franklin (1706–1790)*

When I consider what tremendous consequences come from little
things, I am tempted to think that there are no little things.
—*Bruce Fairchild Barton (1886–1967)*
American author, advertising executive, and politician

Young people tend to waste all attempts of our elders
to relay to us wisdom accumulated over the decades.
—*Ana Castillo (1953)*
Chicana (American-born but of Mexican descent) novelist, poet, short story writer,
essayist, editor, playwright, translator, and independent scholar

Great are those who have not lost their childlike heart.
—*Meng Ke, aka Mencius (372–289 BC)*
Itinerant Chinese philosopher, sage, and eminent interpreter of Confucianism

Whoever gossips to you will gossip about you.
—*Philip Sydney (1554–1586)*
English poet, scholar, and soldier of the Elizabethan Age

No one can make you feel inferior without your own consent.
—*Eleanor Roosevelt (1884–1962)*
This well-known quote points out that freedom of thought
can never be taken from us unless we allow it

Fair play is not blaming others for anything that is wrong with us.
—*Eric Hoffer (1902–1983)*

Surface characteristics that are extreme are always camouflaging a shadow or opposite characteristic. That which we do not confront in ourselves we will meet as fate time and again in a thousand disguises on the paths of life.
—*Carl Jung (1875–1961)*
Swiss psychiatrist, psychoanalyst, author, and direct disciple of Sigmund Freud

I must create a system or be enslaved by another man's.
—*William Blake (1757–1827)*
Innovative English poet, painter, and engraver

You cannot enslave a mind that knows itself.
—*Wangari Maathal (1940–2011)*
Kenyan environmental political activist and Nobel laureate, from *Kaleidoscope*

<u>GREAT MINDS THINK ALIKE: *The Power of Thought*</u>

Day by day, what you choose, what you think and what you do is who you become.
—*Heraclitus (535–475 BC)*

What we steadily, consciously, habitually think we are, we tend to become.
—*Ann Landers (1918–2002)*
Birth name: Esther Pauline "Eppie" Lederer
Advice columnist and celebrity with readership of over 90 million

The consummate truth of life is that we alter our destiny by altering our thoughts.
—*Dennis Deaton (1946)*

GREAT MINDS THINK ALIKE: *Judging Character*

We can judge the heart of a man by his treatment of animals.
—Emanuel Kant (1724–1804)

***You can easily judge the character of a man
by how he treats those who can do nothing for him.***
—Johann Wolfgang von Goethe (1749–1832)

The true test of a person's breeding is how they behave in a quarrel.
—George Bernard Shaw (1856–1950)

When one person tells a lie, countless others tell it as a truth.
—Zen proverb from Zen Wisdom

Maturity of mind is the capacity to endure uncertainty.
—John Huston Finley (1863–1940)
Professor of politics at Princeton University, president of City College
of New York, and NY State commissioner of education

It is possible for ordinary people to choose to be extraordinary.
—Elon Musk (1971)

***Extraordinary people survive under the most terrible circumstances
and become more extraordinary because of it.***
—Robertson Davies (1913–1995)
Canadian novelist, playwright, journalist, and professor

What does not destroy me makes me stronger.
—Friedrich Nietzsche (1844–1900)
Famous phrase from *Twilight of the Idols*

***Life sometimes brings enormous difficulties and challenges that seem
too hard to bear. But bear them you can, and bear them you will,
so your life can have a purpose.***
—Barbara Walters (1929–2022)
American broadcast journalist, author, and television icon known for decades
of high profile interviews, as quoted in *Good News Network*

GREAT MINDS THINK ALIKE: *Defusing Enemies*

He is wise who can make a friend of a foe.
—John Ray (1627–1705)
English author of botany, zoology, and theology books also credited as coining the phrase
"What's good for the goose is good for the gander."

Do I not destroy my enemies when I make them my friends?
—Abraham Lincoln (1809–1865)
President of the United States who was assassinated in the Ford Theatre
shortly after the end of the Civil War

Illusion is in the eye of the beholder.
—Marlo Morgan (1937)
As spoken by Apalie in Morgan's novel *Mutant Message From Forever*

It is when you feel most secure that you become most vulnerable to surprise.
—Sun Tzu (544–496 BC)
From multiple translations of *The Art of War*

Every time reason stands against the human, the human will stand against the reason.
–Thomas Hobbes (1588–1679)
English philosopher who formulated the concept of
the social contract, from *The Ethics of Hobbes*

Where the mind is past hope, the heart is past shame.
—John Lyly (1553–1606)
English poet, dramatist, and courtier

The amount of stress in your life is determined by how much energy you expend resisting your life.
—Gary Zukav (1942)
American spiritual teacher and best-selling author, from *The Heart of the Soul,*
that he co-authored with his wife, Linda Francis

It's as though we have two selves or two natures or two wills with two contrary viewpoints. Your lower self sees you as the center of the universe, while your higher self sees you as a cell in the body of humanity.

—Peace Pilgrim (1908–1981)
Birth name: Mildred Lisette Norman
American spiritual teacher, mystic, pacifist, and peace activist
from *The Sun* magazine April 2012

We are healed by our suffering, only by experiencing it to the full.

—Marcel Proust (1871–1922)
French novelist, critic, and essayist

*We all die. The goal isn't to live forever.
The goal is to create something that will.*

—Voltaire (1694–1778)

*Evil eventually destroys itself. Anyone who employs it
to gain his ends is always himself damaged by it.*

—Wu Wei
A Taoist concept that arose from Confucianism, from *I Ching Wisdom Volumes I and II;*
the author of these books identifies as Wu Wei

*It is looking at things for a long time that ripens you
and gives you a standing.*

—Vincent van Gogh (1853–1890)
Dutch impressionist painter famous for cutting off his own ear.
Great Minds Connect with Leonardo da Vinci on page 157

The eyes see only what the mind is prepared to comprehend.

—Robertson Davies (1913–1995)

It's not what you look at that matters. It's what you see.

—Henry David Thoreau (1817–1862)

Only the mediocre are always at their best.
—Jean Giraudoux (1882–1944)
French diplomat and writer

***One's destination is never a place, but rather
a new way of looking at things.***
—Henry Miller (1891–1980)
in *Ions Noetic Sciences Review* September 2001

The price of greatness is responsibility
—Sir Winston Churchill (1874–1965)
British army officer, two-time British prime minister, lifetime politician, and writer

Habit is stronger than reason.
—George Santayana (1863–1952)

The greatest deception men suffer is from their own opinions.
—Leonardo da Vinci (1452–1519)
The ultimate Renaissance man famous for his inventions, sketches, paintings, architecture,
scientific discoveries, engineering innovations, literature, anatomical drawings, and
observations of natural phenomena; he was considered by many to have been the greatest
genius who ever lived

Empty souls tend to possess extreme opinions.
—William Butler Yeats (1865–1939)
Irish poet and co-founder of the Abbey Theatre

Attention is the rarest and purist form of generosity.
—Simone Weil (1909–1943)
French philosopher, teacher, mystic, and political activist

To preserve what we have, we should give generously.
—I Ching (compiled 1000–500 BC)

It is in giving that we receive.
—*St. Francis of Assisi (1181–1226)*
Birth name: Giovanni di Pietro di Bernardone
Revered Italian Catholic friar, deacon, and mystic

The greatest form of charity is anonymity.
—*George Steinbrenner, III (1930–2010)*
Shipping magnate and outspoken majority owner of the New York Yankees

**Charity is injurious, unless it helps the recipient
to become independent of it.**
—*John D. Rockefeller Sr. (1839–1937)*

**Loneliness is the way by which destiny
endeavors to lead man to himself.**
—*Herman Hesse (1877–1962)*
Nobel Prize-winning German novelist, poet, and painter best known
for his books *Steppenwolf, Siddhartha*, and *Demian*

A luxury once enjoyed becomes a necessity.
—*C. Northcote Parkinson (1909–1993)*
British naval historian and author of 60 books from *The Week* magazine March 24, 2017

We cannot direct the wind, but we can adjust the sails.
—*Bertha Calloway (1925–2017)*
African American community activist, historian, and founder of
the Great Plains Black Museum and the Negro History Society

Too much agreement kills a chat.
—*Eldridge Cleaver (1935–1998)*
African American social activist and writer, who also served as editor of the magazine
published by the Black Panther Party

The more you try to avoid something, the more you tend to attract it.
—*Dennis Deaton (1946)*

Life appears to me too short to be spent in nursing animosity or
registering wrongs.
—*Charlotte Bronte (1816–1855)*
British novelist and poet

A person who pursues revenge needs to dig two graves.
The origin of this phrase is murky, as it has been credited to Confucius but also may be an
English or Japanese proverb; regardless, the concept that revenge also hurts the avenger
is universally accepted

A man's real worth is determined by what he does
when he has nothing to do.
—*Megiddo Message* magazine

Leisure time is for doing something useful.
—*Benjamin Franklin (1706–1790)*

A primary reason people believe life is getting worse is because our
information about the problems of the world has steadily improved.
—*Ray Kurzweil (1948)*
From his book *How to Create a Mind*

Every fish that gets away appears larger than it was.
—*Turkish proverb*

Everything that irritates us about others
can lead us to an understanding of ourselves.
—*Carl Jung (1875–1961)*
From *Memories, Dreams, Reflections*

It is not necessary to understand things in order to argue about them.
—*Pierre Beaumarchais (1732–1799)*
French watchmaker, inventor, playwright, musician, diplomat, publisher, horticulturist,
spy, arms dealer, satirist, financier, and revolutionary both in France and America

Almost anything is easier to get into than to get out of.
—*Agnes Allen (1894–1986)*
This phrase is popularly known as Allen's law. Agnes Allen was the second wife of well-
known historian Frederick Lewis Allen, the long-time editor of *Harper's Magazine*. They
married in 1932 and published many books together. Agnes published a number of books
as Agnes Rogers.

If the only tool you have is a hammer,
you tend to see every problem as a nail.
—*Abraham Maslow (1908–1970)*
From *The Psychology of Science: A Reconnaissance*

I made this letter longer than usual because
I lack the time to make it shorter.
—*Blaise Pascal (1623–1662)*
French mathematician, inventor, physicist, and Catholic
theologian who invented the mechanical calculator

It's human nature to think wisely
and then act in an absurd fashion.
—*Anatole France (1844–1924)*
Nobel Prize-winning French novelist, poet, and journalist

You become what you practice most.
—*Richard Carlson, PhD (1961–2006)*
American psychotherapist, author, and motivational speaker,
from his book *Don't Sweat The Small Stuff*

We have two lives, and the second life begins
when we realize we only have one.
—Confucius (551–479 BC)

Life is not measured by the number of breaths we take,
but by the moments that take our breath away.
—Maya Angelou (1928–2014)
Birth name: Marguerite Annie Johnson
American poet, playwright, screenplay writer, and civil rights activist

To be able to look back upon one's life in satisfaction is to live twice.
—Kahlil Gibran (1883–1931)
Legendary Lebanese American writer and poet, from *The Prophet*

In the end, it is impossible not to become
what others believe you are.
—Julius Caesar (100–44 BC)
Military general and statesman whose rule of Rome led to the rise of the Roman Empire; his colorful life and bloody assassination was immortalized in a play by William Shakespeare

We shall not cease from exploration
and the end of all our exploring will be
to arrive where we started
and know the place for the first time.
—T.S. Eliot (1888–1965)
From his poem *Little Gidding*

We are all better than we know. If only we can be brought to realize
this, we may never be prepared to settle for anything less.
—Kurt Hahn (1886–1974)
German educator with a unique educational philosophy

No one is more profoundly sad than he who laughs too much.
—Jean Paul Richter (1763–1825)
German romance writer of novels and short stories

Greatness lives in one who triumphs equally
over defeat and victory.
—*John Steinbeck (1902–1968)*
Nobel Prize-winning author of numerous classic novels,
from *The Acts of King Arthur and His Noble Knights*

Humans are just like fireflies; even in the darkness everyone has
a light, but each person must choose to let it shine.
—*Jamie Sams (1951)*
From *Dancing the Dream*

Human intelligence evolved because it was useful for survival.
—*Ray Kurzweil (1948)*

Everybody can be great, because everybody can serve.
—*Martin Luther King Jr. (1929–1968)*

Life gives you plenty of time to do whatever you
want to do if you stay in the present moment.
—*Deepak Chopra (1946)*

The advantage of growing old is that you become
aware of your mistakes more quickly.
—*Pierre-Auguste Renoir (1841–1919)*
Renowned French impressionist painter

Children have never been very good at listening to their elders,
but they have never failed to imitate them.
—*James Baldwin (1924–1987)*
From *Nobody Knows My Name*

He who tries to please everybody labors in vain.
—*Latin proverb*

Young people have a very special view of all problems.
They have a certain very healthy recklessness.
—This statement was made by a German educator in
National Geographic's documentary film *Science Fair*

Some people are old at 18 and some are young at 90.
Time is a concept that humans created.
—*Yoko Ono (1933)*
Japanese singer, songwriter, multimedia artist, and peace activist most famous for being
John Lennon's wife. *Great Minds Connect* with Julian Barbour & Deepak Chopra
on page 28 and Lucretius on page 280

If you don't act on your beliefs,
you don't really know if you believe them at all.
—*Victor Hugo (1802–1885)*
French playwright, poet, essayist, and novelist most famous for writing
The Hunchback of Notre Dame and *Les Miserables*

GREAT MINDS THINK ALIKE: *Worry*

My life has been filled with terrible misfortune, most of which never happened.
—*Michel de Montaigne (1533–1592)*
Prominent philosopher, author, and statesman of the French Renaissance

I've had a lot of worries in my life, most of which never happened.
—*Mark Twain (1835–1910)*

Worry means the mind is controlling you. Worry is always pointless.
A solution never comes out of worry.
—*Eckhart Tolle (1948)*
German-born Canadian spiritual teacher and best-selling author

Happy is the man who has broken the chains which hurt the mind,
and has given up worrying once and for all.
—*Ovid (43 BC–17 AD)*

Don't worry, be happy.
—*Bobby McFerrin (1950)*
American jazz and folk vocalist and teacher, from his song of the same name

By forgiving others, the forgiver is the one who is freed...and just as you must learn how to forgive others, you must also learn how to forgive yourself.

Rose, the Aboriginal healer in Gary Holz's novel *Secrets of Aboriginal Healing*

The first step towards getting somewhere is to decide that you are not going to stay where you are.

—J.P. Morgan (1837–1913)

The most iconic financier and banker in American history

The four great settings in which the fundamental values of human existence are played out: truth, beauty, justice and love.

—Luc Ferry (1951)

from *A Brief History of Thought*

Foundations can well be risk-takers on man's cultural and intellectual and humanitarian frontiers.

—William K. Kellogg (1860–1951)

American businessman, breakfast cereal innovator, Arabian horse breeder, and philanthropist who founded the Kellogg Company after revising a cereal created by his brother John at the Battle Creek Sanitarium to develop Corn Flakes. C.W. Post was also a patient at the sanitarium and stole Kellogg's recipes to start the Postum Cereal Company that later evolved into General Foods, now owned by daughter Marjorie Merriweather Post. The resulting feud between Kellogg and C.W. Post lasted more than 20 years.

Between stimulus and response there is a space. In that space is our power to choose our response. In our response lies our growth and our freedom. Our greatest freedom is the freedom to choose our attitude.

—Viktor Frankl (1905–1997)

From his book *Man's Search for Meaning*

Nearly all men can stand adversity, but if you want to test a man's character, give him power.

—Abraham Lincoln (1809–1865)

Gratitude is not only the greatest of virtues,
but the parent of all others.
—*Marcus Tullius Cicero (106–43 BC)*

To children, heaven is being an adult,
and to adults, heaven is being children again.
—*Diane Ackerman (1948)*
Poet, essayist, and prolific author best known for writing *The Zookeepers Wife*
(later adapted into a movie), from her book *Deep Play*

GREAT MINDS THINK ALIKE: *Ancestors*

To understand and reconnect with our stories,
the stories of the ancestors, is to build our identities.
—*Frank Delaney (1942–2017)*
Irish novelist, playwright, and BBC broadcaster

Whatever you are is because of what your ancestors have done.
—*Li Lu (1966)*
Chinese-born American businessman, author, and
philanthropist who founded Himalaya Capital Management

It's in community that our species finds its strength and survival.
Society should be based upon cooperation rather than competition ...
Homo sapiens look a lot like a species that has lost its way.
—*Christopher Ryan (1962)*
From his book *Civilized To Death*.
Great Minds Connect with William Ophuls on page 236. Ryan and Ophuls share the belief
that civilization is moving in a direction that is unhealthy and unsustainable.

The beauty of a woman is seen in her eyes because
that is the doorway to her heart.
—*Audrey Hepburn (1929–1993)*
Belgian-born film and fashion icon who became a prominent humanitarian later in life

Nothing is either good or bad, but thinking makes it so.
—*William Shakespeare (1564–1616)*
From his theatrical classic *Hamlet*

Natural and manmade disasters liberate its surviving victims from an oppressive normalcy.
—Charles E. Fritz (1921–2000)
American scientist and U.S. Army Air Force captain who engaged in extensive disaster research at the end of WWII that revealed the remarkable resilience of survivors

Disaster is sometimes a door back into paradise.
—Rebecca Solnit (1961)
American historian, writer, and activist, from her book *A Paradise Built in Hell: The Extraordinary Communities That Arise in Disaster*. This highlights the fact that disasters often lead to a temporary state of social utopia in which people cooperate, support, and help each other on an ideal level.

There are two great days in a person's life—the day we are born and the day we discover why.
—William Barkley (1907–1978)
Scottish religious scholar, minister, professor, and author of numerous books on religion

Every generation declares war on its parents and makes friends with its grandparents.
—Igor Stravinsky (1882–1971)
Russian composer, pianist, and conductor who was a major force in the evolution of modern music; Stravinsky eventually acquired citizenship in France and then the United States

Most of us spend too much time on what is urgent and not enough time on what is important.
—Stephen Covey (1932–2012)
American educator, author, and keynote speaker, from
The 7 Habits of Highly Effective People

All of humanity's problems stem from man's inability to sit quietly in a room alone.
—Blaise Pascal (1623–1662)
From his posthumously published work *Pensées*

The most basic of all human needs is the need to understand and be understood. The best way to understand people is to listen to them.
—Ralph G. Nichols
Known as the "father of listening," he originated and developed the science of listening

No one rises to low expectations.
—Les Brown (1943)
African American author and motivational speaker

All power is based on perception. If you think you've got it, then you've got it. If you think you don't have it, even if you have it, then you don't have it. In short, you have more power if you believe you have power and view your life's encounters as negotiations.
—Herb Cohen (1938)
American motivational speaker and consultant considered by many to be the world's greatest negotiator, from his book, *You Can Negotiate Anything.* Cohen added:
In geopolitics, the perception that you're willing to take risks and exercise power may prevent opportunism by a potential aggressor.

Self-reverence, self-knowledge, self-control. These three alone lead life to sovereign power.
—Alfred Lord Tennyson (1809–1892)

A lot of times, people don't know what they want until you show it to them.
—Steve Jobs (1955–2011)
Visionary technology pioneer, co-founder of Apple Inc., creator of the iPhone and numerous other computer-driven devices, and driving force behind the rise of Pixar Animation Studios

When you've learned to draw upon your subconscious powers, there's really no limit to what you can accomplish.
—Angela Lansbury (1925–2022)
Irish-British and American actress with a star on the Hollywood Walk of Fame, a Tony Award, and a Golden Globe

You can't change anyone else, but people do change in relationship to your change. All relationships are a system, and when any one part of a system changes, it affects the other part.
–Jack Canfield (1944)

Author of the *Chicken Soup for the Soul* series of books that have been translated into 43 languages in more than 100 countries, and sold more than 500 million copies worldwide

If you change the way you look at things, the things you look at change.
–Dr. Wayne Dyer (1940–2015)

Prolific self-help author and motivational speaker

All that you touch, you change.
All that you change changes you.
The only lasting truth is change.
–Octavia Butler (1947–2006)

Highly acclaimed African American science fiction writer

You don't have to teach people to be human.
You have to teach them how to stop being inhuman.
–Eldridge Cleaver (1935–1998)

Neuroscientists have proved that stories can deeply influence our beliefs and decisions, mainly because stories appeal to our emotions and our capacity for empathy.
–Rebecca Matter

President of the American Writers and Artists Institute, as quoted in an email sent by *Writers Digest*

CONSOLIDATING CHAPTER 5
Observing Human Nature

This chapter encompasses the steaming cauldron that comprises all human activity, with a broad mixture of its splendor and imperfections on full display. All wisdom is intrinsic to human nature, as is all human folly. The phrases of Chapter 5 are insightful observations about the behavior and cogitations of our species throughout history. Although human nature resides at the center of all wisdom disciplines, due to its mercurial tendencies, human nature also reserves the right to ignore all wisdom teachings and flounder in its own imperfection.

If all the categories of this book were a tree, *Observing Human Nature* would comprise the roots and the trunk. All other categories would be branches, with each wisdom phrase serving as a precious leaf. When taking an overall view of Chapter 5, it becomes clear human nature is the hub for all categories, as all human activity arises from our basic nature. It's our basic nature to dream, love, play, and innovate. It's also human nature to seek some degree of spirituality and creativity. The balance between courage and fear often determines our progress. Artistic endeavors evolve from dreams, play, and creativity, as do sports, business, science, and technology. All the above elements operate under the umbrella of human nature. They have combined to create our history and basis for political, governmental, and educational systems, as well as innumerable destructive wars. How we manage these aspects of our nature will determine the destiny of our species.

Essentially, the ultimate purpose of wisdom is to contribute to the improvement of human nature. Due to the vast diversity of our planet, human experiences on different continents and within different social strata lead to disagreements about almost everything, including the veracity of truth and factual information. These differing perspectives also apply to wisdom teachings. Although you may not agree with all statements made in this chapter, it's nonetheless important to be aware of the ideas and concepts they represent. While all humans will never reach full agreement on any issue, increasing awareness and understanding creates a greater likelihood of finding productive compromises and reducing global hostility.

Freedom of thought is a foundational and stabilizing component of human existence. In Eleanor Roosevelt's famous quote, she expresses the universal truth that no one can control your thoughts unless you allow them to. While the accuracy of her statement is universally accepted, many suffer the pain of failing to heed its wisdom.

As the foundation of all other categories, *Observing Human Nature* emerges as a universally connective category, but most directly, human nature drives history and is always in need of *Practical Advice*. Chapter 5 also highlights the importance of thoughtful disagreement, the joy of pleasing others, the necessity of believing in ourselves as a prerequisite for others to believe in us, and how our thoughts shape our health as well as our life paths. This chapter also warns that the concealment of faults is often worse than the faults themselves, and the need to feel important is a major cause of distress in the world. We are also advised about the necessity to push against perceived boundaries when striving to reach our potential. Chapter 5 concludes with Christopher Ryan's concern that humanity is on a hazardous path to self-destruction based on his underlying premise that civilization is not natural to human nature. In his book *Civilized To Death*, Ryan builds a strong case for the theory that we are fundamentally a hunter-gatherer species now finding ourselves entangled in an ever more complicated web of civilized ailments. While it's unrealistic to steer humanity back to hunting and gathering, Ryan's deep dive into the true nature of Homo sapiens offers some valuable hints about how we might redirect aspects of civilization to better serve the modern human condition. Other takeaways from Chapter 5:

- Any path worth taking will have obstacles you must overcome.
- Flexibility is a key component of mental health that helps prevent people and material objects from breaking, which means inflexible opinions are potentially destructive.
- Forgiving others and admitting when we are wrong are signs of strength.
- Indifference has the ability to inflict more pain than hatred.
- Too much laughter is often a telltale sign of unhappiness.
- Turning enemies into friends is a great victory.
- Fully experiencing suffering opens the door to healing.
- Habit often overwhelms reason.
- Greatness brings on responsibility.
- Giving your attention to others is a form of generosity.

Chapter 5 also advises us to embrace criticism as opportunity for growth, never to blame others for our shortcomings, and not let others distort our self-image. When others irritate us, we are advised to take a look inside ourselves to explore our underlying issues. Not surprisingly, human nature works its way into every wisdom category.

WISDOM TRAILS: *Interconnected Categories*
History, Business, Politics, Government, War, Work, Love, Faith, The Arts, Health, Innovation, Technology, Wisdom, Sports, Nature, Happiness, Social Justice

Trails to Other Chapters
- Cicero's list of mistakes humanity has made throughout *History* applies to *Business, Government, Politics and War.*

- Homer's ominous statement that the possession of weapons can cause people to fight is applicable to *Government* and *War.*
- Ray Kurzweil explains why *Technology* causes people to believe life is getting worse.
- Elie Wiesel defines indifference as the opposite of *Love, Art,* and *Faith.*
- Luc Ferry lists the four great settings of human existence as truth, beauty, *Justice,* and *Love.*
- Eric Hoffer discusses fair *Play.*
- William James views craving as the nemesis of *Happiness.*
- Dale Carnegie pits the desire to be important against *Happiness.*
- Lao Tzu reminds us that a thousand-mile journey begins with one step, as does the road to *Success* and the *Education* of a mind.
- Ovid advises that ridding oneself of worry leads to *Happiness.*
- A Latin proverb warns us that trying to please everyone will interfere with achieving *Success.*
- Ray Kurzweil points out human intelligence evolved because it was useful for survival; in this instance, the phrase human intelligence is synonymous with *Creativity.*
- Sun Tzu observes that when people feel secure, they are vulnerable to surprise. This applies to *Sports, Government,* and *War.*
- Bobby McFerrin's song advises us not to worry so we can be *Happy.*
- John Steinbeck finds greatness in defeat as well as victory, which connects with *Sports, Government, Politics,* and *War.*
- Abraham Lincoln's advice on judging character applies to *Work, Business, Leadership, Sports, Politics, Government,* and *War.*
- Frank Delaney and Li Lu discuss the value of studying our ancestors. *(History)*
- Herb Cohen's concept of power directly applies to *Work, Business, Sports, Politics, Government,* and *War.*

CHAPTER 6

COURAGE, FEAR & DOUBT

The secret to happiness is freedom...
and the secret to freedom is courage.
—*Thucydides (460–400 BC)*
Athenian historian who was a general during the Peloponnesian War

You will never do anything in this world without courage.
It is the greatest quality of the mind next to honor.
—*Aristotle (384–322 BC)*

Courage is knowing what not to fear.
—*Plato (429–347 BC)*
Disciple of Socrates, mentor of Aristotle, and founder of The Academy,
the first institution of higher learning in the Western World

GREAT MINDS THINK ALIKE: *What Is Courage?*

Courage is resistance to fear, mastery of fear,
but not absence of fear.
—*Mark Twain (1835–1910)*

Courage is not the absence of fear. It is the making of action in spite
of fear, the moving out against the resistance engendered
by fear into the unknown and into the future.
—*M. Scott Peck (1936–2005)*
From *The Road Less Traveled*

Nothing in life is to be feared, it is only to be understood.
Now is the time to understand more, so that we may fear less.
—*Marie Curie (1867–1934)*

A man of courage is also full of faith.
—*Marcus Tullius Cicero (106–43 BC)*

One man with courage makes a majority.
—*Andrew Jackson (1767–1845)*
Revered soldier, army general, congressman, and
seventh president of the United States

*The dynamic tensions between our drives and our fears
create the theatre of our lives.*
—Dan Millman (1946)

*We can easily forgive a child who is afraid of the dark.
The real tragedy of life is when adults are afraid of the light.*
—Plato (429–347 BC)

GREAT MINDS THINK ALIKE: *Different Sides of Fear*

He who fears he shall suffer already suffers what he fears.
—Michel de Montaigne (1533–1592)

The fear of suffering is worse than the suffering itself.
—Paulo Coelho (1947)
From *The Alchemist*

Fear does not prevent death, it prevents life.
—Naguib Mahfouz (1911–2006)

*Action defeats fear...there is some kind of action for every kind of
fear. Hesitation only magnifies the fear.*
—David J. Schwartz (1927–1987)
From his book *The Magic of Thinking Big*

We have nothing to fear but fear itself.
—Franklin D. Roosevelt (1882-1945)
The only four-time president of the United States served from 1932 until his death
in 1945; his famous statement about fear was inspired by Thoreau's phrase
Nothing is so much to be feared as fear.
—Henry David Thoreau (1817–1862)

*It often takes more courage to change one's opinion
than to stick to it.*
—Georg Christoph Lichtenberg (1742–1799)
The physicist and satirist was the first German to hold a professorship in experimental
physics. *Great Minds Connect* with *Great Minds Think Alike: Change* on page 87

*The bravest are surely those who have the clearest vision of what
is before them, glory and danger alike, and yet notwithstanding,
go out to meet it.*
—Thucydides (460–400 BC)

A man with outward courage dares to die.
A man with inner courage dares to live.
—*Lao Tzu (571–unknown BC)*

I have learned over the years that when one's mind is made up, this
diminishes fear; knowing what must be done does away with fear.
—*Rosa Parks (1913–2005)*
American civil rights activist declared by Congress
to be "the mother of the freedom movement"

Don't ever make decisions based on fear. Make decisions based on
hope and possibility. Make decisions based on what should happen,
not what shouldn't.
—*Michelle Obama (1964)*
Former first lady of the United States, attorney, speaker, and author

There's nothing wrong with fear. The only mistake
is to let it stop you in your tracks.
—*Twyla Tharp (1941)*
From her book *The Creative Habit*

Courage means to seize opportunities
that make certain of victory, without vacillation.
—*Sun Tzu (544–496 BC)*
From *The Art of War*

If you have the courage to begin, you have the courage to succeed.
—*David Viscott (1938–1996)*
American psychiatrist, author, businessman, and media personality

Life shrinks or expands in proportion to one's courage.
—*Anais Nin (1903–1977)*

Have the courage to say no. Have the courage to face the truth.
Do the right thing because it is right. These are the magic keys to
living your life with integrity.
—*William Clement Stone (1902–2002)*
American businessman, philanthropist, and self-help author

May your choices reflect your hopes, not your fears.
—*Nelson Mandela (1918–2013)*

GREAT MINDS THINK ALIKE: *Defeating Fear*

Feeling fear, or not feeling fear is not the issue...
what matters, is not to let the fear stop you.
—*Prince William Marshal, First Earl of Pembroke (1146–1219)*
Legendary Anglo Norman soldier, statesman, and undefeated knight
who served five English kings, as quoted in in *Swordsmen, Saints, and Scholars*

I've been absolutely terrified every moment of my life, but I've never
let it keep me from doing a single thing I wanted to do.
—*Georgia O'Keeffe (1887–1986)*
Painter who was considered the "mother of American modernism"

A good scare is worth more to a man than good advice.
—*Edgar Watson Howe (1853–1937)*
Novelist and newspaper and magazine editor

The desire for safety stands against
every great and noble enterprise.
—*Tacitus (56–120)*

Even in a world that's being shipwrecked, remain brave and strong.
—*Hildegard of Bingen (1098–1179)*
Also known as Saint Hildegard
German abbess, writer, philosopher, mystic, and first known female composer
renowned for her frequent visions

Humans cannot exist if everything that is unpleasant is eliminated instead of understood.
—*Marlo Morgan (1937)*
From her controversial book about Aboriginal Australians, *Mutant Message Down Under*

What you may not realize is that when you judge another person, you do not define them. You define yourself as someone who needs to judge others.
—*Dr. Wayne Dyer (1940–2015)*
From *10 Secrets for Success and Inner Peace*

If we begin with certainties, we shall end in doubts; but if we begin with doubts and are patient, we shall end with certainties.
—*Francis Bacon (1561–1626)*
British viscount, parliamentarian, and philosopher
considered "father of the scientific method"

GREAT MINDS THINK ALIKE: *The Pitfalls of Doubt*

One of the most important skills we can develop is the mental and emotional strength to ignore the doubters and critics, and strive on to achieve our dreams.
—*Dennis Deaton (1946)*
Motivational speaker and founder of Quma learning systems,
from *Quma Inspirations Volume 5, No. 93*

Fear, doubt and worry are among the greatest obstacles not only to success, but to happiness as well.
—*T. Harv Eker (1954)*
From his book *Secrets of the Millionaire Mind*

Doubt is a killer. You just have to know who you are and what you stand for.
—*Jennifer Lopez (1969)*
World-famous American celebrity, singer, dancer, and actress

The trouble with the world is that the ignorant are sure they have the truth, while the intelligent are full of doubt.
—*Bertrand Russell (1872-1970)*
Nobel laureate British philosopher, writer, and political activist

Courage is what it takes to stand up and speak. Courage is also what it takes to sit down and listen.
—*Sir Winston Churchill (1874–1965)*
Although widely attributed to Churchill, there is considerable debate as to whether he ever made this statement

GREAT MINDS THINK ALIKE: *Doubt Can Be Useful*

The beginning of wisdom is found in doubting; by doubting we come to the question, and by seeking we may come upon the truth.
—*Peter Abelard (1079–1142)*

Doubt is not to be feared, but welcomed and discussed, and to demand this freedom is our duty to all coming generations.
—*Richard P. Feynman (1918–1988)*
Nobel prize-winning American theoretical physicist and author, from his book *What Do You Care What Other People Think?* Doubt can serve as constructive dissent. *Great Minds Connect* with *Great Minds Think Alike: Welcoming Dissent* on page 143 and J. Robert Oppenheimer on page 37

I do not know myself. No sooner have I discovered something than I begin to doubt it and I have to destroy it again. What we do is just a shadow of what we want to do, and the only truths we can point to are the ever-changing truths of our own experience.
—*Jean-Paul Marat (1743–1793)*
French political theorist, physician, and scientist who became a journalist and politician during the French Revolution

Courage is the power to let go of the familiar.
—*Dr. Raymond Lindquist (1907–2001)*
Noteworthy Presbyterian minister who served as pastor of the Presbyterian Church of Hollywood for a number of years

The person who risks nothing, does nothing, has nothing, is nothing, and becomes nothing. He may avoid suffering and sorrow, but he simply cannot learn, feel, change, grow or love. Chained by his certitude, he is a slave; he has forfeited his freedom. Only the person who risks is truly free.
—*Leo Buscaglia (1924–1998)*
Bestselling American author, motivational speaker, and professor of special education, also known as Dr. Love. *Great Minds Connect* with Muhammad Ali on page 199 and Mark Zuckerberg on page 128

CONSOLIDATING CHAPTER 6
Courage, Fear & Doubt

Chapter 6 explores the intimate connection between fear and courage. It should be noted that courage and fear are basic elements of human nature, transforming this whole chapter into a significant subdivision of Chapter 5. Doubt was included in this chapter because of its ability to influence fear and courage. This chapter informs us fear arises from the presence of an impending threat or conflict...accompanied by resistance from the perception of some degree of danger, injury, or risk of loss. The quotes in this chapter depict fear as a universal emotion, an emotion we need to master rather than be ashamed of. The key is not to let fear paralyze us. That's where courage enters the scenario as fear's primary antidote capable of preventing fear from becoming a destructive adversary. Interestingly enough, courage is dependent on fear for its existence. If no fear needs to be overcome, then courage has no basis for existence, as courage can only be measured by the amount of fear and danger it encounters. The possibility of fear and courage coexisting in the same moment helps clarify fear as an entity we must manage rather than obliterate. This leads to an interesting relationship between courage and change, because it takes courage to make changes by overcoming the fear of venturing into unfamiliar territory. Such courage requires a spirit of adventure for change to blossom. Another element in this process is the introduction of play. By its ability to lower fear thresholds, play assists courage, thereby allowing creative thought processes to flourish.

The *Doubt* section of Chapter 6 features some differences of opinion among its contributors. This is largely because there is a duality to doubt; it possesses beneficial assets and as well as treacherous pitfalls. Doubt is touted as the beginning of wisdom by Peter Abelard and praised by physicist Richard P. Feynman as a thought process to be welcomed. Francis Bacon also takes a positive stance on doubt, praising its power when combined with patience. Referring back to Chapter 2, J. Robert Oppenheimer describes doubt as an essential component of the scientific method, thereby elevating doubt to a unique position in the productive thought universe. However, *Great Minds Think Alike* in this chapter caution us about the *Pitfalls of Doubt*.

It appears that two key elements in the doubt process are:
1. Be clear about what you are doubting.
2. The degree of your doubt.

Doubting yourself can be a negative, but self-doubt can also be self-correcting. In the final analysis, self-doubt can be humbling and enlightening but also crippling. Additionally, doubt can be used as a weapon to hinder the agendas of others. Then again, doubting the beliefs, decisions, or statements of others can lead to productive debate, especially during the process of innovation. After studying both sides of doubt, it becomes apparent doubt can be a healthy self-regulating process that, much like fear, becomes toxic when extreme. Therefore, arguments on both sides of the doubt debate have valid positions. This exemplifies the duality of doubt.

Clearly, courage is essential for anyone involved in war. Since politics, business, and sports often involve battles of different varieties, courage is a key ingredient for success in these endeavors as well. Government is eternally intertwined with politics and war. This establishes *Government* as a *Wisdom Trail* category for *Courage, Fear,* and *Doubt*, as these three elements exist in every government regime. Chapter 6 fittingly concludes with a forceful statement by Leo Buscaglia, who stresses the necessity of taking risks to achieve anything meaningful in life.

WISDOM TRAILS: *Interconnected Categories*
Happiness, Faith, Politics, Government, Business, War, Sports, Science, Love, Success, Dreams, Creativity, Innovation

Trails to Other Chapters
- Thucydides links courage to freedom, and freedom to *Happiness.*
- Cicero links courage to *Faith.*
- Andrew Jackson's classic quote on courage applies to *Politics, Government,* and *Business.*
- Georg Christoph Lichtenberg notes that changing one's opinion is an act of courage. *(Politics, Government, Sports, Science, War)*
- Rosa Parks provides a method for reducing fear. *(Business, Politics, War)*
- Michelle Obama's advice on fear applies to *Love, Business, The Arts* and *Sports.*
- Sun Tzu's advice on courage applies to *Business, Sports, Politics,* and *War.*
- David Viscott links courage with *Success.*
- *The Pitfalls of Doubt* warns about the debilitating nature of doubt. *(Business, The Arts, Sports, Politics,* and *War).*
- Dennis Deaton's quote in *The Pitfalls of Doubt* also connects with *Dreams.*
- Peter Abelard and Richard Feynman praise the positive attributes of doubt. *(Business, Creativity, Science, Technology, War, The Arts, Government)*
- Leo Buscaglia points out that fear can interfere with our ability to *Love.*

CHAPTER 7

HAPPINESS, SUCCESS & WORK

Happiness is the meaning and purpose of life,
the whole aim and end of human existence.
—Aristotle (384–322 BC)

Very little is needed to make a happy life. It is all within yourself,
in your way of thinking. The happiness of your life depends upon
the quality of your thoughts.
—Marcus Aurelius (121–180)
Roman emperor and Stoic philosopher, from *Meditations*

To be kind to all, to like many and love a few, to be needed and wanted
by those we love, is certainly the nearest we can come to happiness.
—Mary Queen of Scots (1542–1587)
Birth name: Mary Stuart, aka Mary I
She legally became queen of Scotland when only six days old

The one who is happy is he who is ready to be friends with all. He is
not only friendly to persons, but also to objects and conditions.
—Hazrat Inayat Khan (1882–1927)

Most folks are about as happy as they make up their minds to be.
—Abraham Lincoln (1809–1865)

True happiness is…to enjoy the present
without anxious dependence on the future.
—Lucius Annaeus Seneca (4 BC–65 AD)

Getting out of your own way is the first step to happiness.
—Jamie Ducharme
American health correspondent and author quoted in *Time*, January 16, 2023

Let no one ever come to you without leaving happier.
—Mother Teresa (1910–1997)

GREAT MINDS THINK ALIKE: *Pursuing Happiness*

Perfect happiness is the absence of striving for happiness.
—*Chuang Tzu aka Zhuang Zhou or Zhuangzi (369–286 BC)*
Influential Chinese philosopher who wrote one
of the foundational texts of Taoism

The pursuit of happiness is a most ridiculous phrase;
If you pursue happiness, you'll never find it.
C.P. Snow (1905–1980)
Birth name: Charles Percy Snow
British novelist and politician with a PhD in physics

The happiness of a man in this life is determined
by the mastery of his passions.
— *Alfred Lord Tennyson (1809–1892)*

A happy person is not a person in a certain set of circumstances,
but rather a person with a certain set of attitudes.
—*Hugh Downs (1921–2020)*
Broadcaster, television host, news anchor, TV producer, author,
game show host, and music composer

GREAT MINDS THINK ALIKE: *Sharing Grief & Joy*

The best way to cheer yourself up is to cheer someone else up.
Grief can take care of itself, but to get the full value of a joy
you must have someone to divide it with.
—*Mark Twain (1835–1910)*

Shared joy is double joy. Shared sorrow is half a sorrow.
—*Swedish proverb*

Happiness never decreases by being shared.
—*Tony Hsieh (1973–2020)*
Chinese American venture capitalist and Zappos CEO,
from *Delivering Happiness: A Path to Profits, Passion and Purpose*

Friendship improves happiness and abates misery
by the doubling of our joy and the dividing of our grief.
—*Marcus Tullius Cicero (106–43 BC)*

Joy is not in things; it is in us.
—*Richard Wagner (1813–1883)*
German composer and conductor renowned for his operas

Many people think excitement is happiness...
but when you are excited you are not peaceful.
True happiness is based on peace.
—*Thich Nhat Hanh (1926–2022)*
From *The Art of Power*

My mother always told me that happiness was the key to life.
When I went to school, they asked me what I wanted to be
when I grew up. I wrote down "happy."
They told me I didn't understand the assignment,
and I told them they didn't understand life.
—*John Lennon (1940–1980)*
Legendary British musician/singer/songwriter of the Beatles; although widely attributed
to Lennon, there is some question about this quote's true origin

The walls we build around us to keep out the sadness
also keep out the joy.
—*Jim Rohn (1930–2009)*
American entrepreneur, author, and motivational speaker

GREAT MINDS THINK ALIKE: *Making Others Happy*

The noblest art is that of making others happy.
—*P.T. Barnum (1810–1891)*
Internationally acclaimed showman, businessman, author, and philanthropist
famous for his bold promotional methods

The way to be happy is to make others so.
—*Robert Ingersoll (1833–1899)*
American writer and orator nicknamed "The Great Agnostic"
from *The Sun* magazine, May 2009

One is only happy in proportion as he makes others feel happy.
—*Milton Hershey (1857–1945)*
American chocolatier, entrepreneur, and philanthropist who created the town of Hershey,
Pennsylvania to provide a good life for his employees

All happiness comes from the desire for others to be happy.
—*Shantideva (685–763)*
Indian philosopher, Buddhist monk, author and scholar,
as quoted in *The Wisdom of the Tibetan Lamas* by Timothy Freke

Surrender everything...your body, your life, your inner self
—and you will experience peace and inexpressible happiness.
—Yuan Wu (1063–1135)
Chinese monk who compiled the *The Blue Cliff Record*, from *Zen Wisdom*.
Great Minds Connect with David R. Hawkins on page 275

Happiness is the greatest beauty secret.
—Tina Turner (1939–2023)
Birth name: Anna Mae Bullock
Iconic American rock 'n roll singer who made this comment when she was 76 years old

The more deeply sorrow carves into your being,
the more joy you can contain.
—Kahlil Gibran (1883–1931)
From *The Prophet*

Nothing is miserable unless you think it so; and on the other hand,
nothing brings happiness unless you are content with it.
—Boethius (477–524)

It is not how much we have, but how much we love,
that makes happiness.
—Charles Spurgeon (1834–1892)
English Baptist preacher

It is preoccupation with possession, more than anything else
that prevents men from living freely and nobly.
—Bertrand Russell (1872–1970)
British philosopher, logician, mathematician, historian, writer,
social critic, political activist, and Nobel laureate

Strengthen yourself with contentment,
for it is an impregnable fortress.
—Epictetus (55–13 BC)
The Greek philosopher was born a slave in Phrygia (Asian Turkey, formerly Anatolia) and
lived in Rome until banished to Greece; he believed external events are beyond our control
so we should calmly accept whatever happens but that individuals are responsible for
controlling their own actions through rigorous self-discipline

The difference between happiness and fulfillment is the difference between liking something and loving something. Happiness comes from what we do. Fulfillment comes from why we do it.
—Simon Sinek (1973)
British-born American author, motivational speaker, and founder of Optimism Press, from his book *Find Your Why*. Sinek then added:
If you're different at work than you are at home, in one of those two places, you're lying.

GREAT MINDS THINK ALIKE: *What Is Enough?*

To achieve great happiness and success, it is essential to know what is enough.
—I Ching (compiled 1000–500 BC)

Great trouble comes from not knowing what is enough. Great conflict arises from wanting too much.
—Lao Tzu (571–unknown BC)

We never know what's enough until we know what is more than enough.
—Billie Holiday (1915–1959)
Birth name: Eleanora Fagan
Legendary African American jazz singer known as "Lady Day"

Being happy doesn't necessarily mean you're problem-free. It means you make the most of what you have and cherish each day.
—Anonymous
This is the only anonymous quote in the book; although not attributed to any specific person, its message was too good to ignore

Anyone who thinks money will make you happy hasn't got money.
—David Geffen (1943)
American billionaire business magnate, music producer, film studio executive, and philanthropist who co-founded DreamWorks SKG with Steven Spielberg

The more you know, the less you need.
—Yvon Chouinard (1938)
American rock climber, environmentalist, and billionaire who founded the Patagonia brand, from *Let My People Go Surfing: The Education of a Reluctant Businessman*

Happiness resides not in possessions, and not in gold.
Happiness dwells in the soul.
—*Democritus (c.460–c.370 BC)*

Having lots of money while not having inner peace
is like dying of thirst while bathing in the ocean.
—*Paramahansa Yogananda (1893–1952)*
Birth name: Mukunda Lal Ghosh
Hindu monk and yogi from India who spent most of his adult life in the United States teaching Kriya Yoga and is considered by many to be the "father of yoga" in the Western world; Yogananda also founded The Self-Realization Fellowship

GREAT MINDS THINK ALIKE: *Be Satisfied*

To be satisfied with a little is the greatest wisdom;
and he that increaseth his riches increaseth his cares, but a contented
mind is a hidden treasure, and trouble findeth it not.
—*Pharaoh Akhenaten (14th century BC)*
Pharaoh of the 18th dynasty of ancient Egypt who revolutionized his nation's religious order by converting Egyptian society to monotheism from polytheism

Wealth consists not in having great possessions,
but in having few wants.
—*Epictetus (55–13BC)*

Poor is not the person who has too little,
but the person who craves more.
—*Lucius Annaeus Seneca (4 BC–65 AD)*

I make myself rich by making my wants few.
—*Henry David Thoreau (1817–1862)*

To have what we want is riches, but
to be able to do without what we want, is power.
—*George Macdonald 1825–1904)*
Scottish author, poet, and Christian minister who was a pioneer in the field of fantasy novels and fairy tales

I have the greatest of all riches: that of not desiring them.
—*Eleonora Duse (1858–1924)*
Italian actress

Riches enlarge, rather than satisfy the appetite.
—*Thomas Fuller (1608–1661)*
British churchman, historian, and author

Money has never made man happy, nor will it. There is nothing in its nature to produce happiness...A little thought and a little kindness are often worth more than a great deal of money.

—*Cornelius Vanderbilt (1794–1877)*
Premier American railroad owner of the 19th century
who donated funds to build Vanderbilt University

I'd rather want everything and have nothing than have everything and want nothing, because at least when you want something, your life has meaning...it's worthwhile.

—*Vik Muniz (1961)*
Visionary Brazilian artist, sculptor, and photographer who works with
unconventional materials, from the 2010 documentary film *Waste Land*

Concentration is my motto: first honesty, then industry, then concentration.

–*Andrew Carnegie (1835–1919)*
Scottish-American industrialist who was a major player in the steel and railroad industries
before becoming a philanthropist later in life; this quote was Carnegie's formula for success

We need to measure progress against our inner compass, using our feelings and knowledge of ourselves as the ultimate guide. It says happiness can be simple as having something to look forward to in the morning.

—*Linda Weltner (1938)*
Syndicated columnist at *The Boston Globe*, from *No Place Like Home*

Success is getting what you want. Happiness is wanting what you get.

—*Warren Buffett (1930)*
From *The Snowball: Warren Buffett & the Business of Life*

Success is measured not by the position one has reached in life, but by the obstacles he has had to overcome.

—*Booker T. Washington (1836–1915)*
Born into slavery, he became an educator, author, orator, and advisor to U.S. presidents;
from 1890 until 1915, he was the dominant leader in the African American community and
Tuskegee Institute in Alabama as founder of the National Negro Business League

GREAT MINDS THINK ALIKE: *The Law of Attraction*

The greatest teachers who have ever lived have told us that
The Law of Attraction is the most powerful law in the Universe.
—*Rhonda Byrne (1952)*
Australian author and film producer, from her book *The Secret* that has been adapted as a
movie; The Law of Attraction encourages people to alter their thought patterns to clearly
express and attract what they desire

When you know that you want something, and you notice you do not
have it, you assume that there is something outside of yourself that
is keeping it from you, but that is never true. The only thing that ever
prevents you receiving something that you desire is that your habit
of thought is different from your desire.
—*Esther Hicks (1948) and Jerry Hicks (1927–2011)*
Esther Hicks is an inspirational speaker and author who presented workshops and wrote
books about the Law of Attraction with her husband, Jerry, who started his career as a circus
acrobat and professional musician. The above quote is from their book *Ask and It Is Given.*

Success is more permanent when you achieve it
without destroying your principles.
—*Walter Cronkite (1916–2009)*
Iconic broadcast journalist and television news anchorman known as
"the most trusted man in America" during his years as anchor of CBS Evening News

GREAT MINDS THINK ALIKE: *Aiming for Success*

Success usually comes to those
who are too busy to be looking for it.
—*Henry David Thoreau (1817–1862)*

Don't aim at success. The more you aim at it and make it a target,
the more you are going to miss it. For success, like happiness, cannot
be pursued; it must ensue, and it only does so as the unintended side
effect of one's personal dedication to a cause greater than oneself or
as the by-product of one's surrender to a person other than oneself.
Happiness must happen, and the same holds for success: you have to
let it happen by not caring about it.
—*Viktor Frankl (1905–1997)*

Don't aim for success. Just do what you love and believe in,
and it will come naturally.
—*David Frost (1939–2013)*
Television host, interviewer, journalist, and writer

Whether you think you can, or you think you can't...you're right.
—*Henry Ford (1863–1947)*

*What simple action could you take today to produce a new
momentum toward success in your life?*
—*Tony Robbins (1960)*

To do a common thing uncommonly well brings success.
—*Henry J. Heinz (1844–1919)*
Four interesting facts about Henry J. Heinz: (1) His first venture into the food business
was the production of horseradish, which was unsuccessful. (2) He created a mass
production assembly line many years before Henry Ford; Ford studied Heinz's operation
before creating his first assembly line. (3) He successfully lobbied the federal government
to begin regulating the food industry with the 1906 Pure Food and Drug Act. (4) He
established a family tradition of philanthropy that continues to this day.

*He who likes things to be easy will have difficulties.
He who likes problems will succeed.*
—*Laotian proverb*

*If you want to succeed, you should strike out on new paths rather
than travel the worn paths of accepted success.*
—*John D. Rockefeller Sr. (1839–1937)*
One of the wealthiest Americans of all time who made his fortune by revolutionizing and
controlling the petroleum industry in the late 19th century; when his company Standard Oil
was declared a monopoly in 1911, it was dismantled into smaller companies, inadvertently
expanding his fortune to make him the wealthiest American at that time. Later in life, he
became a philanthropist and founded the University of Chicago and Rockefeller University

GREAT MINDS THINK ALIKE: *True Wealth*

A man's true wealth is the good he does in this world.
—*Muhammad (c.570–632)*
Saudi Arabian founder of Islam; this phrase was echoed a thousand years later:

*A man's true wealth hereafter is the good that he does
in this world to his fellows.*
—*Moliere (1622–1673)*
Birth name: Jean-Baptiste Poquelin
French playwright, poet, and actor

I never get tired of being useful.
—Leonardo da Vinci (1452–1519)

The man who dies thus rich dies disgraced.
—Andrew Carnegie (1835–1919)
From his essay *The Gospel of Wealth,* considered a foundational document in the field of philanthropy; this quote officially documented his belief that social responsibility comes with great success

Disciplining yourself to do what you know is right and important, although difficult, is the highroad to pride, self-esteem, and personal satisfaction.
—Margaret Thatcher (1925–2013)
British stateswoman and prime minister of the United Kingdom from 1979 until 1990

The way to true riches is to enrich the soul by the acquisition of virtue. Outside of real heart-virtue there is neither prosperity nor power, but only the appearances of these.
—James Allen (1864–1911)
British philosopher, writer, and one of the pioneers of the self-help movement, from *The Path to Prosperity*; his most famous book is *As a Man Thinketh*

Success requires specialized knowledge plus imagination. Every adversity, every failure, every heartache carries with it the seed of an equal or greater benefit.
—Napoleon Hill (1883–1970)
From his book *Think and Grow Rich*

The amount of time people waste dwelling on failures rather than putting that energy into another project always amazes me.
—Richard Branson (1950)
Founder of Virgin Records, Virgin Airlines, and the spaceflight company Virgin Galactic, from *Losing My Virginity: The Autobiography*

In this world that is changing daily, the only guaranteed to fail is not taking any risks.
—Mark Zuckerberg (1984)
Technology entrepreneur, philanthropist, and co-founder of Facebook. *Great Minds Connect* with Muhammad Ali on page 199, and Leo Buscaglia on page 115

GREAT MINDS THINK ALIKE: *The Many Sides of Failure*

By acknowledging failure,
you take the first step to conquering it.
—*Twyla Tharp (1941)*
From *The Creative Habit*

The season of failure is the best time
for sowing the seeds of success.
—*Paramahansa Yogananda (1893–1952)*

Failure constantly shadows success. Failure offers us
what success never can: The opportunity for correction.
—*Irving H. Buchen (1930)*
American author and business professor at Capella University

Every wrong attempt discarded is a step forward. Failure is the
opportunity to begin again more intelligently. Don't find fault.
Find a remedy.
—*Henry Ford (1863–1947)*
Founder of the Ford Motor Company and pioneer
of the mass production assembly line

It doesn't matter if you try and try and try again, and fail.
It does matter if you try and fail, and fail to try again.
—*Charles Kettering (1876–1958)*
American inventor, engineer, businessman, holder of 186 patents, founder of Delco, head
of research at General Motors from 1920 to 1947, and responsible for the invention of
Freon for refrigeration and air conditioning systems

It is impossible to live without failing at something, unless you live so
cautiously that you might as well not have lived at all, in which case,
you fail by default.
—*J.K. Rowling (1965)*
British author, screenwriter, and producer who created the *Harry Potter* series

Failure is the key to success; each mistake teaches us something.
—*Morihei Ueshiba (1883–1969)*
Japanese martial artist who founded the martial art of aikido

Failure is not a matter of outcome...failure is not trying.
—*Hal Gregersen (1958)*
American researcher, author, motivational speaker, and photographer,
from his book *Questions Are the Answer*

Failure is the fertilizer of success.
—*Denis Waitley (1933)*
American naval aviator turned motivational speaker, consultant,
author, and member of the International Speakers Hall of Fame

Whatever you do, do it with all your might. Work at it early and late, in season and out of season, not leaving a stone unturned, and never deferring for a single hour that which can be done just as well as now.
—P.T. Barnum (1810–1891)

I like what is in work: The opportunity to find yourself.
—Joseph Conrad (1857–1924)
Polish-British novelist and essayist; many of his works have been adapted into major motion pictures, such as *Apocalypse Now*

Work should be something that calls to you as something you want to do. It should be something that gives voice to who you are and what you want to say to the world.
—Kent Nerburn (1946)
American author specializing in Native American history and spirituality, from *Letters to My Son*

GREAT MINDS THINK ALIKE: *What You Do Best*

The best work is not what is most difficult for you; it is what you do best.
—Jean-Paul Sartre (1905–1980),
French existential philosopher, novelist, and playwright who refused to accept the 1964 Nobel Prize for Literature, from *Dirty Hands*

Focus your career around the thing you're good at, not necessarily the things you're trying to get better at.
—David Tisch (1981)
Businessman, angel investor, managing partner of capital firm BoxGroup, and co-founder of TechStars in NYC

The more I help others succeed, the more I succeed.
—Ray Kroc (1902–1984)

The man who does more than he is paid for will soon be paid for more than he does.
—Napoleon Hill (1883–1970)
From *Think and Grow Rich*

Work and play are the same. When you're following your energy and doing what you love all the time, the distinction between work and play dissolves.
—Shakti Gawain (1948–2018)
From her book *Living in the Light*.
Great Minds Connect with quotes about play in Chapter 11

The difference between successful people and others is how long they spend time feeling sorry for themselves.
—Barbara Corcoran (1949)
American businesswoman, author, and investor best known
for her appearances on the television show *Shark Tank*

Tough-minded people become undaunted by difficulty by making the decision to be undaunted by difficulty.
—Dennis Deaton (1946)
From his weekly *Quma Learning Quma Inspirations* emails

Being defeated is often a temporary condition. Giving up is what makes it permanent.
—Marilyn vos Savant (1946)
Birth name: Marilyn Mack
American magazine columnist and author who changed her name after
being awarded the Guinness record for highest intelligence quotient (IQ)

Mental states become traits. Bit by bit, synapse by synapse, you really can build happiness into your brain.
—Rick Hanson, PhD
Neuropsychologist and expert on the subject of self-directed neuroplasticity,
from his book *Hardwiring Happiness*

People today tend to take refuge in overwork to avoid confronting their inner turmoil.
—Thich Nhat Hanh (1926–2022)
From *Be Still and Know*

GREAT MINDS THINK ALIKE: *Shokunin*

Once you decide on your occupation, you must immerse yourself in your work. You have to fall in love with your work. Never complain about your job. You must dedicate your life to mastering your skill. That's the secret of success, and the key to being regarded honorably.

—*Jiro Ono (1925)*

World-renowned Japanese sushi chef and owner of Sukiyabashi Jiro restaurant, which was featured in the movie *Jiro Dreams of Sushi*

Always look ahead and above yourself. Always try to improve on yourself. Always strive to elevate your craft.

—*Yoshikazu Ono (1959)*

The son of Jiro Ono, he apprenticed with his father and works with him at their sushi restaurant; Jiro and Yoshikazu's dedication to the mastery of their craft exemplifies the concept of Shokunin, discussed more fully in the next section of this chapter.

If a man is a streetsweeper, he should sweep streets as Michelangelo painted, Beethoven composed music, or Shakespeare wrote poetry. He should sweep streets so well that all the hosts of heaven and earth will pause to say, "Here lived a great streetsweeper who did his job well."

—*Martin Luther King Jr. (1929–1968)*

From his December 3, 1956 speech at the Holt Street Baptist Church in Montgomery, Alabama; this embodies the concept of Shokunin in a very mundane context

I've learned that "making a living" is not the same as "making a life."

—*Maya Angelou (1928–2014)*

Great Minds Connect with Dolly Parton on page 314

Even a happy life cannot be without a measure of darkness. The word 'happy' would lose its meaning if it were not balanced by sadness.

—*Carl Jung (1875–1961)*

From a 1960 interview

You cannot protect yourself from sadness without protecting yourself from happiness.

—*Jonathan Safran Foer (1977)*

American novelist as quoted in *Oprah Daily* and *The Week* magazine April 8, 2022

*The will to win, the desire to succeed, the urge to reach
your full potential...these are the keys that will unlock
the door to personal excellence.*
—Confucius (535–479 BC)

Great Minds Connect with *Great Minds Think Alike: Extreme Desire* on page 196

GREAT MINDS THINK ALIKE: *Work & Love*

Work is love made visible.
—Kahlil Gibran (1883–1931)

Love and work are the cornerstones of our humanness.
—Sigmund Freud (1856–1939)

The only way to do great work is to love what you do.
—Steve Jobs (1955–2011)

*Success is not the key to happiness. Happiness is the key
to success. If you love what you do, you will be successful.*
—Albert Schweitzer (1875–1965)

*We should deal with one another not as classes but as persons, as
brothers. The more closely we work together, the more effectively
we contribute to the better health of all mankind. This should be
our common objective, and its achievement would make the world a
happier place in which to live.*
—Milton Hershey (1857–1945)

To be a scholar of success, you must be a student of human nature.
—Tom Butler-Bowdon (1967)
Australian-born British researcher and author, while discussing J. Paul Getty
in *50 Success Classics*. Bowdon then added:
*Every great thing starts with a thought
and is powered into realization by a belief.*

*Researchers have concluded again and again that the single most
reliable predictor of happiness is feeling imbedded in a community.*
—Christopher Ryan (1962)
From his book *Civilized To Death*

In order to be successful you have to first want to make other people successful. In order to be loved, you have to first love. In order to be interesting, you have to first be interested. The mere opposite of what you want is what you have to give first, and then you will get back the desired result or outcome in droves.
—*Jay Abraham (1949)*
American business executive, executive coach, and author, as quoted in *The Passion Test*

Whatever happens, I will not let my cheerfulness be disturbed. Why be unhappy about something if you can change it? And if you can't, how will being unhappy help?
—*Shantideva (685–763)*
As quoted in *The Wisdom of the Tibetan Lamas* by Timothy Freke

GREAT MINDS THINK ALIKE: *Happiness Is In Your Mind*

The mind is its own place, and in itself can make a heaven of Hell and a hell of Heaven.
—*John Milton (1608–1674)*
English poet most famous for his poem *Paradise Lost* and its sequel, *Paradise Regained;* Milton was totally blind when composing *Paradise Lost* and had to dictate this epic literary masterpiece and all compositions during his final 22 years

We can think of things like happiness and compassion as skills that are no different from learning to play a musical instrument or tennis...it is possible to train our brains to be happy.
—*Richard Davidson PhD (1951)*

CONSOLIDATING CHAPTER 7
Happiness, Success & Work

Chapter 7 tackles three subjects that consume most of our adult lives:

> *Work, the pursuit of happiness, and the desire for success.*

Contributors to this chapter prescribe a number of different paths to experience happiness, such as making others happy, enduring friendship, being content with what you have, staying healthy, and finding love. Entries in this chapter establish an intriguing connection between love, happiness, and success, with love having a multi-faceted presence including loving others, loving yourself, and loving your work. While work is directly connected to business, it's also intimately connected to our careers, which is why *Work* has been partnered with *Happiness* and *Success* instead of pairing work with *Business*. Although there's only a small distinction between work and business, working for others is not necessarily business, as many workers do not have a command or understanding of the businesses they serve. Conversely, anyone who runs or manages a business is clearly involved in serious work. The intimate relationship between work and business is reinforced by a large number of quotes connecting the two categories. It's also interesting to note how many quotes from *The Lessons of Sports* apply to this chapter.

Of all the categories presented in this book, the greatest consensus by sages of all eras involves the subject of happiness. Great minds throughout history fundamentally concur that wealth and possessions are not the primary determinants of happiness. Wanting less and being satisfied with your place in life are the key deciders of happiness—not success, wealth, or possessions. Making others happy is universally recommended as a route to making yourself happy, and as John Milton and Richard Davidson imply, it appears happiness is primarily an internal issue regulated by our state of mind.

This chapter also points out that even though happiness is a form of success, success does not guarantee happiness. Rather, contentment is the preferred source of happiness, and it's argued happiness is more desirable than success because one can be happy without success, but there's no true success if one is not happy. Chapter 7 also notes that good health is major contributor to achieving happiness. It's not surprising to discover many of the most asked questions in life revolve around the subject of happiness. They include:

> *Are you happy with your job?*
> *Are you happy with your marriage?*
> *Are you happy with where you live?*
> *Are you happy with your car?*

Interestingly enough, the more one studies the wisdom of work, the more it resembles a spiritual activity. The more our work involves spiritual gratification and inspires passion through a sense of play, the greater the chance our career will lead us to a happier life. This supports the notion of work being more than just a career activity, because one's approach to work also represents a philosophy. Hall of Fame NBA basketball coach Phil Jackson encapsulates this concept by saying

To make your work meaningful,
you need to align it with your true nature.

A sparkling example of work as a philosophy is the Japanese concept of *Shokunin*. Sushi chefs Jiro and Yoshikazu Ono have dedicated their lives to mastering the culinary art of making sushi, as depicted in the 2011 movie *Jiro Dreams of Sushi*. Jiro's dedication exemplifies Shokunin, which is defined by both Japanese and Japanese-English dictionaries as "craftsman" or "artisan," but that definition does not fully express Shokunin's deeper meaning of *devotion and pride in one's vocation with relentless dedication to mastery of one's craft.*

Shokunin practitioners also feel a social obligation to give back to their communities and uplift the societal welfare of others by delivering products and services of the highest quality. Shokunin is a way of life, a way of thinking, a personal calling affecting every interaction in a practitioner's world. It demands poise and grace in business as well as all interpersonal relationships. This means practitioners of Shokunin must master both their craft and themselves. Those dedicated to such high standards take on this responsibility without any resistance. The result is a refreshing purity derived from complete surrender to full immersion in the beauty of their craft.

WISDOM TRAILS: *Interconnected Categories*
Compassion, Friendship, Love, The Future, Peace, Education, Nature, Compassion, Business, Spirituality, Creativity, Politics, Play, The Arts, Sports, Observing Human Nature

Trails to Other Chapters
- Mary, Queen of Scots cites kindness and *Love* as sources of happiness.
- Hazrat Inayat Khan focuses on *Friendship* as a source of happiness.
- Lucius Annaeus Seneca finds happiness by not being anxious about the *Future*.
- Cicero connects friendship with *Happiness*.
- Thich Nhat Hahn believes inner peace is the key to happiness. (*Spirituality*)
- John Lennon remembers his strange school experience regarding happiness. (*Education*)

- Yuan Wu offers profound advice on happiness and *Peace*.
- Charles Spurgeon predicates happiness on how much we *Love*.
- Paramahansa Yogananda uses a *Nature* metaphor.
- Cornelius Vanderbilt informs us that kindness is more likely to create happiness than money. (*Compassion*)
- Rhonda Byrne, Esther Hicks, and Jerry Hicks discuss the *Law of Attraction. (Spirituality)*
- James Allen finds riches through enriching the soul. (*Spirituality*)
- Napoleon Hill believes success requires *Creativity*.
- Mark Zuckerberg emphatically proclaims that in an age of accelerating change, failure to take risks guarantees failure. (*Business*)
- P.T. Barnum raises the bar for work ethic and *Business* efforts.
- *The Many Sides of Failure* directly applies to *Business*, as well as *Sports, War, The Arts,* and *Politics*.
- Ray Kroc attributes his *Success* to helping others succeed.
- Shakti Gawain describes the relationship between work and *Play*.
- The practice of Shokunin connects with *Business, The Arts, Philosophy, Love,* and *Sports*.
- Maya Angelou's quote on the issue of work-life balance is applicable to *Extreme Desire*.
- Confucius discusses the will to win and succeed, which connects with *Business, The Arts, Sports, Politics, Government,* and *War*.
- Dennis Deaton advises us to be undaunted by difficulty, which applies to *Business, Creativity, The Arts, Sports, Politics, Government,* and *War*.
- In *Work & Love,* Steve Jobs, Kahlil Gibran, and Sigmund Freud focus on the connection between work and *Love*.
- Milton Hershey suggests a way to improve the *Health* of all mankind by improving *Social Justice*.
- Jay Abraham's advice on success connects with *Spirituality* and *Love*.
- Simon Sinek connects happiness with work and fulfillment with *Love*.

CHAPTER 8

BUSINESS & LEADERSHIP

The purpose of a business is to create customers.
—*Peter F. Drucker (1909–2005)*
Austrian-born American management consultant, educator, and author who invented the
concept of "management by objectives" in *Innovation and Entrepreneurship;*
he is considered by many to be the founder of modern business management

It's easy to think you are the expert on your own product.
But that is a myth. The true experts are your customers.
—*Jamie Wong*
Entrepreneur, investor, and storyteller who founded Vayable

Your most unhappy customers are your greatest source of learning.
—*Bill Gates (1955)*
Founder of Microsoft who has transitioned into an international philanthropist

Business is the ultimate team sport.
—*Jack Welch (1935–2020) & Suzy Welch (1959)*
The ultimate business power couple. Jack: Author and former CEO of
General Electric; Suzy: Author, business journalist, and motivational speaker

Never outsource your main competency.
—*Tony Hsieh (1973–2020)*
From *Delivering Happiness: A Path to Profits, Passion and Purpose*

Perfection is the result of getting all the little things right.
—*Robert Iger (1951)*
Former CEO of the Walt Disney Company, from *The Ride of A Lifetime*

A verbal contract isn't worth the paper it's written on.
—*Sam Goldwyn (1879–1974)*

Be fearful when others are greedy and greedy when others are fearful.
—*Warren Buffett (1930)*
From *The Snowball: Warren Buffett & the Business of Life*

The best time to invest is when there is blood in the streets.
—J.P. Morgan (1837–1913)

Although J.P. Morgan made this phrase famous, it was actually passed on to him by his father, who reportedly heard it spoken by iconic British banker Baron Rothschild

Man is after all, a very finite being in his capacities and powers to do actual work, but when it comes to planning, one mind can, in a few hours, think out enough work to keep a thousand men employed for years.
—Washington Roebling (1837–1926)

Army officer, designer, and builder of NYC's Brooklyn Bridge explaining the power of a chief executive to bring visions to fruition; Roebling supervised the completion of the bridge while confined to a wheelchair in his New Jersey home

The way you do anything is the way you do everything.
—Robert Iger (1951)

From his book *The Ride of A Lifetime*. This seemingly simplistic quote implies that once a good way of doing things has been developed, it can be applied to multiple applications ... pointing out the importance of developing effective principles and protocols to guide all business ventures and life in general. This quote has also been credited to Tom Waits, and Suzanne Evans published a book using this phrase as its title. To further complicate the origin of this phrase, motivational speaker Simon Sinek declares it a Zen Buddhist saying.

Effective negotiators listen far more than they talk.
—William Ury (1953)

Author, academic, anthropologist, negotiation expert, and co-founder of the Harvard Program on Negotiation, from *Getting Past No*

You can find latent potential in any subject if you look hard enough... fortunes have been made in business by people finding the latent potential in a subject and recycling it into something else.
—Michael Michalko (1940)

Internationally acclaimed creativity expert and author, from *Cracking Creativity*

If you want innovation...and you always should, you need to give permission to fail.
—Robert Iger (1951)

Surround yourself with people strong enough to change your mind.
—John Wooden (1910–2010)
Legendary basketball coach, motivational speaker, and the only person in the Basketball
Hall of Fame as both player and coach, from *WOODEN: A Lifetime of Observations and
Reflections On and Off the Court.*
Great Minds Connect with Ray Dalio on page 312

***If Columbus had an advisory committee
he would probably still be at the dock.***
—Arthur Goldberg (1908–1990)
Prominent lawyer who served as a Supreme Court Justice,
Ambassador to the United Nations, and Secretary of Labor

***Innovation is often the result of random conversations...collisions,
where ideas outside your industry are applied to your own. We try
to accelerate those collisions among people.***
—Tony Hsieh (1973–2020)
From *Delivering Happiness: A Path to Profits, Passion and Purpose*

Complicated innovations do not work.
—Peter F. Drucker (1909–2005)
From *Innovation and Entrepreneurship*

***Even old organizations innovate. To engage in a national
conversation, we launched a campaign to give girls skills they need
to be leaders in 25 years.***
—Anna Maria Chavez (1968)
Former CEO of Girl Scouts of America

***When Henry Ford made cheap reliable cars,
people said, "Nah, what's wrong with a horse?"***
—Elon Musk (1971)

You're only as good as the people you hire.
—Ray Kroc (1902–1984)

It is a bad plan that allows for no modification.
—Publilius Syrus (85–40 BC)

The most important thing in communication is hearing what isn't being said...there is nothing so useless as doing efficiently that which should not be done at all.
—Peter F. Drucker (1909–2005)
From *Innovation and Entrepreneurship*

Excessive preparation is often an excuse of procrastination. Preparation should not be neglected, but decisive action must not be delayed.
—Sun Tzu (544–496 BC)
From multiple translations of *The Art of War*

Nothing will ever be attempted if all possible objections must be first overcome.
—Samuel Johnson (1709–1784)
British poet, playwright, essayist, moralist, literary critic, biographer, editor, and lexicographer

Differences enrich us. They are not a threat.
—Anne Wilson Schaef (1934–2020)
From *Native Wisdom for White Minds*

GREAT MINDS THINK ALIKE: *Welcoming Dissent*

Well-managed friction leads to a higher level of consensus.
—Doe Lang

It is often the dissenters who bring about change.
—I Ching (compiled 1000–500 BC)
Great Minds Connect with the *Great Minds Think Alike: Change* on page 87
and *Doubt Can Be Useful* on page 115

**It takes 20 years to build a reputation, but just five minutes to ruin it.
If you think about that, you'll do things differently.**
—Warren Buffett (1930)

**Politeness and civility are the best capital
ever invested in business.**
—P.T. Barnum (1810–1891)
From his book *The Art of Money Getting*

Sequential tasking is better than multi-tasking.
—Scott Belsky (1980)
American entrepreneur, early stage investor, author, and creator of Behance, Inc.,
from *Making Ideas Happen*

GREAT MINDS THINK ALIKE: *Change, Chaos & Opportunity*

In the midst of chaos, there is also opportunity.
—Sun Tzu (544–496 BC)

Whenever there's change, there's opportunity.
—Mark Cuban (1958)
Billionaire businessman, investor, media personality, and owner
of the Dallas Mavericks, while on *Shark Tank* Season 12, Episode 10

**Beneficial changes begin when you can acknowledge
and even embrace your weaknesses.**
—Ray Dalio (1949)
From his book *Principles: Life and Work. Great Minds Connect* with the
Great Minds Think Alike: Change on page 87

Long shots aren't usually as long as they seem.
—*Robert Iger (1951)*
From *The Ride of a Lifetime*

GREAT MINDS THINK ALIKE: *One Step at a Time*

Great and difficult goals are accomplished in simple easy steps.
—*I Ching (compiled between 1000-500 BC)*
Great Minds Connect with Dylan Dreyer on page 50

A thousand mile journey begins with one step.
—*Lao Tzu (571–unknown BC)*

The less work an organization produces,
the more frequently it reorganizes.
—*Arthur Bloch (1948)*
Writer, author, television producer, and author of the *Murphy's Law* books

The speed of the boss is the speed of the team.
—*Lee Iacocca (1924–2019)*
American automobile executive at Ford who later became
CEO of Chrysler, from *Iacocca: An Autobiography.*
Great Minds Connect with Vince Lombardi on page 200

Build your organization from the top down. An organization
is the opposite of a building. Its foundation is at the top.
—*Ray Dalio (1949)*
From his book *Principles: Life and Work*

Once a principle is breached, it's mutated form
propagates like cancer.
—*David R. Hawkins MD (1927–2012)*
From *Power vs. Force*

Rewrite the rules, rather than creating more exceptions to them.
—*Jeffrey Hollander (1954)*
Co-founder of American Sustainable Business Council

GREAT MINDS THINK ALIKE: *Money*

Money never starts an idea.
It is the idea that starts the money.
—*William John (W.J.) Cameron (1879–1953)*
Canadian-born American pharmacist and businessman who founded Cameron's Surgical
Specialty Company, achieving notoriety for his 1928 Kalahari Expedition in Africa

Above all, you want to create something you are proud of.
That has always been my philosophy of business. I can honestly say
that I have never gone into any business to make money.
—*Richard Branson (1950)*

The only purpose of money is to get what you want.
Money is a byproduct of excellence...not a goal.
—*Ray Dalio (1949)*
From his book *Principles: Life and Work*

Allowing workers to dress as they please
instantly increases collegiality.
—*Warren Bennis (1925–2014)*
American scholar, organizational consultant, author, and pioneer
of the contemporary field of leadership

Creative problem solving, planning and strategy sessions will be
far more productive if you incorporate an overnight stay.
—*Michael J. Gelb (1952)*

The main thing that causes companies to fail
is that they miss the future.
—*Larry Page (1973)*
Computer scientist and co-founder of Google (now Alphabet, Inc.)

The product always comes first. No matter what problems or
opportunities arise, never stop focusing on the product.
—*Mark Pincus (1966)*
American internet entrepreneur, tech investor, and founder
of the mobile social gaming company Zynga

Never invest in a business you cannot understand.
—*Warren Buffett (1930)*

The certainty of meaningful and intelligent discussion decreases as the number of people in attendance increases.
—*Gerald A. Michaelson (1929–2004)*
From *Sun Tzu for Success*

There is nothing so small that it cannot be blown out of proportion.
—*Ruckert's Law*
A member of the *Murphy's Law* family of phrases

Strength and growth come only through continuous effort and struggle. No man is ever whipped until he quits in his own mind. A quitter never wins and a winner never quits.
—*Napoleon Hill (1883–1970)*
From *Think and Grow Rich*

Anything less than a total, unqualified commitment to our highest ideals and noblest standards leads not just to mediocrity but the starvation and death of our full potential.
—*Dennis Deaton (1946)*
From his weekly *Quma Learning, Quma Inspirations* emails

Business as usual is a recipe for disaster.
—*Curtis R. Carlson (1945)*
American business executive, technologist, expert consultant on innovation, and economic policy, from his book *Innovation*

The quest for business excellence and the search for personal realization need not be mutually exclusive, and can in fact, be essential to each other.
—*Robert Kegan (1946)*
American developmental psychologist, author, and consultant as quoted in *Principles*

Leadership emerged within mammal and early human bands because it was an efficient survival and social-enhancement mechanism.
—*The Futurist* magazine March–April 2010

Leadership is solving problems. The day soldiers stop bringing you their problems is the day you have stopped leading them. They have either lost confidence that you can help or have concluded you do not care. Either case is a failure of leadership.

—Colin Powell (1937–2021)

Highly decorated Jamaican American four-star general and military strategist who served as secretary of state and chairman of the joint chiefs of staff, as quoted on govleaders.org

Successful leaders outline big, bold and noble visions to cultivate cultures of innovation, unleashing the collective imagination of their teams. Anything is possible when a team of smart dedicated people commit themselves to a common goal. When exceptional leaders paint a compelling vision of the future, and when they expect excellence from their teams, it inspires people to achieve results they never thought possible.

—Carmine Gallo (1965)

American author, keynote speaker, and corporate coach, from his book *The Innovation Secrets of Steve Jobs;* this quote exemplifies the Pygmalion Effect that predicts when excellence is expected, people tend to rise to the occasion. *Great Minds Connect* with his own quote about passionate vision on page 169

True leadership strengthens the followers. It is a process of teaching, setting an example, and empowering others.

—David Niven (1910–1983)

British actor and author who served in the British army before becoming a movie star

In times of uncertainty and fear, leaders must develop the ability to listen and relate to others, to consider alternative approaches, different points of view, entertain new possibilities, and spend time attending to the emotional needs of others.

—Barb Krantz Taylor (1960)

Licensed psychologist and principal consultant at The Bailey Group in Minneapolis, in *Quma Inspirations Volume 3, #6*

Building a team of enthusiastic and talented people is one of the greatest challenges for leaders.

—Scott Belsky (1980)

From his book *Making Ideas Happen*

GREAT MINDS THINK ALIKE: *Seven Keys To Leadership*

A leader can never be happy until his people are happy.
—*Genghis Khan (1162-1227)*

Known as the founder of Mongolia, (Khan means emperor) Genghis Khan was a legendary conqueror who organized numerous Northeast Asian nomadic tribes to form the great Mongol Empire; his brutal rule also expanded cultural exchanges across all of Eurasia.

Learning to listen is the key to good leadership.
—*Beth Ford (1963)*

CEO of Land O'Lakes Butter, Inc. and the first openly gay female CEO of a Fortune 500 company

The main job of a leader is thinking.
—*David J. Schwartz (1927–1987)*

From his book *The Magic of Thinking Big*

The best thing a leader can do for a group is allow its members to discover their own greatness.
—*Warren Bennis (1925–2014)*

Great Minds Connect with Benjamin Disraeli on page 282

Leadership is based on a spiritual quality; the power to inspire, the power to inspire others to follow.
—*Vince Lombardi (1913–1970)*

The first task of a leader is to keep hope alive.
—*Joe D. Batten (1925)*

American motivational speaker and author specializing in management, sales, and leadership, he was the first speaker inducted into the National Speakers Association Hall of Fame, from his book *Tough Minded Leadership*

Innovation is the central job of every leader.
—*A.G. Lafley (1947)*

American businessman, author, and former CEO of Proctor & Gamble, as quoted in *The Innovator's DNA*

Ultimately, leadership is about creating new realities...just being there for others and to listen to them is one of the most important capacities a leader can have. True leadership is about creating a domain in which we continually learn and become more capable of participating in our unfolding future. A true leader thus sets the stage on which predictable miracles, synchronistic in nature, can and do occur.
—*Joseph Jaworski (1934)*

From *Synchronicity: The Inner Path of Leadership*

No man will make a great leader who wants to
do it all himself, or to get all the credit for doing it.
—*Andrew Carnegie (1835–1919)*

Leaders lift others up. They protect the weak. They lead by example.
They choose to be guided by love instead of fear. They confront their
demons to become stronger. They have belief in times of uncertainty,
and never quit when it gets tough.
—*Wim Hof (1959)*
Dutch extreme athlete, motivational speaker, and author known as "The Iceman"

Leadership is the art of getting someone else to do
something you want done because he wants to do it.
—*Dwight D. Eisenhower (1890–1969)*
The 34th president of the United States who previously was supreme commander
of American forces in Europe during WWII.
Great Minds Connect with Daniel Vare on page 229

If your actions inspire others to dream more, learn more,
do more and become more, you are a leader.
—*John Quincy Adams (1767–1848)*
The sixth president of the United States who served as an ambassador prior to his
presidency and as a congressman after his presidency; Quincy, Massachusetts,
is named after his grandfather John Quincy

Visionaries need followers as much as followers need a vision...The
true value of a leader is not measured by the work they do. The true
value of a leader is measured by the work they inspire others to do.
—*Simon Sinek (1973)*
From his book *Together is Better: A Little Book of Inspiration*

In a hierarchy, every employee tends to rise
to his level of incompetence.
—*Lawrence J. Peter (1919–1990)*
Canadian professor and author who was a self-proclaimed "hierarchaeologist," from his
best-selling book *The Peter Principle: Why things Always Go Wrong*

Stay committed to your decisions, but flexible in your approach.
—Tony Robbins (1960)

Entrepreneurship requires an unvanquished spirit
of curiosity, an openness to learning, a letting go
of the Old so you're free to create the New.
—Michael Gerber (1936)
American business consultant and author dedicated to *"transform the state of small business worldwide." Great Minds Connect* with Socrates & Joseph Campbell on page 285

Business is a matter of human service...give them quality.
That's the best kind of advertising in the world.
—Milton Hershey (1857–1945)
Hershey innovated upon Nestle's invention of milk chocolate in that he used fresh dairy milk. Nestle used condensed milk (water removed) to keep the milk from spoiling; the slight bitterness in Hershey's chocolate—that has become their trademark—was due to this spoiling of milk. Hershey decided to put his factory in dairy farm country so that milk was easily accessible. He purchased 1,200 acres, envisioning the construction of a utopian town for his workers before he had finalized his chocolate recipe...a precursor of Walt Disney's initial EPCOT concept.

If you approach a negotiation as if it were a game, you'll be more successful. When it comes to negotiating, you'd be better off acting like you know less, not more. The most powerful words in business are "I don't understand. Help me."
—Herb Cohen (1938)
As quoted in *The Adventures of Herbie Cohen: World's Greatest Negotiator,* authored by his son Rich Cohen (1968) who was a co-creator of the HBO television series *Vinyl*

Tribes are the basic building block of any large human effort. As such, their influence is greater than that of teams, entire companies, and even superstar CEOs. A company is only as strong as the culture of its tribe.
—Dave Logan (1968)
American professor, leadership expert, and author, from his book *Tribal Leadership,* co-authored with co-founder of CultureSync, John King, and healthcare expert, physician, and speaker, Halee Fischer-Wright. To clarify this statement, the authors added:
A small company is a tribe, and a large company is a tribe of tribes.

If you want to rise in a business setting, it's important to understand that every aspect of the business is important, not just the parts that inherently interest you.

−*Clive Davis (1932)*

Iconic American lawyer, record producer and A&R executive who was inducted into the Rock & Roll Hall of Fame for his prominence in developing the careers of major music stars...from his memoir *The Soundtrack of My Life*

Repetition of the familiar leads to stagnation.

—*Henry Kissinger (1923–2023)*

German-born American politician, diplomat, and geopolitical consultant who served as Secretary of State and National Security Advisor for presidents Richard Nixon and Gerald Ford; Kissinger was awarded the Nobel Peace Prize in 1973. This phrase from his book *World Order* warns about the danger of continually reinforcing the status quo.

GREAT MINDS THINK ALIKE: *Expand Your Vision*

Creative thinking is the result of novel experiences and novel ways of looking at common problems...if your vision is to offer an innovative experience in your business, then you should look outside your industry for inspiration.

—*Carmine Gallo (1965)*

An example of this is that Apple, Inc. modeled their retail stores after Four Seasons hotels. This quote supports Tony Hsieh in this chapter and *Great Minds Connect* with Franz Johansson's *Medici Effect* on page 170

The world's most innovative companies prosper by capitalizing on the divergent associations of their founders, executives and employees.

—*Jeff Dyer (1959), Hal Gregersen (1958) & Clayton Christensen (1952–2020)*

Dyer is a business strategy expert, speaker, and author; Christensen was an academic and business consultant who developed the theory of "disruptive innovation"; Gregersen's bio appears with his quote on page 129, from their co-authored book *The Innovator's DNA*. *Great Minds Connect* with Franz Johansson's *Medici Effect* on page 170

Interdisciplinary collaboration is the key to sustainable progress.

—*Ramona Pringle*

Great Minds Connect with *The Medici Effect* on page 170

CONSOLIDATING CHAPTER 8
Business & Leadership

Chapter 8 forms its own circle of relationships by exploring the direct connection of business with work, work with happiness, happiness with love, love with spirituality, and spirituality with work. Begin this circle of connections at any point and you'll end up rotating back to your starting point. It's also possible to slide into the connection between business and politics, with friendship and innovation serving as support factors...and leadership directing traffic. When viewed together, Chapters 7 and 8 form a family. Combining business and work with good leadership creates a dynamic success triangle. If balanced properly with love and spirituality, the resulting blend will likely lead to greater happiness. Interestingly, *Business & Leadership* possesses the most connections to other chapters in this book, an indication these two categories are vitally important to—and intricately entwined with—many facets of contemporary life.

It's important to note that most good business advice is also good advice on how to live our personal lives. When assimilating advice on how to run a business, it's advisable to transfer those lessons into your personal life. Chapter 8 includes a discussion about the need for businesses to embrace change, an issue also pertinent on a personal level, as resistance to change is identified as one of the greatest causes of failure in all aspects of life. Unfortunately, people and businesses often repeat unproductive behaviors in the futile hope negative results will somehow miraculously change.

Four prominent robber barons contribute their wisdom to Chapter 8. Cornelius Vanderbilt, John D. Rockefeller, Andrew Carnegie, and J.P. Morgan were all major players in America's industrial revolution. They helped shape a period in our history known as the Gilded Age. The phrase *Gilded Age* was coined by Mark Twain in reference to the period from the end of the Civil War until 1900 when America experienced stellar industrial growth accompanied by rampant institutional corruption. Vanderbilt came first as a railroad tycoon. He paved the way for the initial ascent of Rockefeller by agreeing to transport Rockefeller's refined oil to expanded markets. Carnegie was to steel production what Rockefeller was to oil refining, and J.P. Morgan eventually purchased Carnegie's steel empire to form U.S. Steel. In their later years, both Rockefeller and Carnegie focused most of their attention on philanthropic activities.

While organizing chapters for this book, there was considerable debate about what category *Leadership* should be partnered with. *Sports, Government,* and *War* were all seriously considered, but in the end, it was decided *Leadership* fit best with *Business* because businesses cannot function without effective leadership. The fact there was so much debate over this decision demonstrates how vital leadership is in sports, government, and war.

A much-overlooked field of leadership is in the arena of education, where teachers function as leaders on a daily basis, both in classrooms and while directing after-school activities. Leadership extends into the performing arts under the titles of director, conductor, and choreographer...especially in movie and theatre productions that assemble large groups of diverse talent. Good leadership is also essential in science and technology, as those endeavors frequently employ teams to explore, research, and build complex machinery and pharmaceuticals. Additionally, successful political campaigns are always composed of teams that require leadership at every level, especially leadership provided by each candidate. In fact, any effort involving more than one person needs good leadership. This includes nuclear families. The vital connection of leadership to so many other categories demonstrates why *Business & Leadership* is an important chapter to study even if you're not particularly interested in business. Regardless of your specific interests, it's advisable to scrutinize phrases describing the valuable traits that comprise effective leadership.

WISDOM TRAILS: *Interconnected Categories*
Sports, Work, Success, Government, Politics, Creativity, Innovation, Courage, Philosophy, War, The Future, Spirituality, Education, Fear, Dreams, Compassion, Curiosity, Play, Native American Wisdom

TRAILS TO OTHER CHAPTERS
- Jack and Suzie Welch describe business as the ultimate team *Sport*.
- Washington Roebling provides a unique outlook on *Work*.
- William Ury offers insight on effective negotiating.
  (Politics, Government)
- Tony Hsieh, Bob Iger, Anna Marie Chavez, and Peter Drucker provide their views on *Innovation*.
- Admiral Hyman Rickover highlights the need for patience in promoting good ideas to overcome the resistance they inevitably encounter.
  (Technology, Science, Innovation, Government, War)
- Richard Branson describes his *Philosophy* of business.
- Sun Tzu reminds us to prepare for success...but also take decisive action. *(War, Politics, Government, Sports)*
- Warren Buffett cautions us about preserving our reputation.
  (Politics, Sports, Government)
- Scott Belsky believes sequential tasking is better than multi-tasking.
  (Work)
- Warren Bennis provides a tip on how to encourage collegiality at *Work*.
- Michael J. Gelb advises leaders to conduct group sessions to achieve superior problem solving results. *(Creativity, Innovation)*

- Jeffrey Hollander's advises rewriting rules instead of making exceptions. (*Government, Work, Sports*)
- Larry Page warns businesses to consider *The Future* when making decisions.
- Robert Kegan combines the quest for business excellence with personal realization. (*Spirituality*)
- Colin Powell describes a symptom of failure of leadership. (*Government, Politics, Sports, War*)
- Carmine Gallo discusses how leadership can encourage *Innovation* by creating visions of *The Future*.
- David Niven describes leadership as a process of teaching. (*Education*)
- Vince Lombardi finds *Spirituality* in good leadership.
- A.G. Lafley names *Innovation* as the core responsibility of all leaders.
- Barb Krantz Taylor believes leaders need to calm *Fear* of their followers by demonstrating *Compassion*.
- Scott Belsky identifies the building of effective teams as a greatest leadership challenge. (*Sports, Government, Politics, Technology*)
- Lee Iacocca knows a leader dictates the speed of the team. (*Sports*)
- Joseph Jaworski believes true leadership is about teaching and helping to create a future where *Miracles* are possible. (*Education, The Future*)
- Wim Hof discusses the connection of leadership to both *Love* and *Fear*.
- John Quincy Adams says leaders should inspire their followers to *Dream*.
- Simon Sinek connects with Barb Krantz Taylor, proclaiming good leadership is about taking care of those you lead. (*Compassion*)
- Warren Bennis believes leaders should help others find their greatness. This applies to *Technology, The Arts, Sports, Education*, and *Government*.
- Michael Gerber states that entrepreneurship requires *Curiosity*.
- Herb Cohen advises us to approach negations as if they are games. (*Play*)
- *Expand Your Vision* explains why companies prosper when they encourage *Creativity & Innovation*.
- Dave Logan connects tribal leadership with business. (*Native American Wisdom*)
- Henry Kissinger's warning about repeating the familiar applies to *Government, Politics, Sports, Technology, Science*, and many other walks of life.
- Carmine Gallo's advice connects *Innovation* with the *Medici Effect*.

CHAPTER 9

CREATIVITY, INNOVATION & CURIOSITY

Creating is the essence of life.
—*Julius Caesar (100–44 BC)*

Creativity is a part of our spiritual DNA.
—*Julia Cameron (1948)*
American author, teacher and filmmaker best known for her book *The Artist's Way*

Creativity is a drug I cannot live without.
—*Cecille B. DeMille (1881–1959)*
Filmmaker, director, producer, one of the founding fathers of American cinema, and a co-founder of Paramount Pictures

Innovate or die.
—*Roon Arledge (1931–2002)*
Iconic television sports and news producer who developed ABC's Wide World of Sports, created Monday Night Football, Nightline, ABC World News Tonight, and 20/20

There is nothing that can stop the creative. If life is full of joy, joy feeds the creative process. If life is full of grief, grief feeds the creative process …the creative process is a spiritual path.
—*Stephen Nachmanovitch (1950)*
From his book *Free Play*

Creativity is not just for artists. It's for businesspeople looking for a new way to close a sale; it's for engineers trying to solve a problem; it's for parents who want their children to see the world in more than one way.
—*Twyla Tharp (1941)*
From *The Creative Habit: Learn It and Use It for Life*

Organizations of the future will increasingly depend on creativity to survive.
—*Warren Bennis (1925–2014)*

GREAT MINDS THINK ALIKE: *Gestation*

Men of lofty genius sometimes accomplish the most when they work the least, for their minds are occupied with their ideas and the perfection of their conceptions to which they afterwards give form.
—*Leonardo da Vinci (1452–1519)*

This statement was in response to a church prior's complaint to Ludovico Sforza—the duke of Milan who had commissioned Leonardo to produce a work of art in his church—that Leonardo had spent a number of days sitting on a hill looking at the church while sipping wine. Leonardo was explaining that it takes time to marinate a great work of art; he was fully engaged in fulfilling his commission while sitting on the hill. This story depicts the essence of a gestation period. *Great Minds Connect* with Vincent van Gogh on page 93

If you're working all the time, you don't have the perspective to see your problem with fresh eyes.
—*Reed Hastings (1960)*

American businessman and a co-founder of Netflix. In his book *No Rules Rules,* Hastings embellished on this quote with the following:

Time off provides mental bandwidth that allows you to think creatively and see your work in a different light.

No idea is so antiquated that it was not once modern. No idea is so modern that it will not someday be antiquated.
—*Ellen Glasgow (1873–1945)*
Pulitzer Prize-winning American novelist

Invention is often the mother of necessity, and not vice versa.
(Inversion of the phrase: "*Necessity is the mother of invention.*")
—*Jared Diamond (1937)*
American geographer, historian, anthropologist, ornithologist, and Pulitzer Prize-winning author explaining how innovation can create products that become indispensable, from his book on evolutionary biology *Guns, Germs, and Steel*

Observation followed by creativity is our greatest ally.
—*John Chester (1971)*
From the documentary film *The Biggest Little Farm*

Great ideas and great successes all begin with a passionate vision, and it's just as important for individuals as it is for corporations.
—*Carmine Gallo (1965)*
From his book *The Innovation Secrets of Steve Jobs*

GREAT MINDS THINK ALIKE: *The Power of Ideas*

You can imprison a man, but not an idea.
You can exile a man, but not an idea.
You can kill a man, but not an idea.
—*Benazir Bhutto (1953)*
The first woman to head a democratic government in a Muslim country
by serving as prime minister of Pakistan

An invasion of armies can be resisted,
but not an idea whose time has come.
—*Victor Hugo (1802–1885)*

Man's mind, once stretched by a new idea,
never regains its original dimensions.
—*Oliver Wendell Holmes, Sr. (1809–1894)*
Ralph Waldo Emerson uttered a remarkably similar quote:
The mind, once stretched by a new idea
never returns to its original dimensions.

Your mind is like a parachute. If it isn't open, it doesn't work.
—*Buzz Aldrin (1930)*
American fighter pilot and Apollo 11 astronaut who was the second man to walk on the
moon—after Neil Armstrong. Considerable research into the origins of this quote reveals
that Aldrin did not originate this phrase, nor did musician *Frank Zappa (1940-1993)*
who is often credited with coining it. Substantial controversy over its origin dates back to
distiller *Lord Thomas Dewar (1864–1930)* who uttered a slightly different version as early
as 1928. There is also evidence of this phrase dating back to 1927 in the
Louisville Times with no author credited.

You can't use up creativity. The more you use, the more you have.
—*Maya Angelou (1928–2014)*

Creativity is something you are, not only something you do.
It's a way of moving through the world, every minute, every day.
–*Rick Rubin (1963)*
American record producer and co-founder of Def Jam Records,
from his book *The Creative Act: A Way of Being*

GREAT MINDS THINK ALIKE: *Connecting Things*

Creativity is just connecting things.
—*Steve Jobs (1955–2011)*

**Creativity is about taking the facts, fictions and feelings
we store away and finding new ways to connect them.**
—*Twyla Tharp (1941)*
From *The Creative Habit: Learn It and Use It for Life*

**The human mind has an uncanny ability to make creative
connections between seemingly random or irrelevant stimuli.**
—*Bryan Mattimore (1955)*
American innovation leader, author, and "Chief Idea Guy" at
the Growth Engine Company, from his book *Idea Stormers*

The best way to have a good idea is to have lots of ideas.
—*Linus Pauling (1901–1994)*

**The act of moving forward creates the next step.
Every creative move you make creates the next possibility.**
—*Nancy Hillis*
American existential psychiatrist and abstract artist, from *The Artist's Journey*

**Creativity can be manifested in medicine, in propaganda,
in teaching poetry, in designing a house or an atom bomb.
Unfortunately, the same capacity for play and experiment
that gives rise to our finest achievements has also resulted in
the invention of ever more refined methods of mass destruction.**
—*Stephen Nachmanovitch (1950)*
From his book *Free Play*

**The problem is never how to get new innovative thoughts
into your mind, but how to get old ones out. Every mind is
a building filled with archaic furniture. Clean out a corner
of your mind, and creativity will instantly fill it.**
—*Dee Hock (1929–2022)*
Founder and former CEO of Visa International who was inducted into the Business Hall
of Fame in 1991. *Ray Kurzweil* reiterated this quote in his book *How to Create a Mind*.
Great Minds Connect with *Great Minds Think Alike: Clearing Space* on page 301

159

GREAT MINDS THINK ALIKE: *What's the Problem?*

No problem can withstand the assault of sustained thinking.
—*Voltaire (1694–1778)*

A problem adequately stated
is a problem well on its way to being solved.
—*R. Buckminster Fuller (1895–1983)*
American architect, inventor, futurist, and prolific author

The more specifically you define your challenge,
the easier it is to generate ideas.
—*Michael Michalko (1940)*
From *Cracking Creativity*

No problem can be solved until it is reduced to some simple form.
The changing of a vague difficulty into a specific, concrete form
is an essential element in thinking.
—*J.P. Morgan (1837–1913)*

When we distance ourselves from the problem
at hand, we can judge it more clearly.
—*Igor Grossman*
Social-cognitive scientist who serves as director of the *Wisdom and Culture Lab* at the
University of Waterloo, quoted when discussing a phrase he coined, *Solomon's Paradox,*
that observes people tendency to be wiser when reasoning about problems of others than
problems of their own. His main research objective is to understand processes that enable
individuals to think and act wisely. A world traveler, Grossman was born
in the Soviet Union, raised in the Ukraine and Germany, attended college at the
University of Michigan, and now lives in Canada.

Thought is constantly creating problems, and then trying to solve
them. But as it tries to solve them, it makes it worse because it doesn't
notice that it's creating them, and the more it thinks, the more
problems it creates.
—*Dr. David Bohm (1917–1992)*
American theoretical physicist and philosopher who was a major contributor on the
subject of quantum physics, from *Thought as a System*

Some problems are so complex that you have to be highly intelligent
just to be undecided about them.
—*Lawrence J. Peter (1919–1990)*
This quote is a good example of wisdom with a touch of humor

GREAT MINDS THINK ALIKE: *The Art of the Question*

*The art and science of asking questions
is the source of all knowledge.*
—*Thomas Berger (1924–2014)*
American novelist who authored the novel *Little Big Man* that was adapted
into a major motion picture starring Dustin Hoffman and Faye Dunaway

*If you want more and better answers to your creative challenges,
start by asking more and better questions.*
—*Bryan Mattimore (1955)*
From his book *Idea Stormers*

One cannot pose a question unless the answer already exists.
—*David R. Hawkins, MD (1927–2012)*
From his book *Power vs. Force*

Understanding a question is half an answer.
—*Socrates (470–399 BC)*

A wise man's questions contain half the answer.
—*Solomon ibn Gabirol (c.1022–1070)*
Spanish poet and religious philosopher

*The question "Why?" is the most powerful invention of the human
mind. When you use it to discover your own beliefs, you can become
self-creative and sculpt your own reality.*
—*Charles Case (1945–2016)*
American anthropologist, educator, and philosopher, as quoted in *Socrates Way*

*The creative process is forming questions that cause answers
that in turn lead to better answers.*
—*Viki King*
Writer, script consultant, and lecturer, from her book *How To Write A Movie in 21 Days*

*All questions are the frame into which the answers fall...by changing
the frame, you radically change the range of possible solutions.*
—*Tina Seelig (1958)*
American educator and author specializing in creativity and innovation,
from the Stanford Management, Science & Engineering website in 2013

*Great questions break down assumptions. Without changing
your questions, you cannot get beyond incremental progress
on the same path you've been pursuing.*
—*Hal Gregersen (1958)*
Gregersen advises that reframing questions provides the potential to make them
catalytic and give them power to excite the imagination

The need to be right all the time is the biggest bar to new ideas.
It is better to have enough ideas for some of them to be wrong than
to be always right by having no ideas at all.
—*Edward de Bono (1933–2021)*
From his book *Lateral Thinking*

The first and simplest emotion which we discover
in the human mind, is curiosity.
—*Edmund Burke (1729–1797)*
Irish statesman

Creativity flows when curiosity is stoked.
—*Neil Blumenthal (1980)*
CEO and co-founder of Warby Parker

Curiosity is the essence of human existence. Who are we? Where are
we? Where do we come from? Where are we going? I don't know. I
don't have any answers to those questions. I don't know what's over
there around the corner. But I want to find out.
—*Gene Cernan (1934–2017)*
American Aeronautical engineer, fighter pilot, and astronaut
who was (Apollo 17) the 11th person to walk on the moon

My favorite words are possibilities, opportunities and curiosity.
If you are curious, you create opportunities, and then if you open
the doors, you create possibilities.
—*Mario Testino (1954)*
Internationally known Peruvian fashion and portrait photographer

At a child's birth, if a mother could ask a fairy godmother to endow it
with the most useful gift, that gift should be curiosity.
—*Eleanor Roosevelt (1884–1962)*

Be curious, not judgmental.
—*Walt Whitman (1819–1892)*
One of America's foremost poets, best known for his collection *Leaves of Grass*

All there is to thinking is seeing something noticeable,
which makes you see something you weren't noticing,
which makes you see something that isn't even visible.
—*Norman Maclean (1902–1990)*
American author, scholar, and professor of English literature

As long as the mind can envision the fact
you can do something, you can do it.
—*Arnold Schwarzenegger (1947)*
Austrian American actor, filmmaker, businessman, author, politician, and
seven-time Mr. Universe who was governor of California from 2003 to 2011

GREAT MINDS THINK ALIKE: *Creativity & Happiness*

Happiness lies in the joy of achievement
and the thrill of creative effort.
—*Franklin D. Roosevelt (1882–1945)*

Problem solving is the source of a long and happy life.
—*Steve Chandler (1944)*
An author of 30 books that have been translated into over 25 languages,
his coaching, public speaking, and business consulting services have been used
by CEOs, top professionals, major universities, and Fortune 500 companies

Satisfaction of one's curiosity is one of
the greatest sources of happiness in life.
—*Linus Pauling (1901–1994)*
Nobel Prize-winning American chemist who was also awarded the Nobel Peace Prize;
he is considered one of the twenty most influential scientists in history

The ultimate creative thinking technique is to think like God.
If you're an atheist, pretend you know how God would do it.
—*Frank Lloyd Wright (1867–1959)*
Pioneering architect, interior designer, and writer

Human anatomy is a byproduct of creativity.
To think is to practice brain chemistry.
—*Deepak Chopra (1946)*
Spoken during his appearance on the *Dr. Oz* television show November 26, 2012

GREAT MINDS THINK ALIKE: *The Value of Imagination*

Imagination is more important than knowledge.
—Albert Einstein (1879–1955)

Imagination is the warship of your mind capable of turning mind energy into accomplishment and wealth.
—Napoleon Hill (1883–1970)
Self-help author, from his book *Think and Grow Rich*

Imagination means nothing without doing.
—Charlie Chaplin (1889–1977)
Acclaimed as the greatest silent movie actor and filmmaker in history who also composed music for his films; later in his career, Chaplin also created and appeared in talking films

Without curiosity, the creative process never has the raw material it needs.
—Bryan Mattimore (1955)
From his book *Idea Stormers*

Satori is the sudden flashing into consciousness of a new truth hitherto undreamed of. It is a flash of intuition deep enough and wide enough to break the barriers of thought in the mind.
—D.T. Suzuki (1870–1966)
Author, lecturer, and scholar of Zen Buddhism, from *Zen Wisdom*

An epiphany is the sudden realization of a significant truth, often arising out of a commonplace event. At that special moment, a life's meaning becomes clear...an insight into your personality, a discovery of something you value or believe in, an acute sense of where you are in life. Such moments can determine the course of your life.
—Robert U. Akeret (1928–2016)
Swiss psychoanalyst and author who lived in the United States, from *Family Tales, Family Wisdom*

If you are seeking creative ideas, go out walking. Angels whisper to a man when he goes for a walk.
—Raymond Inmon
German born mathematician and physicist
Great Minds Connect with Steven Spielberg on page 51

164

GREAT MINDS THINK ALIKE: *Wild Ideas*

Good ideas are always crazy, until they're not.
—*Larry Page (1973)*
This quote is also attributed to Elon Musk and Ashlee Vance (in Page's biography of Elon Musk), although it appears that Larry Page said it first

Every vision is a joke until the first man accomplishes it.
Once realized, it becomes commonplace.
—*Robert Goddard (1882–1945)*
American physicist and inventor credited with creating and building the world's first liquid-fueled rocket

When you're brainstorming, you have to accept wild ideas.
—*Jeff Bezos (1964)*
Founder and CEO of Amazon, founder of the aerospace company Blue Origin, and one of the wealthiest people in the world

If it's a good idea, it doesn't matter where it comes from.
—*Mark Goodson (1915–1992)*
American television producer best known for producing successful game shows, as quoted in *Alex Trebek: The Answer Is...*

It is easier to tone down a wild idea than to think up a new one...
most ideas are step-by-step children of other ideas.
—*Alex F. Osborn (1888–1966)*
Legendary American advertising executive and author hailed as the "father of brainstorming," from *Your Creative Power*

A good idea is never lost. Even though its originator or possessor
may die, it will someday be reborn in the mind of another.
—*Thomas Alva Edison (1847–1931)*

It's the freedom that craziness provides that can lead you to create
the best ideas of all.
—*Bryan Mattimore (1955)*

The people who are crazy enough to think they can change the world
are the ones who do.
—*Steve Jobs (1955–2011)*
One of his pet phrases when discussing innovation

What you think, you become. What you feel, you attract.
What you imagine, you create.
—*Buddha (563–483 BC)*

As a rule, I always look for what others ignore.
—*Marshall McLuhan (1911–1980)*
Canadian philosopher and expert on media theory

GREAT MINDS THINK ALIKE: *Simplicity*

Out of intense complexities, intense simplicities emerge.
—*Sir Winston Churchill (1874–1965)*

Simplicity is the ultimate sophistication.
—*1977 Apple Computer ad for the Apple II.*
This quote was mistakenly attributed to Leonardo da Vinci in a 2000 Compari ad.
It coincides with the following quote in the 2016 book *Oil and Marble*:
Simplicity is the ultimate sophistication...
the path to true complexity.
—*Stephanie Storey (1975)*
American art historian, producer, director, editor, and novelist. A similar phrase
with an identical thrust appeared in the 1931 short story *Stuffed Shirts*.

The height of sophistication is simplicity.
—*Clare Boothe Luce (1903–1987)*
American author, playwright, journalist, politician, and ambassador

It's the open mindedness to little things that brings human success.
The greatest minds think in simple terms.
—*Russell Cromwell (1843–1925)*
Baptist minister, lawyer, and author who founded Temple University.
Great Minds Connect with William of Ockham on page 320

A vision is meaningless if it does not have the power to persuade.
—*Mark Benioff (1964)*
American billionaire internet entrepreneur and philanthropist who co-founded Salesforce
and also owns *Time*. Benioff has donated hundreds of millions of dollars to
a variety of causes. Another Benioff quote is:
You need to have a beginner's mind to create bold innovation.

One simple truth about creativity: It's a self-fulfilling prophecy.
If you define yourself as creative, are motivated strongly enough,
and persist long enough to generate a host of creative ideas...
then the prophecy comes true.
—*Bryan Mattimore (1955)*
From his book *Idea Stormers*

GREAT MINDS THINK ALIKE: *Collaboration*

Complex problems are best solved collaboratively.
—*David M. Kelley (1951)*
Founder of the global innovation and design company IDEO, from the company's website.

The power of human thought grows exponentially with the number of minds that share that thought. Multiple minds working in unison magnify a thought's effect exponentially.
—*Dan Brown (1964)*
American author famous for his books that have been turned into movies;
this quote is from *The Lost Symbol*.

I just looked at what worked for me and decided to share it with everyone else...this process that I use for everything now: it's observe, brainstorm, research, build, communicate.
—*Gitanjali Rao (2005)*
American scientist, inventor, engineer, and author who was awarded *Time's* first Kid of
the Year (2020) at the age of 15, as quoted in the December 14, 2020 issue of *Time*

When inspiration does not come to me, I go half way to meet it.
—*Sigmund Freud (1856–1939)*

The essence of creativity is not the possession of some special talent, it is much more the ability to play.
—*John Cleese (1939)*
English actor, producer. and screenwriter,
as quoted in *On Becoming A Leader* by Warren Bennis

A key aspect of creativity is the process of finding great metaphors.
—*Ray Kurzweil (1948)*

Any time you can experiment, you ought to do it, because you never know what will happen.
—*Walt Disney (1901–1966)*

Resisting change is as futile as resisting weather, and change is our weather now.
—*Warren Bennis (1925–2014)*
From his book *On Becoming A Leader*

Keeping your mind open in the face of uncertainty is the single most powerful secret of unleashing your creative potential...the ability to thrive with ambiguity must become part of our everyday lives.

—Michael J. Gelb (1952)
From his book *How To Think Like Leonardo Da Vinci*

The limit is not the sky. The limit is the mind.

—Wim Hof (1959)
From his book *The Wim Hof Method*

An abnormal reaction to an abnormal situation is normal behavior.

–Viktor Frankl (1905–1997)
From his book *Man's Search for Meaning*. For those who question the appearance of this quote under the category of Creativity, please revisit it after reading this brief explanation: Rather than paralleling the concept of *"two wrongs make a right,"* this phrase paves the way for innovation as a survival mechanism for coping with abnormal situations... especially those that are potentially dangerous. Therefore, this phrase can be interpreted as the process describing how humans have adapted to the perils of life throughout the ages. Although radical at first, once established, certain adaptive behaviors eventually become viewed as normal.

I like nonsense. It wakes up the brain cells.

—Dr. Seuss (1904–1991)
Birth name: Theodor Seuss Geisel

The best ideas are created by those who are following their dreams. Passion is the fuel that gives you energy to reach your dreams, but vision provides the roadmap. Passion is meaningless without vision...Innovation means nothing unless you can get people excited about it.
—Carmine Gallo (1965)
From his book *The Innovation Secrets of Steve Jobs*

When confronted with places never seen before, the brain must create new categories. It is in this process that the brain jumbles around old ideas with new images to create new syntheses.
—Gregory Berns, MD & PhD (1964)
American neuroscientist, neuroeconomist, psychologist, and best-selling author from his book *Iconoclast*

There is no doubt that creativity is the most important human resource of all. Without creativity, there would be no progress, and we would be forever repeating the same patterns.
—Edward de Bono (1933–2021)

There's nothing more dangerous than the right answer to the wrong question.
—Peter Drucker (1909–2005)
This is a very important phrase for the brainstorming process that directly connects to *The Art of the Question*. If the wrong question is discussed, participants end up solving the wrong problem. This can lead companies and individuals down the wrong path, as a correct answer to the wrong question is destined to lead everyone astray.

GREAT MINDS THINK ALIKE: *The Power of Language*

Language shapes thought, and thought shapes action.
—Tony Robbins (1960)
This concept comes from Tony Robbins's background in neurolinguistic programming

We create our reality with language. When a person looks out at the world, he sees it filtered through a screen of his words, and this process is as invisible to him as water is to a fish.
—Dave Logan (1968)
From his book *Tribal Leadership*, co-authored with John King and Halee Fischer-Wright

Creativity in some industries thrives on copying...
invention is collective.
—Alexa Clay (1984) and Kyra Maya Phillips
From their book *The Misfit Economy;* this quote embodies the rationale for
open-source software and technologies that aim to stimulate diverse innovation

For good ideas and true innovation, you need
human interaction, conflict, argument and debate.
—Margaret Hefferman (1955)
Business executive, author, keynote speaker, expert on leadership,
and business development

GREAT MINDS THINK ALIKE: *Failure, Creativity & Success*

An essential part of creativity is not being afraid to fail.
—Edwin Land (1909–1991)
American scientist, inventor, and co-founder of the Polaroid Corporation who invented
the Polaroid instant camera and accumulated 535 patents during his career

Fail soon to succeed sooner.
—IDEO company mantra
The founder of IDEO is David Kelley; this phrase acknowledges that failure is
a natural part of the innovation process and fear of failure limits innovation.

If you're not prepared to be wrong,
you'll never come up with anything original.
—Sir Ken Robinson (1950–2020)
British author, lecturer, and expert on the role of the arts in education and
a proponent of encouraging creativity in the educational process;
Robinson was knighted in 2003 for his work in this field

An explosion of insight happens at the intersection of different fields,
cultures, and industries. When you step into an intersection of fields,
disciplines, or cultures, you can combine existing concepts into a
large number of extraordinary ideas.
—Franz Johansson
Swedish American writer, entrepreneur, and public speaker from his book *The Medici
Effect.* The term *Medici Effect* refers to the significant contribution of the Medici family
to the onset of the European Renaissance. The Medici family summoned to their court
a diverse array of craftsmen, artists, scientists, architects, philosophers, and scholars,
thereby creating a cross-cultural intersection that resulted in an explosion of creativity and
innovation. Recognizing this phenomenon as relevant today, the *Medici Effect* explains
how input from diversely populated teams representing a variety of disciplines leads to
superior innovation. *Great Minds Connect* with Jeff Dyer, Hal Gregersen,
and Clayton Christensen on page 151

CONSOLIDATING CHAPTER 9
Creativity, Innovation & Curiosity

Chapter 9 gets to the heart of the creative process by highlighting its key components and applications. On its most basic level, creativity is an adaptive mechanism of the human brain that facilitated survival of humans as a species during the millennia of prehistory, paving the way for our rise to domination of the animal kingdom. This is an example of what may be called the *Law of Evolutionary Dysfunction* or *Survival of the Weakest,* based on the fact that a weak species must innovate to survive. Since weaker species either utilize creativity or perish, prehistoric humans needed to become creative while fighting for survival in the prehistoric animal kingdom. On the opposite end of this spectrum, sharks never needed to be creative since they have always been superior predators. Now that humans have created modern technological societies, our challenges are far different than the scenarios prehistoric humans faced. Looking beyond survival in the wild, Warren Bennis believes creativity will be the primary survival tool for organizations of the future because innovation is the only way to cope with the inevitability of constant change. That's why Roon Arledge bluntly declares, "Innovate or die."

In Chapter 9, we learn about numerous dimensions of the creative process:

- Creativity as a survival skill can be equated to resourcefulness, and resourcefulness is at the heart of innovation.
- The underlying inspiration for both creativity and innovation is curiosity. When combined with great dreams and creativity, curiosity perpetually expands your potential.
- Curiosity, creativity, and innovation form the core impetus for societal evolution...the basis for development of science, technology, the arts, education, sports, and business.
- Good questions fuel the creative process.
- There are two kinds of creativity: practical and artistic. Everyone innately possesses practical creativity.
- Gestation periods are productive for idea formation; they're an integral component of the creative process.
- Idea generation flourishes when many ideas are considered. A diversity of inputs usually leads to superior results.
- Creativity and innovation have the power to expand both the greatness and folly of human nature. This power culminates in an ability to establish and transform civilizations.

At this point, it's important to clarify the difference between *practical creativity* and *artistic creativity*. Practical creativity is the innate human ability to be adaptive and innovative...to solve problems and make adjustments. All humans are capable of learning and developing practical creativity, which serves as a facilitator of resourcefulness separate from artistic creativity. Artistic creativity is much more specialized and involves the development of specific skill sets. Although practical creativity supports artistic creativity, a person need not be artistic to possess practical creativity, and those who are artistic often lack practical creativity. The possession of both practical and artistic creativity is characteristic of many great achievers in the arts, business, and sports. Understanding the difference between practical and artistic creativity crystallizes the understanding we all can cultivate some form of creativity to enrich our lives. Twyla Tharp supports this concept by explaining why creativity is not just for artists. Stephen Nachmanovitch provides examples by stating, "*Creativity can be manifested in medicine, propaganda, poetry, house design and even weapons of mass destruction.*" This quote hints at creativity's potential to also be used in a harmful manner.

Chapter 9's study of the creative process includes Franklin D. Roosevelt, Linus Pauling, and Steve Chandler promoting the creative process as a great source of happiness. Walt Disney urges everyone to experiment whenever possible, and Carmine Gallo finds that great ideas and success begin with passionate visions. Buzz Aldrin utilizes the parachute as a metaphor for keeping our minds open at all times, a metaphor supported by Michael Gelb, who states that keeping the mind open despite uncertainty is a key to unleashing inner creativity. Victor Hugo and Benazir Bhutto cite the immense power of ideas, and Linus Pauling asserts the best way to find great ideas is to propose lots of them. The generation of numerous new ideas is the underlying rationale for brainstorming sessions, and David M. Kelley supports this process by telling us complex problems are best solved collaboratively. Brainstorming utilizes questions as a primary mechanism, a process addressed in *The Art of the Question* (see page 161) where a number of great minds discuss the extraordinary power of good questions. Using a metaphor of archaic furniture, Dee Hock suggests it's necessary to remove old thoughts to make room for newer and more innovative ones. Once old thinking is removed, there is space for new ideas to enter. That's where Albert Einstein muses about the importance of imagination, and Arnold Schwarzenegger optimistically declares we can create anything we can envision. *Great Minds Think Alike: Wild Ideas* then tells us how wild suggestions can be extraordinarily productive when tamed. Revealing another vital aspect of the creative process, Leonardo da Vinci and Reed Hastings both recommend the use of gestation periods for generating and expanding ideas. Focusing on the development of creative skills, Twyla Tharp and Alex Trebek remind us that preparation is a vital component of the creative process.

The foremost use of practical creativity is in solving problems. To address that aspect, five contributors combine to provide insight and advice on problem-solving in the section *What's the Problem?* The question then becomes: *Where does creativity come from?* Chapter 9 tells us curiosity is the main source by serving as a proverbial bubbling brook capable of continually generating creativity. Astronaut Gene Cernan defines curiosity as the essence of human existence, while Bryan Mattimore emphatically states curiosity is necessary for the creative process to function. Walt Whitman advises us to be curious but not judgmental, and Eleanor Roosevelt declares curiosity to be a child's most useful gift. Bryan Mattimore then describes creativity as a self-fulfilling prophecy, explaining that combining persistence with the belief you are creative is the surest path to innovative ideas.

Franz Johansson concludes Chapter 9 by introducing the *Medici Effect*. This eclectic concept explains the explosive creativity that occurs at intersections of different fields, cultures, and industries, thereby placing extreme value on obtaining a diversity of inputs during any creative process, a concept providing the foundation for breakthrough thinking.

WISDOM TRAILS: *Interconnected Categories*
Spirituality, Business, The Arts, Science, Technology, Feng Shui, The Future, Success, Work, Observing Human Nature, Practical Advice, Happiness, Government, Play, Dreams, Fear, Health

Trails to Other Chapters
- Julius Caesar declares creativity is the essence of *Human Nature.*
- Julia Cameron believes creativity is part of our *Spiritual* DNA.
- When Roon Arledge says *"Innovate or die,"* he is talking about *Business.*
- Twyla Tharp explains why creativity is not just for *The Arts*...it's also for *Business* and *Technology.*
- Warren Bennis tells us creativity is an organizational necessity for *The Future.*
- Carmine Gallo views passionate vision as an integral ingredient for *Success.*
- Leonardo da Vinci and Reed Hastings tout the value of gestation periods in creative *Work.*
- Bryan Mattimore highlights the human brain's ability to make creative connections. *(Observing Human Nature)*
- Quotes in *What's the Problem?* directly apply to *Business, Work, Science,* and *Technology.*
- Dee Hock uses the metaphor of clutter-clearing and archaic furniture as a way to pave the way for innovation. *(Feng Shui)*
- Quotes in *The Art of the Question* also apply to *Science, The Arts, Business, Government, Politics,* and *War.*

- Stephen Nachmanovitch describes the creative process as a *Spiritual* path. He also connects creativity with *The Arts, Science, War,* and *Health.*
- Gene Cernan calls curiosity the essence of *Human Nature.*
- Walt Whitman provides *Practical Advice* about being curious.
- Franklin D. Roosevelt connects creativity with *Happiness.*
- Arnold Schwarzenegger insists if the mind can envision something, it can be accomplished.
  (Business, The Arts, Sports, Science, Technology, Politics)
- Steve Chandler claims problem-solving is the key to *Happiness.*
- Linus Pauling believes satisfaction of curiosity is the key to *Happiness.*
- Robert U. Akeret's quote about epiphanies relates to *Spirituality.*
- Quotes about *Wild Ideas* apply to *Business, Science, Technology, Government,* and *War.*
- Mark Benioff notes that visions are useless if they lack the power to persuade. *(Business, Government, Politics)*
- Russell Cromwell highlights the need for open-mindedness to achieve *Success.*
- Walt Disney urges everyone to experiment.
  (Science, Technology, Business, The Arts, Sports, and *Government)*
- Dan Brown's quote establishes a rationale for the creation of teams in all arenas of life. *(Business)*
- John Cleese declares the essence of creativity is the ability to *Play.*
- Carmine Gallo finds the best ideas come from pursuing *Dreams.*
- Peter Drucker warns about the danger of asking the wrong questions.
  (Business, Government, Science, Technology)
- Alexa Clay and Kyra Maya Phillips note that copying is often a form of innovation. *(Business, Technology)*
- Edwin Land, IDEO, and Sir Ken Robinson agree *Fear* of failure is the main adversary of creativity and innovation. *(Success)*
- Franz Johansson connects ideas to intersections of numerous disciplines, fields, and cultures.
  (Science, Technology, Business, The Arts, Sports, Government)

CHAPTER 10

THE ARTS & LITERATURE

Study the science of art and the art of science.
—*Leonardo da Vinci (1452–1519)*

Art is a powerful tool in opening up our consciousness to new possibilities. It isn't just engineers who drive research possibilities. It is artists as well.
—*Alexa Clay (1984) and Kyra Maya Phillips*
This quote refers to the fact that science fiction writers and artists often create visions leading to scientific advances and breakthrough exploration. From their book *The Misfit Economy*

Art imitates life and in turn life imitates art, making art an ideal catalyst for envisioning a sustainable future.
—*Ramona Pringle*
From her article in *The Futurist* magazine, July–August 2013

A true artist is not one who is inspired but one who inspires others.
—*Salvador Dalí (1904–1989)*
Spanish surrealist painter

Art is studied in Japan not only for art's sake, but for spiritual enlightenment.
—*D.T. Suzuki (1870–1966)*
Japanese author, lecturer, and scholar of Zen Buddhism

A man who works with his hands is a laborer; a man who works with his hands and his mind is a craftsman; but a man who works with his hands and his brain and his heart is an artist.
—*Thomas Aquinas (1225–1274)*
Italian Dominican friar, philosopher, Catholic priest, and influential theologian

We love objects of art for the doors that they open into universal beauty.
—*Simone Vay, aka Simone Veil (1927)*
Prominent French female politician

Historically, it has been the artist's role to make manifest the beautiful inherent in all the objects of nature and man.
—Arshile Gorky (1904–1948)
Armenian surrealist and abstract expressionist painter who spent his later years in the United States, as quoted in *The Artist's Mentor*

There is, at this point in history, a desperate need for a resurgence of humanism, a reawakening of values. I believe that art—art of any kind—can play a significant part in the reaffirming of humanity.
—Ben Shahn (1898–1969)
Lithuanian-born American artist, as quoted in *The Artist's Mentor*

Music feeds math, feeds science, feeds painting. The only way to create something unique is to make connections between seemingly disparate things. If I focus only on art, the art will die. Chaos erupting into beauty...that's art!
—Stephanie Storey (1975)
From her book *Oil and Marble*

The meaning of life is to find your gift. The purpose of life is to give it away. Painting is a blind man's profession. He paints not what he sees, but what he feels...what he tells himself about what he has seen.
—Pablo Picasso (1881–1973)
Iconic Spanish artist, sculptor, and stage designer who co-founded Cubism

The Earth as the paradise of the gods. That is what I want to paint... art is about emotion; if art needs to be explained, it is no longer art.
—Pierre-Auguste Renoir (1841–1919)

There is little of more importance to the future of our country and civilization than full recognition of the place of the artist. For art to nourish the roots of our culture, society must set the artist free to follow his vision wherever it takes him.
—John F. Kennedy (1917–1963)
World War II hero and 35th president of the United States, who was assassinated in 1963

Creative art is for all time and is therefore independent of time. It is of all ages, of every land...by this we mean the creative spirit in man which produces a picture or a statue is common to the whole civilized world, independent of age, race and nationality.
—Alma Thomas (1891–1978)
African American artist and teacher, as quoted in *The Artist's Mentor*

The greatest works of literature, film, dance, theater, music and art reflect our human condition since the beginning of time— all our emotions, struggles, elations, decisions, crises, dreams predicaments...everything in our life that's meaningful to us.
—Nancy Hillis
As quoted in *The Artist's Journey*

All truly profound art requires its creator to abandon himself to certain powers which he invokes but cannot altogether control.
—André Malraux (1901–1976)
French novelist, art theorist, and minister of cultural affairs, as quoted in *The Artist's Mentor*

Emotional content is an image's most important element. The best images are the ones that retain their strength and impact over the years regardless of the number of times they are viewed.
—Anne Geddes (1956)
Australian-born photographer whose books and posters have been printed in 83 countries; her creative baby photograph collections have sold more than 18 million books and 13 million calendars

Music gives wings to the imagination. Through its evocative nature, it provides the complex infrastructure to stimulate and contain the multiple metaphors of the inner self.
—Carol A. Bush
Author of *Healing Imagery & Music*

The full flowering of the arts and sciences typically follows a civilization's economic and political decline.
From *The Law of Evolutionary Potential* courtesy of University of Michigan Press (1960)

Music is what feelings sound like.
—*Georgia Cates (1974)*
Best-selling American romance author

Listening is the real secret of making music with others.
—*Robert Gass (1948)*
Leadership coach, seminar leader, musician, and composer
who holds a doctorate of organizational and clinical psychology

This will be our response to violence: To make music more intensely, more beautifully, more devotedly than ever before.
—*Leonard Bernstein (1918–1990)*
Famous symphony conductor and composer of *West Side Story*

Great works are performed not by strength, but perseverance.
—*Samuel Johnson (1709–1784)*
English poet, playwright, essayist, moralist, literary critic, biographer,
editor, and lexicographer

I invent nothing. I rediscover.
—*Auguste Rodin (1840–1917)*
French sculptor who created the famous sculpture *The Thinker*

No effort made to attain something beautiful is ever lost.
—*Helen Keller (1880–1968)*

We learn by practice. Whether it means to learn to dance by practicing dancing or to learn to live by practicing living, the principles are the same. One becomes in some area an athlete of God. Practice means to perform, over and over again in the face of all obstacles, some act of vision, of faith, of desire. Practice is a means of inviting the perfection desired.
—*Martha Graham (1894–1991)*
Dancer, choreographer, and dance instructor whose technique transformed American dance and is taught worldwide. *Great Minds Connect* with Babe Didrikson on page 195

GREAT MINDS THINK ALIKE: *The Search for Truth*

That's what artists do. They lie in their search for the truth.
—Bruce Springsteen (1949)
American musician, singer, and songwriter who has sold more than 135 million records
worldwide, won 20 Grammy Awards, two Golden Globes, an Oscar, and Tony Award

A novelist is a person who invents the truth.
—Elizabeth Bowen (1899–1973)
Irish novelist and short story writer

You write what you strive to be...not what you are.
—John Mellencamp (1951)
American rock musician, singer-songwriter, painter, and actor

Chemical synthesis is entirely a creative activity where art, design, imagination & inspiration play predominant roles.
—Robert B. Woodward (1917–1979)
Nobel Prize-winning American chemist specializing
in the synthesis of complex natural products

Be steady and well-ordered in your life so you can be fierce and original in your work.
—Gustave Flaubert (1821–1880)
Prominent French novelist specializing in literary realism

I dream of painting and then I paint my dream.
—Vincent van Gogh (1853–1890)

If people knew how hard I worked to get my mastery, it wouldn't seem so wonderful at all.
—Michelangelo (1475–1564)
Birth name: Michelangelo di Lodovico Buonarroti Simoni
Italian sculptor, artist, and poet who created some of the most iconic creations
in the history of the world. He also coined this famous phrase about sculpture:
Every block of stone has a statue inside it, and it is the task of the sculptor to discover it.

GREAT MINDS THINK ALIKE: *Painting & Poetry*

**Painting is poetry that is seen rather than felt,
and poetry is painting that is felt rather than seen.**
—*Leonardo da Vinci (1462–1519)*
Leonardo seems to be echoing a quote from Plutarch's *Moralia* attributed to Simonides:

**Painting is silent poetry, and poetry is painting
with the gift of speech.**
—*Simonides of Ceos (556–468 BC)*
Greek lyric poet who also invented some of the letters of the Greek alphabet

**The courage of the poet is to keep ajar
the door that leads into madness.**
—*Christopher Morley (1890–1957)*
American journalist, novelist, essayist, poet, and college lecturer
who also produced stage productions

We make poetry out of our quarrel with ourselves.
—*William Butler Yeats (1865–1939)*

Movements of the soul are made known by movements of the body.
—*Leon Alberti (1404–1472)*
Italian Renaissance polymath who was an author, artist, architect, poet, priest,
linguist, philosopher, and cryptographer, from his book *On Painting*

**The good painter has to paint two principle things:
Man, and the intention of his mind.
Movements should announce the motions of the mind.**
—*Leonardo da Vinci (1452–1519)*

If I close my eyes, I see things better than with my eyes open.
—*Henri Matisse (1869–1954)*
French painter and sculptor known as one of the founders of the
modern art movement; Matisse was Pablo Picasso's favorite artist

**The difference between fiction and reality?
Fiction has to make sense.**
—*Tom Clancy (1947–2013)*
American novelist whose books have sold more than 100 million copies

Write drunk, edit sober.
—Ernest Hemingway (1899–1961)
Nobel Prize-winning American novelist and short story writer
who lived an intriguing life before committing suicide

**If one cannot understand the usefulness of the useless, and the
uselessness of the useful, one cannot understand art.**
—Eugene Ionesco (1909–1994)
Romanian-born French playwright known for his avant-garde style

**Graffiti is arguably as old as cave paintings. Its existence
in public rest rooms and on mass transit is a timeless part
of the urban landscape.**
—Phoebe Hoban
American journalist and biographer, as quoted in *The Artist's Mentor*

**Songwriting is about getting the demon out of me. It's like being
possessed. You try to sleep, but the song won't let you. So you have
to get up and make it into something. So, letting go is what
the whole game is.**
—John Lennon (1940–1980)

**Our ability to grow is directly proportional to
our ability to entertain the uncomfortable.**
—Twyla Tharp (1941)
From her book *The Creative Habit*

A first rate soup is more creative than a second-rate painting.
—Abraham Maslow (1908–1970)

**Every child is an artist. The problem is
how to remain an artist once we grow up.**
—Pablo Picasso (1881–1973)

You must master yourself to reach your destiny as an artist.
—Nancy Hillis

To send light into the darkness of men's hearts—
that is the duty of the artist.
—Robert Schumann (1810–1856)
Revered German pianist and composer of the Romantic era who lived a very colorful life
full of turbulent love affairs, political exile, and bouts of poverty

The ability to simplify means to eliminate the unnecessary,
so that the necessary may speak.
—Hans Hoffman (1880–1966)
German-born American abstract impressionist painter and renowned art teacher.
Although Hoffman was referring to simplicity in artwork, this philosophy is just as
applicable to Creativity and Innovation in Business, Science, and Technology.
Great Minds Connect with *Great Minds Think Alike: Simplicity*
on page 166 as well as Isaac Newton on page 86

The goal of art isn't to attain perfection. The goal of art
is to share who we are. And how we see the world...
Great art is created through freedom of expression
and received with freedom of individual interpretation.
Great art opens conversation, rather than closing it...
Great art is an invitation, calling to creators everywhere
to strive for still higher and deeper levels.
—Rick Rubin (1963)
From his book *The Creative Act: A Way of Being*

CONSOLIDATING CHAPTER 10
The Arts & Literature

Chapter 10 contains analysis of and advice on numerous aspects of the visual arts, performing arts, and literary arts...much of which is also applicable to other genres, especially *Work*. Contributors to this chapter note that the arts interpret history by commemorating notable events, social conditions, and extraordinary people. We are told the arts are rooted in passionate creativity driven by dreams, as creativity pulses through the heart of all artistic ventures.

For those who desire careers in the arts, Twyla Tharp emphasizes that dedicated practice is essential, aligning *The Arts* with *Work, Business, The Lessons of Sports,* and *Education*. At their highest levels, all art forms become business, which explains the term show *business*. As with sports, the arts are enjoyed by both hobbyists and spectators. For those who seek to build successful careers in the arts or sports, these genres become serious work reaching into the core of their humanity.

For the purposes of this chapter, the arts encompass film, theatre, dance, music, painting, sculpture, and all forms of literature. These pursuits are vibrant components of a healthy society, even though they are often misunderstood and perpetually undervalued in the United States. Most overlooked is the arts' contribution to local and national economies. A great example is the Broadway theatre district's impact on the economy of New York City. Broadway theatres attract tourists from around the world, thereby supporting hotels, restaurants, and New York City's other tourist attractions, in addition to providing tens of thousands of job opportunities. The same holds true for music concerts at Lincoln Center and Madison Square Garden, as well as art exhibits at the city's numerous museums. While these locations are examples of the arts contributing to one particular city's economy, the same holds true for cultural centers of most major cities worldwide.

Chapter 10 features numerous famous members from arts communities of the past 800 years. The chapter begins with Leonardo da Vinci connecting art with science, followed by Pablo Picasso's belief that the meaning of life is to find your gift, and the purpose of life is to give that gift away. Contributors to this chapter provide a variety of opinions on the underlying purposes of creating art, such as inspiring others, providing beauty, reaffirming our humanity, reflecting the human condition, depicting historic events, envisioning the future, stimulating creativity, and as composer Robert Schumann eloquently states, sending "light into the darkness of men's hearts."

WISDOM TRAILS: *Interconnected Categories*

Science, Technology, Work, Spirituality, Love, History, The Future, Creativity, Observing Human Nature, Faith, Sports, Extreme Desire, Creativity, Courage, Dreams

Trails to Other Chapters

- Leonardo da Vinci finds art in science and *Science* in art.
- Thomas Aquinas differentiates between laborers, craftsmen, and artists. *(Work)*
- D.T. Suzuki informs us that in Japan, art is studied for its *Spiritual* qualities.
- Simone Vay connects the arts with *Love*.
- Arshile Gorky and Ben Shahn discuss the historical role of artists in society. *(History)*.
- Stephanie Storey connects music to math and *Science*.
- Ramona Pringle views art as a catalyst for envisioning *The Future*.
- John F. Kennedy believes recognizing the value of the arts is essential to our nation. (*Government*)
- Alma Thomas notes the timelessness of *Creativity* and art.
- Nancy Hillis describes how the arts commemorate the human condition. *(Observing Human Nature)*
- Pierre-August Renoir talks of painting "the Earth as the paradise of the gods," which connects the arts with *Nature*.
- Martha Graham delivers a dissertation on practicing that connects with *Faith, Sports, Extreme Desire,* and *Work*.
- Leonard Bernstein injects the arts into *Social Justice*.
- Robert Woodward salutes the role of *Creativity* in the arts.
- Gustave Flaubert gives advice on how to be at our best while at *Work*.
- Christopher Morley discusses the *Courage* of the poet.
- Michelangelo's comment about extreme effort applies to *Work, Business,* and *Sports*.
- Leon Alberti finds *Spirituality* in soulful movements of the body.
- Vincent Van Gogh tells us he paints his *Dreams*.
- Phoebe Hoban refers to the roots of cave paintings and graffiti. *(History)*
- Robert Schumann insists the duty of the artist is to bring light into dark hearts. (*Love, Compassion*)

CHAPTER 11

THE POWER
OF PLAY

It is a happy talent to know how to play.
—*Ralph Waldo Emerson (1803–1882)*

Our brains are built to benefit from play no matter what our age.
—*Theresa A. Kestly*
American clinical psychologist, educator, play therapist,
and author of *The International Neurobiology of Play*

You can discover more about a person in an hour of play
than in a year of conversation.
—*Plato (429–347 BC)*

GREAT MINDS THINK ALIKE: *Creativity & Play*

Almost all creativity involves purposeful play.
—*Abraham Maslow (1908–1970)*

The creation of something new is not accomplished
by the intellect, but by the play instinct.
—*Carl Jung (1875–1961)*

Play is the highest form of research...combinatory play is the act of
opening up one mental channel while dabbling in another.
—*Albert Einstein (1879–1955)*

GREAT MINDS THINK ALIKE: *Don't Grow Old*

People do not quit playing because they grow old;
they grow old because they quit playing.
—*Oliver Wendell Holmes, Sr. (1809–1894)*
This maxim is also attributed to George Bernard Shaw
with slightly different wording:

We don't stop playing because we grow old;
we grow old because we stop playing.
—*George Bernard Shaw (1856–1950)*

In our play, we reveal what kind of people we are.
—*Ovid (43 BC–17 AD)*

<u>GREAT MINDS THINK ALIKE:</u> *Learning from Play*

Play is the foundation of learning, creativity,
self-expression and constructive problem solving.
It's how children wrestle with life to make it meaningful.
—*Susan Linn (1948)*
American psychologist, author, lecturer, research associate,
and ventriloquist who also works as a children's entertainer

The most powerful learning is that which is most like play.
—*Warren Bennis (1925–2014)*
From *On Becoming A Leader*

Children learn as they play. Most importantly,
in play children learn how to learn.
—*O. Fred Donaldson (1943)*
American play specialist, author, and lecturer who invented the *Original Play*
game protocol that he has used with both children and wild animals

Play is the way that human beings learn about the world.
That's how we discover how things work.
—*Katie Salen (1969)*
American game designer, educator, author, and proponent of transformative play; Salen
envisions play as a tool for exploring the world...a way to create change

Play is far older than humans...Play is widespread among animals
because it invites problem solving, allowing a creature to test its
limits and develop strategies. The more an animal needs to learn in
order to survive, the more it needs to play. Without play, humans
and many other animals would perish...Social play establishes
rank, mate-finding and cooperation when needed. Play is an activity
enjoyed for its own sake...It is our brain's favorite way of learning
and maneuvering.
—*Diane Ackerman (1948)*
From her book *Deep Play*

Play is not only fundamental to the cognitive and
physical development of children, but was also a
foundation for hunter-gatherers social existence.
—*Peter Gray (1946)*
American psychologist, researcher, scholar, and author specializing
in the relationship between education and play

*When enough people raise play to the status it deserves
in our lives, we will find the world a better place.*
—*Dr. Stuart Brown (1933)*
American medical doctor, psychiatrist, clinical researcher, and author who founded
the National Institute for Play. When his initial research discovered that many murderers
and felony drunk drivers suffered from a lack of play during their childhoods, Brown
launched a lifelong study of the benefits of healthy play, calling it "a developmentally
important human process."

*Play offers an evolutionary advantage to animals, including
humans, by enhancing health and improving the ability to survive
and reproduce...play is essential for the growth and development of a
healthy, fully functional brain.*
—*Chris Kresser*
American educator and author in the fields of functional medicine and ancestral health

*Play is different from game. Play is the free spirit of exploration
doing and being for its own pure joy. Game is an activity defined by a
set of rules, like baseball...play is an attitude, a spirit, a way of doing
things ...when the most challenging labors are undertaken from
the joyous work spirit, they are play... without play, learning and
education are impossible.*
—*Stephen Nachmanovitch (1950)*
From his book *Free Play*

*Leila is cosmic play...play for the sake of playing like a child...
play for play's sake...pure play...everlastingly purposeless play...
play that is and end in itself.*
—*Aldous Huxley (1894–1963)*
From his book *Island*

*Transformational Play provides a lighthearted atmosphere
in which people learn to be in creative flow with others...an
unforgettable and optimal learning environment appears.*
—*Angela Halvorsen Bogo*
Norwegian social technologies facilitator, singer, and storyteller,
from her website transformationalplay.net

The best athlete wants his opponent at his best.
The best general enters the mind of his enemy.
The best businessman serves the communal good.
The best leader follows the will of the people.
All of them embody the virtue of non-competition.
Not that they don't love to compete, but they do it
in the spirit of play.
—*Tao Te Ching, verse 68*
As translated by Stephen Mitchell

Once you see your life as a game, and the things you strive for as no
more than pieces in that game, you'll become a much more effective
player...you must consider other people as players with as much at
stake as yourself, if not more. If you understand their motivations,
you can control the action. Focus less on yourself and more on
others. Your real world is a negotiating table, and like it or not,
you're a participant.
—*Herb Cohen (1938)*
As quoted in *The Adventures of Herbie Cohen: World's Greatest Negotiator.*
In his book *You Can Negotiate Anything,* Cohen offers a shorter quote on this subject*:*
Try to regard all encounters and situations...
including your job, as a game.

CONSOLIDATING CHAPTER 11
The Power of Play

Chapter 11 informs us about the benefits of play by describing how play enhances creativity, facilitates learning, and even slows the aging process. This is in addition to the aerobic benefits of playful physical activities such as sports. Further research on the benefits of play finds broad agreement that play stimulates brain activity, improves body health, enhances cooperation, reduces stress, assists problem-solving, and builds relationships. Play is also a major component of most leisure activities. A deeper dive into how far the tentacles of play extend finds comedians playing with words to make us laugh, dramatic films and theatre playing with our emotions, poets playing with words to arouse our passions, and accountants playing with numbers to minimize their clients' tax liabilities.

Two important takeaways from Chapter 11 are that play is an important part of a healthy lifestyle and also a vibrant aspect of serious business. When combined with intention, play has the potential to transform lives, as *play with a purpose* transcends pure recreation. In so doing, play demonstrates a spiritual aspect. The specifics of what we choose to play, who we decide to play with, and how proficient we are at playing is not nearly as important as the amount of enjoyment and benefit we derive from our playful activities. On a deep level, play inspires the beneficial habits of practice, resilience, innovation, and cooperation. For those skilled enough to make a living by playing a sport or working in the arts, it's vital to continue enjoying the play aspect of those professions once they become businesses.

Of all the categories in this book, *Play* was originally the most nomadic. At first, *Play* was paired with *Sports* because all sports are deeply rooted in the spirit of play. However, it was decided *Extreme Desire* was the best partner for *Sports* because of all the quotes about desire already in the *Sports* category. It was then decided *Play* would be best paired with *Education* because injecting play into education makes children more receptive to learning. However, it was also argued that injecting play into *Work* is good for *Business*. Reviewing all these viable options actually diluted each one of them, making it clear *Play* should have its own category. As soon as that decision was finalized, *The Power of Play* emerged as a central player in a variety of human endeavors.

Further discussion unveiled play as much more than a frivolous human activity; it's a fundamental human need. Chris Kresser enumerates the evolutionary advantages play provides to all species who engage in it, while Carl Jung pinpoints the play instinct as a primary source of creativity. Humans need to recreate to relieve tension and shed nervous energy, but beyond those surface benefits of play, there are many deeper benefits. When conceived and guided properly, play becomes a concept...an independent art form.

Chapter 11 notes there are numerous types and levels of play. The most basic type is *pure play*; the play enjoyed by young children who simply frolic without guidance or structure. Then there is *the playing of games*, with each game possessing its own unique set of rules. There are physical games described as sports, board games such as *Monopoly*, card games, casino games, puzzles, trivia games and television game shows such as *The Price Is Right*...plus it would be remiss not to mention chess and checkers. There are also games such as tag and hopscotch that are physical but aren't sports. When reviewing even this incomplete list, it becomes clear *play* is just as much a mental activity as it is physical. This is what makes the subject of play so intriguing.

Since the beginning of time, humans have been creating new and different ways to play. Quotes in this chapter inform us that most other species in the animal kingdom also indulge in play, especially when young. Nature documentaries have recorded a wide variety of species—from dolphins to baby bears to puppies—engaging in what the Sanskrit language calls *leila*, or *divine play*. Stephen Nachmanovitch defines this type of play as "the free spirit of exploration doing and being for its own pure joy." Such play is cavorting in ocean waves at the beach, ice-skating on a frozen pond, climbing a mountain just to yodel into the canyon below, flying a kite, or a brisk hike to nowhere. Play is also a puppy tearing the stuffing out of a sofa cushion after an hour of fetching sticks, a pig rolling in mud on a hot day, two hawks coasting on thermals high above the tree tops, cooking without a recipe, an ecstatic dance with a toddler, wildly splashing paint across a stretched canvas, juggling three apples, or stopping to watch a glorious sunset. Play is boundless and obeys no clock. It needs no destination and reserves the right to reinvent or morph itself at any moment, always offering a unique ability to enrich our lives. Play offers an infinite array of modalities and possibilities as avenues for self-expression. It symbolizes the celebration of being fully alive by bestowing a special type of freedom on all those who indulge in its pleasures.

Pure play establishes the foundation for competition in games and sports, which are initially played for the joy of playing them. The compulsion to win and a lust for glory are elements that subsequently rise up from our basic human nature. The evolution of the arts follows a similar arc, as most art forms evolve from aspects of play. While play nurtures the roots of sports and the arts, there are numerous other productive applications of play. Surprising benefits are realized when play is mixed into other genres. As elements of play are injected into a work environment, frequently, the result is higher productivity. Injecting play into education results in accelerated and deeper learning. However, a caution must be included, as too much or misdirected play can degenerate into chaos.

A profound dimension of *The Power of Play* is the concept of *play with a purpose*. Play with a purpose attaches goals to playful activities. In sports and games, this can be as simple as wanting to win, but as a character trait, *play with a purpose* becomes a way of life. The final quote in Chapter 11 uses the phrase *transformational play,* previously defined by Katie Salen as *transformative play.* These two similar phrases focus on play's ability to facilitate powerful positive change. When combined with intention and focus, transformational play becomes an independent art form demonstrating it's possible to utilize the art of play to achieve significant growth in numerous fields of endeavor. Targeted play strategies are capable of reshaping businesses, teams, and interpersonal relationships, thereby helping us all move closer to achieving our goals.

WISDOM TRAILS: *Interconnected Categories*

Happiness, Observing Human Nature, Creativity, Innovation, Science, Education, History, Health, Sports, War, Leadership, Business, Love, Work, Politics

Trails to Other Chapters

- Ralph Waldo Emerson believes knowing how to play contributes to *Happiness.*
- Plato learns about people by observing them play. *(Observing Human Nature)*
- Abraham Maslow and Carl Jung connect *Creativity* with play.
- Albert Einstein considers play to be the highest form of research. *(Science)*
- Quotes in *Learning From Play* explore the importance of play in *Education, History,* and *Creativity.*
- Stephen Nachmanovitch differentiates *play* from *game,* as in *Sports.*
- Ovid views play as the essence of *Human Nature.*
- Angela Halvorsen Bogo creates a playful atmosphere to facilitate learning and *Creativity. (Education)*
- The Tao Te Ching connects play with *Sports, Business, Politics, Leadership,* and *War.*
- Herb Cohen advises us to view all of life as a game, thereby injecting the element of play into all human interactions, especially *Work, Business, Politics,* and *Sports. (Observing Human Nature)*

CHAPTER 12

THE LESSONS
OF SPORTS
& EXTREME DESIRE

Sport is life and life is sport. Sport really mirrors life.
—Venus Williams (1980)
Former #1 female tennis player in both singles and doubles,
during an *ESPN* interview on August 27, 2021

What athletics teach is the self-discipline of hard work and sacrifice
necessary to achieve a goal. There are no shortcuts to success...only
temporary success is achieved by taking short cuts. Life is the same
as athletics. Nothing good comes in life or athletics unless a lot of
hard work has preceded the effort...you have to work to accomplish
anything.
—Roger Staubach (1942)
Heisman Trophy winner and star quarterback of the Dallas Cowboys

You miss 100% of the shots you don't take.
—Wayne Gretzky (1961)
Considered by most the greatest professional hockey player ever;
Gretzky also coined another famous phrase:
I skate to where the puck is going to be...not where it has been.

The formula for success is simple: practice and concentration,
then more practice and more concentration.
—Babe Didrikson (1911–1956)
Full name: Mildred Ella Didrikson Zaharias
One of the greatest multi-sport female athletes of all time Didrikson, won Olympic
gold medals in track & field in 1932 before becoming a professional golfer and winning
numerous LPGA championships. *Great Minds Connect* with Martha Graham on page 179

Whatever your goal in life, be proud of
every day you work in that direction.
—Chris Evert (1954)
Hall of Fame tennis player who holds the highest career winning percentage in
the history of women's tennis; she currently is a tennis television commentator for ESPN

To be an innovator, you can't be worried about making mistakes.
—Julius Erving (1950)
Hall of Fame basketball player best known as "Doctor J"

You can't get much done in life if you only
work on the days you feel good.
—*Jerry West (1938)*
Hall of Fame basketball player who transitioned into being
an elite basketball executive and talent evaluator

GREAT MINDS THINK ALIKE: *Extreme Desire*

Desire! That's the one secret of every man's career.
Not education. Not being born with hidden talents.
Desire!
—*Bobby Unser (1934–2021)*
Legendary auto racer and author

What is the single most important quality in a champion?
I would have to say Desire. It comes down to the mental aspect.
All champions have that quality. They don't give up, they dig into
something extra. That's a necessity if you want to be considered
a champion.
—*John McEnroe (1959)*
Seven-time Grand Slam singles champion tennis player and television commentator with
77 singles titles and 78 doubles titles, as quoted in *Winning* by Michael Lynberg

It is not always the strongest person who wins the fight, the fastest
one who wins the race, or the best team that wins the game. In most
cases it's the one who wants it the most, the one who has gone out
and prepared, who has paid the price.
—*Tommy Lasorda (1927–2020)*
Hall of Fame manager of the Los Angeles Dodgers
who spent 69 years in different capacities with that team.
Great Minds Connect with Confucius on page 133

Adversity makes the weak weaker and makes the strong stronger.
You have to pick and choose what side you want to be on.
—*Saquon Barkley (1997)*
NY Giants star running back, discussing his serious knee injury

Champions keep playing until they get it right.
—*Billy Jean King (1943)*
Former #1 American tennis player and Grand Slam champion,
as quoted in *Quma Inspirations Volume 3, #41*

The great ones never take fundamentals for granted.
—*Twyla Tharp (1941)*

Failing to prepare is preparing to fail.
—*John Wooden (1910–2010)*
From *WOODEN: A Lifetime of Observations and Reflections*
On and Off the Court; Wooden failed to mention he was quoting Benjamin Franklin,
its original author, who stated
By failing to prepare, you are preparing to fail.
Great Minds Connect with *Great Minds Think Alike: Preparation* on page 168

*As soon as it hurts, the beginner thinks about stopping. I work
beyond that point. The body isn't used to ten, eleven, or twelve reps
with a maximum weight. No human body was ever prepared for this.
The last few reps are what make muscle grow, an area of pain that
divides the champion from someone who is not a champion. That's
what most people lack, having the guts to go through the pain
no matter what.*
—*Arnold Schwarzenegger (1947)*

*I suppose it's just human nature, but we all have the tendency to
practice the things we already do pretty well. In truth, we should do
just the opposite if we hope to improve.*
—*Nancy Lopez (1957)*
Four-time LPGA golfer of the year who won 48 LPGA events and was inducted
into the World Golf Hall of Fame in 1987, as quoted in *Winning* by Michael Lynberg

*The first thing is to know your faults and then take on a systematic
plan of correcting them. You know the saying about a chain being
only as strong as its weakest link. The same can be said of the chain
of skills a man forges.*
—*Babe Ruth (1895–1948)*
Birth name: George Herman Ruth
Legendary Hall of Fame baseball player known as the Sultan of Swat.
Babe Ruth also said:
It's hard to beat a person who never gives up...
Never let the feat of striking out get in your way.
Great Minds Connect with *Great Minds Think Alike: Defeating Fear* on page 113

You are really never playing an opponent. You are playing yourself, your own highest standards, and when you reach your limits, that is real joy.

—Arthur Ashe (1943–1993)
First African American tennis player to win Wimbledon, Australian, and U.S. Open titles

I could not retreat from a challenge. If the chance was there, no matter how difficult it appeared, if it meant winning, I was going to take it. It was the sweetness of the risk that I remember, and not its dangers. You must play boldly to win.

—Arnold Palmer (1923–2016)
One of the most popular professional golfers of all time, as quoted in *Winning* by Michael Lynberg. *Great Minds Connect* with *Great Minds Think Alike: Be Bold* on page 60

I'm a firm believer in the theory that people only do their best at things they truly enjoy. It's difficult to excel at something you don't enjoy.

—Jack Nicklaus (1940)
One of the greatest professional golfers of all time, he holds the record for most major tournament wins

The best way to teach isn't by preaching to somebody. It's by sharing stories. I call it creative education.

—Kobe Bryant (1978-2020)
One of the greatest professional basketball players of all time who tragically died in a helicopter crash. *Great Minds Connect* with a Red Lake Ojibwe elder on page 267

GREAT MINDS THINK ALIKE: *Winning from Losing*

*Losing strengthens you.
It reveals your weaknesses so you fix them.*

—Pat Summit (1952–2016)
Women's college basketball coach with the most wins in history when she retired

I've learned that something constructive comes from every defeat.

—Tom Landry (1924–2000)
Innovative Hall of Fame coach of the Dallas Cowboys for 29 years. *Great Minds Connect* with *Great Minds Think Alike: The Many Sides of Failure* on page 129

He who is not courageous enough to take risks
will accomplish nothing in life.
—*Muhammad Ali (1942–2016)*
American boxer, media icon, social activist, and philanthropist who
was considered by many to be the greatest heavyweight champion ever.
Great Minds Connect with Leo Buscaglia on page 115 and Mark Zuckerberg on page 128

The most important measure of how good a game I played
was how much better I made my teammates play.
—*Bill Russell (1934–2022)*
Hall of Fame basketball player who won 11 NBA championships in his 13-year career; one
of the greatest defensive players in history, he was the heart and soul of the Boston Celtic
dynasty in the 1960s

GREAT MINDS THINK ALIKE: *Teamwork*

You will never get the same effort from one man seeking
glory as from a group of men pulling for a shared goal.
—*Bo Schembechler (1929–2006)*
University of Michigan head football coach for 21 years
and a member of the College Football Hall of Fame

Individual commitment to a group effort is what makes a team work,
a company work, a society work, a civilization work.
—*Vince Lombardi (1913–1970)*
Legendary head coach of the Green Bay Packers

You always have to focus in life on what you want to achieve.
—*Michael Jordan (1963)*
Acclaimed by most as the greatest basketball player of all time,
Jordan is also an immensely successful businessman and author of
For the Love of the Game: My Story and *Driven from Within.*
Another Michael Jordan quote is:
If you run into a wall, don't turn around and give up.
Figure out how to climb it, go through it, or work around it.

The difference between the possible and the impossible lies in a man's
determination. Set your goals in life, and go after them with all the
drive, self-confidence, and determination you possess.
—*Tommy Lasorda (1927–2020)*

Fear is the greatest obstacle to learning. It's like fire. If you learn to control it, you let it work for you. If you don't learn to control it, it'll destroy you and everything around you...Heroes and cowards feel exactly the same fear. Heroes just react differently to it.

—Cus D'Amato (1908–1985)

Boxing manager of heavyweight champions Floyd Paterson and Mike Tyson.

Mike Tyson (1966) developed his own version of this phrase:

Fear is your best friend or your worst enemy. It's like fire. If you control it, it can cook for you; it can heat your house. If you can't control it, it will burn everything around you and destroy you.

What is right is more important than who is right...A leader is interested in finding the best way, not in having his own way. The goal is to create correct habits that can be produced instinctively under great pressure.

—John Wooden (1910–2010)

From *WOODEN: A Lifetime of Observations and Reflections On and Off the Court.*

Great Minds Connect with Harry Truman on page 225

GREAT MINDS THINK ALIKE: *Resilience*

Our greatest glory is not in never failing, but in rising every time we fail.

—Confucius (551–479 BC)

It's not whether you get knocked down. It's whether you get up.

—Vince Lombardi (1913–1970)

The strength of the group is the strength of the leader.

—Vince Lombardi (1913–1970)

From *Bart Starr: When Leadership Mattered*

Great Minds Connect with Lee Iacocca on page 144

Try not to do too many things at once; know what you want. Persevere and get it done.

—George Allen (1918–1990)

NFL Hall of Fame coach of the Washington Redskins and the Los Angeles Rams

To have long term success as a coach, or in any position
of leadership, you have to be obsessed in some way.
—*Pat Riley (1945)*
Professional basketball player, championship coach,
author, and motivational speaker; Riley also popularized the phrase:
You prove your worth with your actions, not your mouth.
Although often credited to Pat Riley, it appears that
this quote's original author was the German romantic writer
Johann Paul Friedrich Richter better known as Jean Paul...see page 98

The quality of a person's life is in direct proportion to their
commitment to excellence, regardless of their chosen field of
endeavor. The difference between a successful person and
others is not a lack of strength, not a lack of knowledge,
but rather in a lack of will.
—*Vince Lombardi (1913–1970)*

GREAT MINDS THINK ALIKE: *Perfection*

Perfection is not attainable, but if we chase perfection,
we can catch excellence.
—*Vince Lombardi (1913–1970)*

Perfection is what you are striving for, but perfection
is an impossibility. However, striving for perfection
is not an impossibility.
—*John Wooden (1910–2010)*
From *WOODEN: A Lifetime of Observations and Reflections On and Off the Court*

Success is perishable and often outside our control.
In contrast, excellence is something that's lasting,
dependable, and largely within a person's control.
—*Joe Paterno (1926–2012)*
Penn State head football coach from 1966 until 2011; his teams won 409 games,
the most wins for any college football coach

It is much more difficult to break a habit
when there is no adequate replacement for it.
—*Timothy Gallwey (1938)*
American tennis player, coach, and author, from his book *The Inner Game of Tennis*

You never get ahead of anyone as long as you're trying to get even.
—Lou Holtz (1937)
The only college football coach to lead six different schools to bowl games, Holtz is a member of the College Football Hall of Fame who also worked as an ESPN sports analyst

A lot of parents think kids learn responsibility from work, and I've always said: Baloney. Kids learn leadership and organization from games, from having fun.
—John Madden (1936–2021)
Hall of Fame pro football coach and sports commentator who won 16 Sports Emmy Awards, as quoted in *Winning* by Michael Lynberg

Good thoughts have much to do with good rowing. It isn't enough for the muscles of the crew to work in unison; their hearts and minds must also be as one. To see a winning crew in action is to witness a perfect harmony in which everything is right... That is the formula for endurance and success.
—George Yeomans Pocock (1891–1976)
British-born racing shell builder, coach of the 1956 USA Olympic Champion rowing team, and mentor for numerous champion oarsmen and coaches

A life is not important except in the impact is has on other lives. Life is not a spectator sport. If you spend your whole life in the grandstand just watching what goes on, you're wasting your life.
—Jackie Robinson (1919–1972)
Hall of Fame baseball player who became the first African American to play in the major leagues when he broke the "color barrier" in 1947

The first step in creating an improved future is developing the ability to envision it.
—Jim Tressel (1952)
Former Ohio State University football coach, from his book *The Winners Manual for the Game of Life*

It's harder to stay on top than it is to make the climb. Continue to seek new goals.
—Pat Summit (1952–2016)

Sporting expeditions are in certain respects like religious pilgrimages...sport, by ordering and sublimating our energies and by closing off the world's drudgery and confusion, can evoke our spiritual depths like a work of art or a monastic discipline.
—*Michael Murphy (1930)*
Co-founder of Esalen Institute and author of books about human potential

Learning focus of attention is a master skill that has unlimited application. Focus of attention is at the heart of doing anything well.
—*Timothy Gallwey (1938)*
From his book *The Inner Game of Tennis*

Work like you don't need the money. Love like you've never been hurt. Dance like nobody's watching.
—*Leroy "Satchel" Paige (1906–1982)*
The oldest Major League rookie in history, first Negro League player
to pitch in a World Series, and the first Negro League player to be inducted
into the baseball Hall of Fame

It's essential for athletes to learn to open their hearts so that they can collaborate with one another in a meaningful way...The first thing I did with the Bulls was teach the players an abbreviated version of mindfulness meditation based on the Zen practice I'd been doing for years. I developed a number of strategies to help them quiet their minds and build awareness so they could go into battled poised and in control. I also introduced the players to yoga, tai chi and other Eastern practices to help them balance mind, body and spirit. Our goal was to bond the players together so they would experience what we called "one breath, one mind"... I talked about basketball as a spiritual game...so I devoted one of our practice sessions to talking about the Buddha's thinking and how it applies to basketball... That's what gives you strength and energy in the midst of chaos.
—*Phil Jackson (1945)*
Hall of Fame NBA coach who won 11 Championships...two as a player with the NY Knicks, and nine while coaching the Chicago Bulls and Los Angeles Lakers; in his book *Eleven Rings*, Jackson describes his eclectic and sophisticated style of leadership as "controlled improvisation"

CONSOLIDATING CHAPTER 12
The Lessons of Sports & Extreme Desire

Lessons learned from sports serve as metaphors for an array of human endeavors. The number of connections sports has to other arenas of life is impressive. Chapter 12 highlights the significant contribution of sports to other walks of life by documenting its multitude of connections with *Happiness, Work, Politics, War, Business,* and *Leadership.* Notably, there are no win-win scenarios in competitive sports; when one team wins, the other team loses. This differentiates sports from business, as the best business transactions result in win-win scenarios. The same is true for interpersonal relationships. On the other hand, the absence of win-win scenarios in sports aligns it with politics and war, causing those two categories to resemble sports competitions. That's why *Sports* is such a vibrant and volatile category; its lessons vary greatly depending on the genre they are applied to.

All sports begin with play. Initially, children play sports purely for the love of playing. Later in life, playing sports becomes either a hobby or a career. At some point, playing to win becomes serious for elite athletes, and for supremely elite athletes, serious play develops into a business. Even then, the element of play must remain for professional success to be enjoyed. If playing a sport feels solely like work, it can become tedious, wearisome, and overly repetitive...thereby eroding happiness. This is also true in business, which is the reason large corporations frequently spend fortunes on offsite meetings featuring sports-related activities.

It's important to differentiate between playing sports for pure joy and aspiring to create careers as professional athletes. Another consideration is the nature of each particular sport, as every sport presents its own unique challenges. In all sports, athletes are challenging their own limitations and mental barriers plus dealing with the physical demands of competition. Most sports involve competing against someone or an opposing team, but sports like golf force players to compete against the golf course and each players' own internal demons. Arthur Ashe eloquently broaches this dimension of sports by revealing that in individual sports like tennis and golf, players are essentially playing against themselves.

Sports share intimate relationships with creativity, business, and the performing arts. A linguistic connection between sports and the arts is that participants in theatrical productions are called *players*...as are movie moguls in Hollywood, major business executives, and adversaries in chess matches. Political campaigns frequently resemble extended sport seasons, as campaigns conclude with confrontations between the two strongest candidates. This conjures up the similarity of sports to war and politics...especially when extreme desire for victory becomes an obsession. Sports, politics, and war all require effective strategies and good leadership. Leaders in sports are identified as managers, coaches, and captains, with politics and the military using different terminologies to identify those types of leadership roles.

As explained in Chapter 7, it's vital to love our work. It's also important to feel camaraderie with work colleagues. This leads to another differentiation between various sports: *team sports versus individual sports.* Collaboration and teamwork have deep roots in both sports and work. The wisdom derived from sports extends to business, the arts, government, and war as well as science and technology, where teams of scientists and engineers are formed to work on complex endeavors. In return, technology has become increasingly important in sports; technological developments have altered the playing field in almost every sport...such as bobsled design, football helmets, concussion protocols, medical treatments and surgeries, etc. This connects sports with science and health, a connection beyond the obvious need for athletes to have healthy diets and exercise routines.

The Extreme Desire Controversy

The type of desire discussed in this chapter is *extreme desire*; desire breeding a willingness to disregard all collateral damage to achieve a passionately coveted goal. While such desire is widely praised in the world of sports, a very different analysis of desire exists in the realms of spirituality and happiness. This leads to what shall be called *The Extreme Desire Controversy,* a controversy simmering throughout the worlds of sports, business, work, success, and the arts before infiltrating into science, technology, and any endeavor demanding extreme desire as an element of great success. On the flip side of extreme desire is an acceptance of what is...satisfaction with what you have, not being attached to the outcome as much as the process, enjoying teamwork, preparation, and excellence as ends in themselves...a belief that *the journey is the destination,* with a desire for inner peace as a primary goal.

The Extreme Desire Controversy has many sides to it, with implications seeping into every aspect of life. All levels of desire are drivers of passion, thereby establishing desire as one of the main motivators of all human exploits. Unbalanced desire can become dangerous, but then again, it can also propel a person or organization to greatness. In so doing, desire transforms itself into a sort of necessary evil. This is where the road splits and the trail becomes tangled in multiple layers of debate. To excel in sports, extreme desire is mandatory, as proclaimed by numerous quotes in this chapter. In fact, rampant desire to succeed at all costs is part of the blueprint for greatness in sports. The same is true for business, science, and the arts, as passionate desire fuels a determination to persevere against all odds. Unfortunately, such desire is often accompanied by equally great unhappiness. When desire becomes all-consuming, it's helpful to pause and seek a better perspective on where you're headed on a personal level, because overwhelming desire can entangle personal lives much like it entangles professional ones. This leads to Maya Angelou's phrase about the difference between *making a living* and *making a life*. The more aware we are of all dimensions of our passionate endeavors, the more likely we are to emerge fulfilled and happy, a concept about mastering passions addressed by Alfred Lord Tennyson on page 120. This is why extreme desire is identified in Buddhism as a cause of suffering...so the *extreme desire* debate becomes about happiness, which applies to all arenas of life.

The point of conflict is that moderating desire to create balance in one's life can be a hindrance to exhilarating success. For example, to become champions, athletes must train and work at their craft with a focused dedication bound to cause imbalances. The same holds true for anyone attempting to create a major business, a great work of art, or run for political office. Each individual and each business must understand that achieving the exceptional requires a rebalancing of priorities and creation of healthy balances between the competing forces of desire, happiness, and health.

It's important to acknowledge another dimension of extreme desire: the desire for material possessions and wealth, a side of desire garnering universal scorn from this book's contributors who tell us why *less becomes more* and how gluttony is the surest path to unhappiness. This debate reaches the roots of happiness, with voices from every era of history reiterating the same advice:

The key to happiness is not about having more, it's about desiring less. Wealth and possessions command little respect when evaluating how happy a person will be, as many poor people who live simple lives with few possessions turn out to be the happiest of all. This seemingly contradictory reality views desire as a form of craving that is clearly an unhealthy mental state.

Please bear in mind, extreme desire is complex, with multiple levels, such as:

- Extreme desire for personal glory
- Group desire...the desire to collaborate and function as a team.
- Extreme desire to excel at something...to be the best you can; in extreme states, this can develop into an obsession to be better than everyone else...ultimately, to be the best of all time
- The desire to win...to become a champion, get elected, win a battle, win a war, build a business, conquer another nation
- Extreme desire to control others
- Extreme desire for possessions and wealth
- Extreme desire to help others is very different from self-centered desires, but a passion nonetheless. Passionate philanthropy is a manifestation of such desire.

The following list summarizes the predominant effects of extreme desire.

- *How extreme desire helps:* Energizes, inspires practice rituals, develops skills and stamina, overrides insecurities, provides clear goals to pursue.
- *How extreme desire hurts:* Creates imbalances, can lead to isolation, can justify being inconsiderate, can hurt the ones who love you, can narrow perspective and limit peripheral vision.

- *What diminishes negative aspects of desire:* Compassion, a sense of humor, self-awareness, and surrender combined with collegiality.
- *What increases negative effects of desire:* Blind ambition, lack of discipline, impatience, loss of perspective.

Impatience can become problematic if it interferes with practice, which is an essential part of skill development for athletes and artists. Ravenous desire has a tendency to demand immediate results, which is counterproductive to practice because practice focuses on the process more than the result. Sophisticated practice demands disciplined faith and patience to sustain incremental growth and a polishing of skills...a taming of extreme desire. Once tamed, extreme desire can enhance practice by increasing stamina and focus. The issue of patience directly applies to business, where "the grind" replaces the word *practice*.

Extreme desire can also stimulate social interaction. Even individual sports require teams of support personnel and interaction with a myriad of people. This explains why professional athletes in individual sports such as golf and tennis have support teams to interact with on a regular basis. Team sports feature a combination of individual desire and team desire by employing a variety of support personnel to supplement supportive teammates and coaches. This combines desire for self-improvement with a collaborative desire to create collective success. A big part of success in professional sports is surrender to the process... without a lessening of desire. An intriguing merger of Buddhist principles with overwhelming desire was implemented by basketball coach Phil Jackson (see pag 203), known as the *Zen Master* when he coached legendary basketball players Michael Jordan and Kobe Bryant. These two athletes were consumed by raging desire but simultaneously embraced Jackson's Buddhist principles to further empower their efforts. Although desire is considered a source of suffering in Buddhism, Jackson's marriage of these two opposing forces created a swirl of entropic energy that surrounded his players, leading them to greater heights. Since overwhelming desire requires sacrifice, a major question becomes: *What—and how much— are you willing to sacrifice to manifest your dreams and achieve your goals?*

In the final analysis, extreme desire is not necessarily good or evil. It's a mental and emotional state everyone experiences in varying degrees. Although *Sports* is the category sparking *The Extreme Desire Controversy*, this matter is a widespread human issue relevant to numerous facets of life. What becomes clear is that desire must be harnessed and focused to provide best results. Passionate desire inspires creative solutions capable of evolving on a spiritual level. Finding balance to mitigate the potential hazards of extreme desire, combined with a flexible mixture of compassion, friendship, and love appears to be the formula for establishing and maintaining a happy, productive life.

WISDOM TRAILS: *Interconnected Categories*

Success, Work, Innovation, Education, Business, Politics, Observing Human Nature, Courage, Government, Fear, Leadership, The Future, Spirituality

Trails to Other Chapters

- Roger Staubach, Chris Evert, and Jerry West connect *Sports* with *Work*.
- Babe Didrikson provides her formula for *Success*.
- Bobby Unser rates desire as more important than *Education*.
- Tommy Lasorda's quote on preparation and desire also applies to *Business, Politics, War,* and *The Arts*.
- Julius Erving pinpoints fearlessness as a necessity for *Innovation*.
- Nancy Lopez discusses *Human Nature*.
- Babe Ruth's advice about systematically correcting faults applies to any endeavor...especially *The Arts, Business, Politics, Government,* and *War*.
- Arthur Ashe discusses aspects of sports that create *Happiness*.
- Jack Nicklaus cites the need to enjoy our *Work*.
- Kobe Bryant believes the best way to *Educate* is by telling stories.
- Quotes in *Winning From Losing* highlight the silver lining of defeat, aligning with *Business* advice about overcoming failure to achieve *Success*. *(War)*
- Muhammad Ali touts the virtues of *Courage*.
- Quotes in *Teamwork* apply to *Business, War, Government,* and *The Arts*.
- Michael Jordan stresses the need for focus to achieve *Success*. *(Work)*
- Cus D'Amato discusses how *Fear* can be either an ally or an enemy.
- John Wooden discusses *Leadership*.
- Quotes in *Resilience* apply to *Business, Science, Politics, War,* and *Success*.
- Vince Lombardi notes the importance of *Leadership*. *(Business, Politics, War)*
- Pat Riley observes that great *Leaders* are often obsessed.
- Joe Paterno reminds us *Success* is perishable.
- Timothy Gallwey highlights a quirk in *Human Nature*.
- John Madden believes kids learn *Leadership* from *Play* better than from *Work*.
- George Yeomans Pocock explains why rowing teaches great lessons for *Success*.
- Jim Tressel offers advice in how to create a better *Future*.
- Michael Murphy connects sports with *Spirituality*.
- Satchel Paige offers advice on dancing, *Love,* and *Work*.
- Phil Jackson connects sports with *Spirituality* to achieve *Success*.

CHAPTER 13

EDUCATION

Education is the most powerful weapon
we can use to change the world.
—Nelson Mandela (1918–2013)

The value of education is not the learning of many facts
but the training of the mind to think.
—Albert Einstein (1879–1955)

GREAT MINDS THINK ALIKE: *Education & Democracy*

The foundation of every state is the education of its youth.
—Diogenes (412–323 BC)
Turkish-born Greek philosopher who was a very colorful character, one of the founders of
Cynic philosophy, and thought to be the first person to use the word "cosmopolitan" when
he declared himself a citizen of the world rather than identifying with his country

Education is the cornerstone of a democracy.
—Abraham Lincoln (1809–1865)

Civic responsibility should be taught in elementary school.
—Donna Brazile (1959)
American community activist, educator, and author who was the
first African American woman to lead a presidential campaign

Wherever you are...that is the entry point.
—Kabir (1440–1518)
Indian mystic poet and saint. Although not readily apparent, this quote brings up a vital
aspect of teaching...the importance of finding an entry point into the minds of students to
teach them effectively; this is the key to maximizing the receptivity of each student.

To know that we know what we know, and to know that we
do not know what we do not know, that is true knowledge.
—Nicolaus Copernicus (1473–1543)
Polish mathematician, astronomer, physician, scholar, translator, governor, and diplomat
most famous for his pioneering statement that the Earth rotated around the sun

Education is not the filling of a pail, but the lighting of a fire.
—William Butler Yeats (1865–1939)

***If you think education is expensive,
wait till you find out the cost of ignorance.***
—Barack Obama (1961)
Attorney, United States Senator, and first African-American president of the United States

***Civilization is not inherited; it has to be learned and earned by each
generation answer; if the transmission should be interrupted for one
century, civilization would die, and we should be savages again.
So our finest contemporary achievement is our unprecedented
expenditure of wealth and toil in the provision of higher education
for all.***
—Will Durant (1885–1981) & Ariel Durant (1898–1981)
From their co-written book *The Lessons of History*

***Skepticism is as much the result of knowledge
as knowledge is of skepticism.***
—Homer (unknown, c. 1250–850 BC)

The greatest education in the world is watching the masters at work.
—Michael Jackson (1958–2009)
Megastar singer-songwriter, dancer, and choreographer,
from autobiography, *Moonwalk*

***The delicate balance of mentoring someone is not creating them
in your own image, but giving them the opportunity to
create themselves.***
—Steven Spielberg (1946)

The true textbook for the pupil is his teacher.
—Mohandas (Mahatma) Gandhi (1869–1948)
From his autobiography *The Story of My Experiments with Truth*

***Live as if you were to die tomorrow.
Learn as if you were to live forever.***
— Mohandas (Mahatma) Gandhi (1869–1948)

*The whole art of teaching is the art of awakening
the natural curiosity of young minds for the purpose
of satisfying them afterwards.*
—Anatole France (1844–1924)

The average teacher is prone to kill imagination in the young.
—Charles D. Aring, MD (1929–1998)
Prominent American neurologist, from his 1977
Journal of the American Medical Association article

GREAT MINDS THINK ALIKE: *Knowing It All*

*Once the heart learns to admit "I don't know,"
that's when the real learning can begin.*
—Maimonides (1138–1204)

It is what you learn after you know it all that counts.
—John Wooden (1910–2010)
From *WOODEN: A Lifetime of Observations and Reflections On and Off the Court*

When the student is ready, the teacher will appear.
—Lao Tzu (571–unknown BC)

GREAT MINDS THINK ALIKE: *Great Teachers*

*There are no great teachers or great students...
it's the meeting of the two together.*
—Luciano Pavarotti (1935–2007)
World famous Italian operatic tenor, as quoted by Madelyn Renee

*The great teachers do not tell you what to do,
they show you how to be.*
—Roger Jahnke (1947)
Master teacher, healer, and author of books on the practice
of Qi Gong, from *The Healing Promise of Qi*

*The mediocre teacher tells. The good teacher explains.
The superior teacher demonstrates. The great teacher inspires.*
—William Arthur Ward (1924–1994)
Prolific American motivational writer

To teach is to learn twice.
—Joseph Joubert (1754–1824)
French essayist and moralist whose works were all published posthumously

**Knowledge is power only when organize
and put into a plan of action.**
—Napoleon Hill (1883–1970)
From *Think and Grow Rich*

Repetition is the mother of learning.
—T. Harv Eker (1954)
From his book *Secrets of the Millionaire Mind.*
Great Minds Think Alike: with Martha Graham about practice on page 179

**When I learn something new, and it happens every day,
I feel a little more at home in the universe.**
—Bill Moyers (1934)
American journalist, author, and political commentator, from *A World of Ideas*

**All the genius I have lies in this: When I have a subject in hand,
I study it profoundly. Day and night it is before me. I explore it
in all its bearings. My mind becomes pervaded with it. Then the effort
I have made is what people call the fruit of genius. The fruit of genius
is the fruit of labor & thought.**
—Alexander Hamilton (1757–1804)
A founding father of the United States and one of George Washington's
most trusted colleagues, Hamilton was killed in a historic duel with Aaron Burr
and is now immortalized in a Broadway musical

**Educating the mind without educating the heart
is no education at all.**
—Aristotle (384–322 BC)
Great Minds Connect with Mahatma Gandhi on page 275

The desire to know is natural to all good people.
—Leonardo da Vinci (1452–1519)

To educate a man in mind and not in morals
is to educate a menace to society.
—*Theodore Roosevelt (1858–1919)*
Statesman, conservationist, author, governor of New York,
and former president of the United States

Learning is as much an attitude as it is an activity.
—*Frank Sonnenberg (1955)*
Award-winning author named one of America's Top 100
Thought Leaders and Most Influential Small Business Experts

GREAT MINDS THINK ALIKE: *The Grandeur of Reading*

The reading of all good books is like conversation
with the finest minds of past centuries.
—*Rene Descartes (1596–1650)*
French philosopher, mathematician, and scientist
eternally famous for coining the phrase, *"I think, therefore I am"*

Books are uniquely portable magic
that bind together people of different lifetimes.
—*Stephen King (1947)*
American author of horror, supernatural fiction, suspense, and fantasy novels
whose books have sold more than 350 million copies; several of which
have been adapted into feature films or television series

There is frequently more to be learned from the unexpected questions
of a child than from the discourses of men.
—*John Locke (1632–1704)*
English political philosopher often referred to as the "father of liberalism"

One remains young as a long as one can still learn,
can still take on new habits, can bear contradictions.
—*Marie von Ebner-Eschenbach (1830–1916)*
Austrian writer of psychological novels

Change is the end result of all true learning.
—*Leo Buscaglia (1924–1998)*
Great Minds Connect with the *Great Minds Think Alike: Change* on page 87,
as well as Mark Cuban on page 143

Subject content has been mastered when you can successfully teach it to others.
—Gerald A. Michaelson (1929–2004)
From *Sun Tzu for Success*

If you can't explain it simply, then you don't understand it well enough.
—Albert Einstein (1879–1955)

Your brain has a capacity for learning that is virtually limitless, which makes every human a potential genius.
—Michael J. Gelb (1952)

Everybody is a genius, but if you judge a fish by its ability to climb a tree, it will live its whole life believing that it is stupid.
—Albert Einstein (1879–1955)

True ignorance is not the absence of knowledge, but the refusal to acquire it.
—Karl Popper (1902–1994)
Austrian-born British philosopher best known for his writings
about science, politics, and social issues

Rather than a linear accumulation of facts, knowledge can be seen as the replacement of one worldview with another... paradigms do not only exist in science, but are the natural human way of comprehending the world.
—Tom Butler-Bowdon (1967)
From his book *50 Philosophy Classics*

The true aim of education is to awaken real powers of perception and judgment in relation to life and living. For only such an awakening can lead to true freedom.
—Rudolph Steiner (1861–1925)
Austrian philosopher, writer, lecturer, and social reformer
who founded anthroposophy as well as the Waldorf schools

GREAT MINDS THINK ALIKE: *Learning From Questions*

Education shouldn't be about delivering answers.
It should be about asking more questions.
—*John Lloyd*
American educator with a PhD in special education

Once you learn to ask questions...relevant, appropriate and
substantial questions...you have learned how to learn, and no one
can keep you from learning whatever you want or need to know.
—*Neil Postman (1931–2003) and Charles Weingartner (1922–2007)*
Postman and Weingartner were educators and authors who collaborated on a
number of books on the subject of education, including *Teaching as a Subversive Activity*.
Great Minds Connect with *The Art of The Question* on page 161

Schools have to periodically change the way they do business
if they want to be the heart of the community.
—*Jacqueline von Edelberg*
American political science Fulbright Scholar, author, and social entrepreneur
who helped revive the Nettelhorst School in a Chicago suburb

We learn best when we have a deadline.
—*M. Scott Peck (1936–2005)*
From *Further Along The Road Less Traveled*

Intelligence is something we are born with.
Thinking is a skill that must be learned.
—*Edward de Bono (1933–2021)*
De Bono was a proponent of schools teaching students *how* to think in addition to
standard fact-based curriculums. To avoid any possible confusion, it's necessary to
differentiate teaching *how* to think from teaching *what* to think, which can be interpreted
as brainwashing. Teaching students "thinking skills" aims to improve their abilities to learn.

The most essential prerequisite to understanding is to
be able to admit when you don't understand something.
—*Richard Saul Wurman (1935)*
American architect, graphic designer, author of 90 books, and cofounder of the TED
(Technology, Entertainment, Design) conferences that connect ideas across multiple
disciplines, aligning them with the *Medici Effect*. This quote is from *Information Anxiety 2*.

The most important thing parents can teach their children
is how to get along without them.
—*Frank A. Clark (1860–1935)*

An education capable of saving humanity is no small undertaking;
it involves the spiritual development of man, the enhancement of
his value as an individual, and the preparation of young people to
understand the times in which they live.
—*Maria Montessori (1870–1952)*
Italian physician and educator famous for creating the Montessori method of teaching, from a collection of her lectures published as *Education and Peace*. Montessori's strong opinions on the education of children are exemplified by the following two statements:
If teaching is to be effective with young children
it must assist them to advance on the way to independence.
From *The Discovery of the Child*
One test of the correctness of educational procedure
is the happiness of the child.
From *What You Should Know About Your Child*

The measure of teachers are their students.
—*Dan Millman (1946)*
From his book *Peaceful Heart, Warrior Spirit*

The less instruction interferes with the process of learning built into
your very DNA, the more effective your progress is going to be …the
less fear and doubt are embedded in the instructional process, the
easier it will be to take the natural steps of learning. Natural learning
is from the inside out, not vice versa…it is your individual internal
learning process that ultimately governs your learning.
—*W. Timothy Gallwey (1938)*
From his book *The Inner Game of Tennis*

Our progress as a nation can be no swifter
than our progress in education.
—*John F. Kennedy (1917–1963)*

Becoming one with his physical environment was a natural to an Indian child's education as learning to read and write was to an American boy.

—Bob Drury and Tom Clavin

From their book about Red Cloud and the struggles of 19th-century Native American life, *The Heart of Everything That Is*. Drury is a prolific American journalist and author; Clavin is the author of 18 nonfiction books about military history, sports, and entertainment

Education through art may be especially important, not so much for turning out artists or art products, as for turning out better people.

—Abraham Maslow (1908–1970)

Maslow's humanistic philosophy believes the purpose of education is to help create better human beings; it views college as a place where students discover their identity and vocation. From *The Farther Reaches of Human Nature*

Knowledge is the superpower of the 21ˢᵗ century. Even the smartest people alive when I was born did not know what 10-year-olds today have available to them. That is truly cause for hope.

—Sylvia Earle (1935)

American marine biologist, explorer, and author, as quoted in the November 8, 2021 issue of *Time*

Preventing war is the work of politicians, establishing peace is the work of educationists.

—Maria Montessori (1870–1952)

This philosophy gained the attention of Mahatma Gandhi and helped to forge a supportive friendship between them

CONSOLIDATING CHAPTER 13
Education

Education helps build the foundation for all societies...modern or ancient, advanced or primitive. Chapter 13 informs us that education is the primary method utilized by contemporary cultures to pass traditions on to future generations. While most tribal cultures continue to pass on ancestral knowledge and cultural rituals through oral traditions, modern societies increasingly rely on written materials and technology. Though transmission methods vary widely, all cultures educate their young in some manner. Regardless of the chosen methods, education preserves the historical roots that bind societies together. In modern societies, education also functions as the foundation for science, technology, the arts, and all forms of work and business. Ideally, educational institutions provide moral integrity, inspire curiosity, develop creativity, and foster an atmosphere of collegiality. Simply put, the overarching purpose of general education is to produce upstanding citizens who will perpetuate societal norms, with higher education and vocational schools preparing students for productive careers. Diogenes, Abraham Lincoln, and Will and Ariel Durant all view good education as a vital component of healthy nations, a view reinforced by Sylvia Earle who believes knowledge is the superpower of the 21st century. Not to be outdone, Maria Montessori bestows education with the power to inspire spiritual growth capable of restoring world peace to save civilization from self-destruction.

Public education ideally helps create the fabric of modern societies by providing a system for nations to instill broad knowledge and traditional values into their youth. An important unstated benefit gained from healthy educational cultures is that students learn to peacefully coexist with each other while also gaining a perspective on how their societies function. This valuable enculturation factor of education is potentially more important for youth than their preparation for future careers.

Education interfaces with all aspects of life. In the broadest sense, education takes place everywhere, especially in tribal cultures. If approached with openness, life can become a perpetually educational experience. Parents and elders serve as teachers and role models for children, and in modern societies, many individuals learn more about life when out of school than during classes. This is especially true for vocational skills best learned on the job. Education is the conduit through which human achievement must travel on its way to fulfillment. It's an integral part of the maintenance and growth of civilizations. Formal education is not the whole picture...the dissemination of truth throughout tribes and nations is essential for societies to retain stability. In modern societies, we gather information from various media and daily conversation. This connects education to government, politics, and social justice through an assortment of media.

Chapter 13 tells us education is best when students are taught *how to think* and are inspired to grow both intellectually and socially. Education has many operational elements, as it can be viewed from the viewpoint of teachers, students, government and/or business. Since public education is dependent on funding from government and politicians, it unfortunately becomes ensnared in partisan bickering. In addition, institutions of higher learning are vulnerable to outside pressures due to eternal dependence on financial support from wealthy alumni, large corporations, and government grants.

This chapter displays a connection with Chapter 11 by pointing out the importance of play in educational processes. The *Great Minds Think Alike: Learning From Play* on page 188 features insightful quotes about the role of play in enhancing students' ability to think productively. This brings us to the true heroes of education: the teachers. Teachers are education's foot soldiers responsible for creating healthy learning environments. Although they're rarely adequately recognized or rewarded for their roles as leaders and role models, teachers who inspire curiosity and instill compassion in their students are providing an invaluable service. Kabir gets to the heart of all learning when he indicates that finding an entry point into each student's mind is the foundational challenge of teaching...the delicate combustion point of education where the mind of each student meets the mind of each teacher. This transient intersection determines the depth and quality of a student's learning experience. Once a student's entry point is discerned, the art of teaching proceeds to Lao Tzu's Chapter 5 quote about a thousand-mile journey beginning with one step, which encourages the education process to break down each learning challenge into a series of achievable steps. A combination of identifying entry points and implementing a "chip away" approach to learning fortifies the teaching process.

Anatole France calls teaching an art, Aristotle reminds teachers to also educate the heart, and Theodore Roosevelt insists we should teach morality to all students. On page 198, Kobe Bryant views storytelling as an educator's greatest asset, and John Lloyd advises us to ask more questions. Meanwhile, Dr. Charles Aring offers a note of caution, warning that average teachers are prone to stifle the imagination of their students. Michael Gelb informs us every person has the potential to become a genius, and Alexander Hamilton tells us intense focus is what helped him achieve lofty cerebral states. Joseph Joubert's eclectic comment "to teach is to learn twice" implies teaching is an educational experience for teachers as well as students. This statement reflects the fact that a teacher's depth and understanding of a subject grows during the act of transmitting knowledge. Steven Spielberg concludes Chapter 13 by identifying the importance of mentoring students to create their own identities, rather than attempting to uniformly mold them based on some predetermined concept.

WISDOM TRAILS: *Interconnected Categories*

Government, History, Work, Curiosity, Success, Compassion, Observing Human Nature, Business, Spirituality, Happiness, Fear, Doubt, Native American Wisdom, The Arts, The Future, War, Peace

Trails to Other Chapters

- Diogenes and Abraham Lincoln believe education is a vital component of a healthy society. (*Government*)
- Donna Brazile believes civic responsibility should be taught in school. *(Government)*.
- Will and Ariel Durant explain why higher education is historically important to maintain civilizations. *(History, Government)*
- Michael Jackson puts supreme educational value on watching the masters at *Work*.
- Anatole France calls teaching the *Art* of inspiring *Curiosity*.
- Alexander Hamilton declares that the fruit of genius comes from labor and thought. *(Work, Creativity, Success)*
- Aristotle's quote about educating the heart (*Compassion*) also establishes a strong connection between education and *Spirituality*.
- Theodore Roosevelt insists education must include the teaching of morals. (*Spirituality*)
- Quotes in the *Grandeur of Reading* connect education with *History*.
- Tom Butler-Bowdon's quote about fact, knowledge, and paradigms connects with *Science*. *(Observing Human Nature)*
- Jacqueline von Edelberg focuses on the *Business* of education.
- Timothy Gallwey warns about the negative effects of *Fear* and *Doubt*.
- John F. Kennedy views education as essential for national progress. *(Government)*
- Bob Drury and Tom Clavin compare educational practices in American schools with *Native American* tribal education.
- Abraham Maslow recommends education through *The Arts*.
- Sylvia Earle believes knowledge will be the superpower of the 21st century, which is *The Future*.
- Maria Montessori highlights the need for education to enhance *Spirituality*. It's also her belief that education is essential for the maintenance of *Peace* in the world and the *Happiness* of children.
- Richard Saul Wurman connects learning with the *Medici Effect*.
- Abraham Maslow promotes *The Arts* as a valuable component of education.

CHAPTER 14

GOVERNMENT, POLITICS & SOCIAL JUSTICE

***The care of human life and happiness, and not their destruction,
is the first and only legitimate object of good government.***
—Thomas Jefferson (1743–1826)
Echoing James Madison's statement in his 1788 *Federalist No.62,* this quote appeared
in Jefferson's March 31, 1809 letter to Republicans of Washington County

Government exists to protect us from each other.
—Ronald Reagan (1911–2004)
Movie actor, corporate spokesman, president of the Screen Actors Guild,
governor of California, and 40th president of the United States

***The whole history of the world is summed up in the fact that,
when nations are strong, they are not always just, and
when they wish to be just, they are no longer strong.***
—Winston Churchill (1874–1965)

Officeholders are the agents of the people, not their masters.
—Grover Cleveland (1837–1908)
The only United States president to serve two terms that were not consecutive

***He who molds public sentiment, goes deeper than he who
enacts statutes or pronounces decisions. He makes statutes
and decisions possible or impossible to be executed.***
—Abraham Lincoln (1809–1865)

***Being all equal and independent, no one ought to harm another in his
life, health, liberty, or possessions...the end of law is not to abolish or
restrain, but to preserve and enlarge freedom***
—John Locke (1632–1704)
This quote from *Second Treatise of Government* is significant because
of its influence on the drafting of the Declaration of Independence

***Bureaucracy defends the status quo long past the time
when the quo has lost its status.***
—Lawrence J. Peter (1919–1990)
A cleverly turned phrase pointing out a fundamental truth about governments that
also holds true for many businesses because it's a basic tendency of human nature

GREATMINDS THINK ALIKE: _Lawmaking_

_A state is better governed which has few laws,
and those laws are strictly observed._
—Rene Descartes (1596–1650)

Useless laws diminish the authority of necessary ones.
—Jesse C. Hart (1864–1933)
Arkansas Supreme Court Justice commenting on the
1923 litigation of _Pugsley v. Sellmeyer_

_In the ideal state, laws are few and simple. In the corrupt state, laws
are many and confused. The ideal state is that in which an injury
done to the least of its citizens is an injury done to all._
—Solon (638–558 BC)
Ancient Greek politician, poet, and innovative lawmaker who established
the foundation for the creation of Athenian democracy

_You can choose whatever name you like for the two types of
government. I personally call the type of government, which can be
removed without violence "democracy", and the other is tyranny._
—Karl Popper (1902–1994)
As quoted in _The Economist_

_We have always held to the hope, the belief, the conviction
that there is a better life, a better world, beyond the horizon._
—Franklin D. Roosevelt (1882–1945)

_An imbalance between rich and poor is the oldest
and most fatal ailment of all republics._
—Plutarch (46–120)

_One has to try to find compromises with mutual respect,
but also with a clear opinion. That's politics—always looking
to find a common way forward._
—Angela Merkel (1954)
Chancellor of Germany and leader of the European Union from 2005 to 2021

GREAT MINDS THINK ALIKE: *The End of Civilization*

*A great civilization is not conquered from without
until it has destroyed itself within.*
—*Ariel Durant (1898–1981)*
Pulitzer Prize-winning American writer, historian, and philosopher,
from *The Story of Philosophy*

*Whole societies have been reduced to ruin
because they tolerated the intolerable.*
—*M. Scott Peck (1936–2005)*
This quote from *Abounding Grace* also applies to interpersonal relationships

*We're in a giant car heading toward a brick wall,
and everyone is arguing over where they're going to sit.*
—*David Suzuki (1936)*
Canadian professor, writer, science broadcaster, and environmental activist
with a PhD in zoology

*The end of the human race will be that
it will eventually die of civilization.*
—*Ralph Waldo Emerson (1803–1882)*

*Do not think your single vote does not matter much. The rain that
refreshes the parched ground is made up of single drops.*
—*Kate Sheppard (1848–1934)*
New Zealand's most famous suffragette

*It is amazing how much can be accomplished
when you don't care who gets the credit.*
—*Harry S. Truman (1884–1972)*
Great Minds Connect with John Wooden on page 200

I love an opposition that has convictions.
—*Frederick the Great (1712–1786)*
King of Prussia from 1740 until his death, and a proponent of enlightened absolutism

*The great bulwark against a potential dictator is
an informed people attached to a government of laws.*
—*Abraham Lincoln (1809–1865)*

Despotism corrupts the person who submits to it
far more than the person who imposes it.
—*Alexis de Tocqueville (1805–1859)*
French aristocrat, diplomat, political scientist, author, and historian

Unlimited power is apt to corrupt the minds of those who possess it;
and this I know my lord, that where laws end, tyranny begins.
—*William I, aka William the Conqueror (1028–1087)*
The first Norman King of England is best known for winning the
1066 Battle of Hastings that ended Anglo-Saxon rule in England

You can't maintain yourself as a power for any length of time
without corrupting yourself.
—*E.L. Doctorow (1931–2015)*
American novelist and professor best known for his
historical novels, from *Bill Moyers: A World of Ideas*

Resolved, that the women of this nation in 1876, have greater cause
for discontent, rebellion and revolution than the men of 1776.
There never will be complete equality until women themselves
help to make laws and elect lawmakers.
—*Susan B. Anthony (1820–1906)*
Women's rights activist who led the women's suffrage movement

The harder the conflict, the more glorious the triumph.
—*Thomas Paine (1737–1809)*
English-born American political activist, philosopher, political theorist,
revolutionary, and author of *Common Sense*

The government, which was designed for the people, has got into the
hands of the bosses and their employers, the special interests. An
invisible empire has been set up above the forms of democracy.
—*Woodrow Wilson (1856–1924)*
American lawyer, president of Princeton University, governor of New Jersey, and
president of the United States from 1912 until 1920 who was a leading architect in the
creation of the League of Nations, the unsuccessful predecessor of the United Nations

If lies can show the truth, they can become the truth, they can cause the truth, so I may build an empire on lies, but they are the truth.
—Genghis Khan (1162–1227)

Those who make peaceful revolution impossible make violent revolution inevitable.
—John F. Kennedy (1917–1963)

The seed of revolution is repression.
—Woodrow Wilson (1856–1924)

Every generation needs a new revolution.
—Thomas Jefferson (1743–1826)

The sloppier the rebel uniform, the more likely the overthrow of the existing government.
—Arthur Bloch (1948)

GREAT MINDS THINK ALIKE: *After the Revolution*

Nothing is clearer in history than the adoption by successful rebels of the methods they were accustomed to condemn in the forces they deposed. Violent revolutions do not so much redistribute wealth as destroy it...The only real revolution is in the enlightenment of the mind and the improvement of character, the only real emancipation is individual, and the only real revolutionists are philosophers and saints.
—Will Durant (1885–1981) & Ariel Durant (1898–1981)
From their co-written book *The Lessons of History*

The most radical revolutionary will become a conservative the day after the revolution.
—Hannah Arendt (1906–1975)
German American philosopher, political theorist, and author, as quoted in *The Week* magazine, who credited *The New Yorker* as their source

Revolutions are the locomotives of history. Workers of the world unite; you have nothing to lose but your chains.

—Karl Marx (1818–1883)

German philosopher, writer, political theorist, and social revolutionary famous for authoring *The Communist Manifesto*

Remember, democracy never lasts long. It soon wastes, exhausts, and murders itself. There was never a democracy yet that did not commit suicide.

—John Adams (1735–1826)

Lawyer, diplomat, and statesmen who was the first vice president under George Washington before becoming the second president of the United States; father of John Quincy Adams and grandfather of John Adams

Women belong in all places where decisions are being made. It shouldn't be that women are the exception.

—Ruth Bader Ginsburg (1933–2020)

Lawyer, women's rights advocate, and Supreme Court Justice

Never negotiate out of fear but never fear to negotiate.

—John F. Kennedy (1917–1963)

From his inaugural address on January 20, 1961

If we expect to inherit the blessings of our Fathers, we should return to their primitive simplicity of manners.

—Abigail Adams (1744–1818)

Wife of president John Adams and mother of president John Quincy Adams

No man will ever bring out of the Presidency the reputation that carried him into it.

—Thomas Jefferson (1743–1826)

The day before my inauguration President Eisenhower told me, "You'll find that no easy problems ever come to the President of the United States. If they are easy to solve, someone else has solved them." I found that hard to believe, but now I know it is true.

—John F. Kennedy (1917–1963)

Diplomacy is the art of letting someone else have it your way.
—Daniel Vare (1880–1956)
Italian diplomat and author who lived many years in China.
Great Minds Connect with Dwight Eisenhower on page 149

Flattery is the infantry of negotiation.
—Hugo von Hofmannsthal (1874–1929)
Austrian novelist, librettist, poet, dramatist, narrator, essayist,
and author of the *Lord Chandos Letter*

GREAT MINDS THINK ALIKE: *Liberty*

Liberty consists less in doing one's own will than in not being subject to that of another; it consists further in not subjecting the will of others to our own.
—Jean-Jacques Rousseau (1712–1778)

Liberty has never come from the government. Liberty has always come from the subjects of the government. The history of government is a history of resistance. The history of liberty is the history of the limitation of government, not the increase of it.
—Woodrow Wilson (1856–1924)

Liberty means responsibility. That is why most men dread it.
—George Bernard Shaw (1856–1950)

Though liberty is established by law, we must be vigilant, for liberty to enslave us is always present under that very liberty.
—Marcus Tullius Cicero (106–43 BC)

***When liberty destroys order,
the hunger for order will destroy liberty.***
—Will Durant (1885–1981)

When people are free to choose, they choose freedom.
—Margaret Thatcher (1925–2013)

Freedom is never more than one generation away from extinction. We didn't pass it to our children through the bloodstream. It must be fought for, protected, and handed on for them to do the same.
—Ronald Reagan (1911–2004)

Freedom without law is license, which soon degenerates
into anarchy, and shortly thereafter into tyranny.
—*Peter F. Drucker (1909–2005)*
From *Innovation and Entrepreneurship*

Pardoning the bad is injuring the good.
—*Benjamin Franklin (1706–1790)*

You cannot separate peace from freedom because
no one can be at peace until he has his freedom.
—*Malcolm X (1925–1965)*
Legendary leader of the Black Power movement of the 1960s
and author of the best-selling book *Autobiography of Malcolm X*

Congress is so strange. A man gets up to speak and says nothing.
Nobody listens, and then everybody disagrees.
—*Boris Marshalov (1902–1967)*
Russian observer after attending a session of the
United States House of Representatives

Politics have no relation to morals.
—*Niccolo Machiavelli (1469–1527)*
Italian diplomat, politician, historian, philosopher, author, playwright,
and poet who is the acknowledged "father of modern political science"

Good politics is the art of compromise.
—*Alex Trebek (1940–2020)*
From his book *Alex Trebek: The Answer Is...*

Practical politics consists of ignoring facts.
—*Henry Adams (1838–1918)*
Grandson of John Quincy Adams, Henry Adams was a historian and political journalist
posthumously awarded a Pulitzer Prize for his memoir

In politics, the middle way is none at all...
Always stand on principle...even if you stand alone.
—*John Adams (1735–1826)*

Politics is the hottest, most dangerous subject in the land.
It's not only a conversation-wrecker, it's a friendship-wrecker,
a family-wrecker, a job-wrecker and a future wrecker.
—*Barbara Walters (1929–2022)*
From her book *How to Talk with Practically Anybody About Anything*

There are no facts, only interpretations.
—*Friedrich Nietzsche (1844–1900)*

Taxes are the price we pay for a civilized society.
I like to pay taxes. With them, I buy civilization.
—*Oliver Wendell Holmes, Jr. (1841–1935)*
Revered judge, jurist, and legal scholar who served on the United States Supreme Court
from 1902 to 1932; Holmes was also a lieutenant colonel in the army during the Civil War.

If you're not out front defining your vision,
your opponent will spend gobs of money to define it for you.
—*Donna Brazile (1959)*

Justice is a complex set of passions to be cultivated, not an abstract
set of principles to be formulated and imposed upon society. Our
knowledge of justice begins with our experience of our own place
in the world. Our sense of justice has origins in such emotions as
resentment, jealousy, outrage, and revenge as well as in compassion.
—*Robert C. Solomon (1942–2007)*
Professor of philosophy who wrote more than 45 books, from *A Passion for Justice*

True patriotism hates injustice in its own land
more than anywhere else.
—*Clarence Darrow (1857–1938)*
Legendary lawyer of high-profile cases including the Scopes trial

It is not possible to found a lasting power upon injustice.
—*Demosthenes (384–322 BC)*
Statesman and orator of ancient Athens

GREAT MINDS THINK ALIKE: *Stand Up for Justice*

*The price good people pay for indifference
to public affairs is to be ruled by evil men.*
—Plato (429–347 BC)

*Our lives begin to end the moment we become silent
about things that matter.*
—Martin Luther King Jr. (1929–1968)

*The world is a dangerous place, not because of those who do evil,
but because of those who look on and do nothing.*
—Albert Einstein (1879–1955)
Great Minds Connect with Herb Cohen's quote on aggression on page 246

*Whenever one person stands up and says, "Wait a minute,
this is wrong," it helps other people do the same.*
—Gloria Steinem (1934)

*A people who elect corrupt politicians, imposters, thieves
and traitors are not victims, but accomplices.*
—George Orwell (1903–1950)
Birth name: Eric Arthur Blair
Famous American author who wrote *War of the Worlds* and *1984*

*We have justice whenever those who have not been injured by
injustice are as outraged by it as those who have been.*
—Solon (638–558 BC)

Injustice anywhere is a threat to justice everywhere.
—Martin Luther King Jr. (1929–1968)

Return evil with justice.
—Confucius (551-479 BC)

Justice without force is powerless. Force without justice is tyranny.
—Blaise Pascal (1623–1662)

Force without legitimacy leads to defiance, not submission.
—Malcolm Gladwell (1963)
Canadian journalist, author, and public speaker

You can't hold a man down without staying down with him.
—Booker T. Washington (1836–1915)

That old law about "an eye for an eye" leaves everybody blind.
—Martin Luther King Jr. (1929–1968)
Dr. King was paraphrasing Mahatma Gandhi in his book *Stride Toward Freedom*

GREAT MINDS THINK ALIKE: *Equal Is Not Always Equal*

The worst form of inequality is trying make unequal things equal.
—Aristotle (384–322 BC)
Aristotle may have been taught this concept by Plato. A modern form of this phrase is:

Nothing is more unequal than the equal treatment of unequal people.
—Christopher Ryan (1962)
American author, who in his book *Civilized to Death*,
provides an example of this concept:
Giving the same gift to people of unequal wealth is unequal.
Fulfilling the existing need is the key barometer of effectiveness.
If one person has $1,000 and another person has $100,000,
then a gift of $100 to both is obviously of unequal proportion.

Real social progress isn't achieved through plans or predictions. It's achieved by keeping systems open to new ideas & opinions.
—Alex Bogusky (1963)
Designer, author, and consumer advocate

The pursuit of truth does not permit violence on one's opponent. True nonviolence is impossible without the possession of unadulterated fearlessness...nonviolence is the greatest force at the disposal of mankind. It is mightier than the mightiest weapon of destruction.
—Mohandas (Mahatma) Gandhi (1869–1948)
Gandhi urged his followers to always practice the principles of *ahimsa* and *satyagraha*, upon which all his actions were based. Ironically, after practicing nonviolence for decades, Gandhi was violent assassinated.

Right action is better than knowledge; but in order to do what is right, we must know what is right.
—Charlemagne (748–814)
Also known as Charles the Great, Charlemagne was king of the Franks, king of the Lombards, and emperor of the Romans as he united most of Western Europe for the first time since the fall of the Western Roman Empire

The time is always right to do what is right.
—*Martin Luther King Jr. (1929–1968)*

If all men were angels, no government would be necessary.
—*James Madison (1751–1836)*
Statesman, diplomat, and fourth president of the United States who was instrumental in drafting the Constitution and establishing the structure of America's federal government by authoring *The Federalist Papers* under the pseudonym Publius

We win justice quickest by rendering justice to the other party.
—*Mohandas (Mahatma) Gandhi (1869–1948)*
From his autobiography *The Story of My Experiments with Truth*

The first requisite of civilization is that of justice.
—*Sigmund Freud (1856–1939)*

GREAT MINDS THINK ALIKE: *How to Judge a Nation*

We should judge the quality of life in a society not by looking at the way the rich in that society live, but by the way the lowest percentile of the people live their lives.
—*Muhammad Yunus (1940)*
Nobel Peace Prize-winning entrepreneur who founded the Grameen Bank in Bangladesh that has lent billions of dollars to help the poor rise out of poverty; Yunus is a pioneer in the concepts of microcredit and microfinance

No one truly knows a nation until one has been inside its jails. A nation should not be judged by how it treats its highest citizens, but its lowest ones.
—*Nelson Mandela*
From his autobiography *Long Road To Freedom*

This country will not be a permanently good place for any of us to live in unless we make it a reasonably good place for all of us to live in.
—*Theodore Roosevelt (1858–1919)*
From one of his Chicago speeches in 1912

Law applied to its extreme is the greatest injustice.
—*Marcus Tullius Cicero (106–43 BC)*

The best way to get a bad law repealed is to enforce it strictly.
—Abe Lincoln (1809–1865)

All justice movements are intertwined with one another.
They are threads that make up the fabric of the American
story. Progress today is possible because of the groundwork
laid by trailblazers who stood up for what was right,
even when it was dangerous.
—Amanda Nguyen (1991)
American civil rights activist who created the civil rights organization Rise,
from her March 16, 2020 article in *Time*

I never answered the questions asked me.
I only answered the questions I wish were asked me.
—Robert S. McNamara (1916–2009)
Former Secretary of Defense under presidents John F. Kennedy and Lyndon Johnson,
who provides a profound lesson in how politicians can manipulate interviews!

GREAT MINDS THINK ALIKE: *Stages of Acceptance*

First they ignore you. Then they ridicule you.
And then they attack you and want to burn you.
And then they build monuments to you.
—Nicholas Klein (1884–1951)
American lawyer and labor union advocate from his career-defining speech
to the Amalgamated Clothing Workers of America.
A few years later, Mahatma Gandhi wrote:

First they ignore you, then they laugh at you,
then they attack you, then you win.
—Mahatma Gandhi (1869–1948)
The above phrases identify the predictable stages of ridicule, repression,
and respect experienced by powerful social movements

The world of politics is always twenty years behind
the world of thought.
—John Jay Chapman (1862–1933)
American lawyer who became a politically active essayist and speaker

The degree of inventiveness and innovation in a society
is the main driver of its productivity.
–Ray Dalio (1949)
From his book *Principles for Dealing with The Changing World Order*

Revolutions, no matter how sweeping, need to be consolidated
and in the end adapted from a moment of exultation to what is
sustainable over a period of time.
–Henry Kissinger (1923–2023)
From his book *World Order*. Kissinger added:
A society is fortunate if its leaders
can occasionally rise to the level of wisdom.

Civilization is by its very nature, a long-running Ponzi scheme. It
lives by robbing nature and borrowing from the future, exploiting its
hinterland until there is nothing left to exploit, after which it implodes
...would a panel of the wise–Confucius, Gautama Buddha, Lao Tzu,
Rumi, and Socrates conceivably approve of our current way of life?
—William Ophuls (1934)
American political scientist, ecologist, and author, from *Apologies to the Grandchildren*.
This quote is just the beginning of Ophul's passionate rant on the evils of civilization.
Great Minds Connect with Christopher Ryan on pages 43 and 102. Ryan and Ophuls
share the belief that civilization is moving in an unhealthy and unsustainable direction.

For all its cruelties, civilization is precious, an experiment worth
continuing...Those who don't like civilization and can't wait for it
to fall on its arrogant face, should keep in mind that there is no
other way to support humanity in anything like our present numbers
or estate.
—Ronald Wright (1948)
From his book *A Short History of Progress*

CONSOLIDATING CHAPTER 14
Government, Politics & Social Justice

While there are no politics in wisdom, hopefully someday there will be more wisdom in politics. It's quite apparent most politicians become significantly wiser immediately after retiring from politics, as the political process distorts their logic while they are immersed in it. The quotes of Chapter 14 inform us politics never function perfectly, as politicians continually stray from the goal of maximizing societal benefits of government and improving the quality of life for all constituents. Politics is the recipient of quotes from many other wisdom disciplines, although that wisdom is usually ignored. Chapter 14 features a parade of past United States presidents along with many other notable politicians and historical world leaders. Presidents Washington, Jefferson, John Adams, James Madison, John Quincy Adams, Andrew Jackson, Lincoln, Grover Cleveland, Woodrow Wilson, Franklin Roosevelt, Truman, Eisenhower, Kennedy, Reagan, and Obama all weigh in to create a formidable presidential summit complemented by other notable leaders from the past two millennia.

Presidential quotes in this chapter are by men who governed during mostly turbulent times. George Washington's presidency was anything but smooth, although history has glossed over its rough spots. During the Washington administration, the role of president was still undefined, as was the whole structure of our national government. Huge issues were debated, including whether a federal government was even necessary. During his presidency, Thomas Jefferson negotiated the Louisiana Purchase from France, but also dealt with numerous treacherous challenges including Barbary pirates, British interference with our nation's commerce, the forced removal of Native Americans from newly acquired lands, and the issue of slavery. Andrew Jackson fought valiantly during both the American Revolution and War of 1812 prior to being elected president. As president, Jackson fought government corruption and was deeply involved in the expansion of our country into Native American lands by brutally enforcing the Indian Removal Act. He also survived the first attempted presidential assassination. Abraham Lincoln's presidency was a rollercoaster from his first week in office, as the Southern states immediately seceded and the Civil War commenced, ending only days before his assassination. Teddy Roosevelt was catapulted into the presidency by the assassination of William McKinley during a period of dynamic upheaval in our government's relationship with big business. Woodrow Wilson struggled with our nation's preference for neutrality at the outset of World War I, eventually realizing the inevitability of American involvement in that bloody conflict. Although he presided over military victory, Wilson's presidency ended with a failed attempt to establish the League of Nations. Furthermore, Wilson suffered a debilitating stroke and finished his second term in office as an invalid. Franklin Roosevelt battled the crippling effects of polio during most of his political life, inherited the Great Depression, and then presided over our country's participation in

World War II, a war navigated by Dwight Eisenhower in Europe and Douglas MacArthur in the Pacific. Early in his fourth term as president, Roosevelt died, leaving the presidency to Harry Truman, who presided over the conclusion of WWII by dropping atomic bombs on Japan. Truman soon found himself embroiled in a bitter feud with General McArthur regarding the unwinnable Korean War. Dwight Eisenhower's two terms in office seemed peaceful on the surface, but he presided over the early years of our Cold War with the Soviet Union. John F. Kennedy inherited the Cold War from Eisenhower, presided over the disastrous Bay of Pigs invasion, and was assassinated in 1963. Ronald Reagan's presidency struggled mightily until he was seriously wounded during an assassination attempt. Reagan's heroically cheerful demeanor during his recovery revitalized his presidency and made him immensely popular, although a stock market crash and Contra scandal at the end of his second term became problematic. The life-altering experience of serving as president of the United States seasoned these men's views on government and expanded their horizons as they observed our nation from a unique vantage point.

In a perfect democracy, the pure purpose of government would be to help everyone. Although governments frequently become weak links in the social justice chain, they always possess the potential to generate significant positive change. Unfortunately, in our imperfect world, government and politics tend to digress into partisan battles over elections, power, and money. The unfortunate truth is that political bickering often becomes the chief adversary of good government. The hostility of recent partisan politics in the United States has tarnished most people's view of how our country is governed, obscuring the fact that through the years, many fine people have populated our political landscape. The subjects of *Government* and *Politics* have purposely been placed immediately after *Sports* to inspire a discussion of what is one of the most dangerous misconceptions pulsing through modern times:

The confusion of winning in politics versus winning in sports. Sports require winners and losers to accurately punctuate each competition. Winning and losing in sports creates undeniable truths that prevail over any rhetoric or "spin" about the outcome of an event. The critical difference between sports and politics is that regardless of who wins a political campaign, when the election is over, all players are theoretically on the same team. Once elections are concluded, political parties are expected to come together in serving their cities, states, and nations, whereas sports rivalries do not require conciliation of any sort. When this difference is obscured, political dysfunction is the result. Politicians who win elections are elected to serve everyone in their domain, not just the people who voted for them. Unfortunately, partisan politics sweep this fundamental truth under the rug, thereby stalling societal progress. The more political rivalries resemble bitter sports rivalries, the more a nation will suffer. While clear winners and losers must be validated by elections, this is where the political line needs to be drawn. When a candidate loses an election, it does not mean his or her ideas are all wrong. Many times, losing candidates have some very good ideas. The rhetoric of partisan politics seriously blurs all attempts to clearly evaluate ideas because so much of most campaigns boils down to issues unrelated to policy. Personal attacks and spin doctors inject poisonous arguments into debates that often leave excellent candidates in disarray and electorates in a state of confusion about where basic truths are located. The lack of accepted definitive truth creates an ever-widening gulf between opposing sides of every issue. As a result, issues of great importance become locked in insufferable debates with little or no movement toward a solution.

After taking a closer look at political gridlock and histrionics, it becomes clear political bickering resembles family bickering, as interpersonal dysfunction in politics mimics family dysfunction. Interestingly enough, this transactional model also applies to business, especially large corporations. Politics and workplaces are often where extreme desire shows its ugly side by morphing into blind ambition. While it's easy to identify and analyze deleterious political realities, it's far more difficult to untangle them. Not only are these pernicious dynamics deeply imbedded in lineages of animosity, they are also inherent in any power struggle. At best, the hope is to calm down both sides of a political battle to find middle ground that enables a negotiated agreement. For any government or business relationship to function, both sides must believe it's in their best interest to act in a bipartisan manner. This is the greatest challenge of any democratic system, a challenge governments worldwide currently struggle with.

This leads to what can be called *The Bear Trap of History*, where all efforts to control meet with the universe's drift toward greater entropy. History is replete with examples demonstrating that the greater the effort to control, the greater the eventual chaos before the chaos finally resolves into a new form of organization. The repercussions of large-scale control often take time to manifest. That lag time often seduces despots and authoritarian leaders into shortsighted power grabs that lead to an inevitable demise of their regimes and empires. The more a nation or empire seeks to control, the deeper its eventual ruin will be. It may take years, decades, or even centuries, but history assures us it will happen. Meanwhile, the collateral damage can be devastating. History teaches us that the quicker the rise to power by a despot, the quicker the fall. Napoleon and Hitler are prime examples of authoritarian leaders who rose quickly and went down in flames within relatively short periods of time. The Roman Empire is an example of an empire that lasted many centuries, mainly because it had mitigating egalitarian tendencies woven into its methods of control. From this lesson, we can surmise that the more ruthless a rise to power, the greater the carnage of its disintegration... hence the famous phrase,

Those who live by the sword, die by the sword.

This paraphrases the Bible's Gospel of Mathew
where Jesus is quoted as saying:

Put up again thy sword into his place:
for all they that take the sword shall perish with the sword.

In democratic societies, "the sword" serves as metaphor for painful election defeats as opposed to bloody military conflicts. Anyone rising to power needs to understand that the seeds of destruction are always planted in one's ascension. Unfortunately, those in possession of power are usually too preoccupied with the preservation of their immediate needs to heed this inevitable truth.

In the 1940s, Mahatma Gandhi introduced the principle of *ahimsa* to the world stage as the cornerstone of his nonviolent protest against the inequities of British rule in India. These nonviolent protests he organized eventually succeeded in bringing an end to British rule. Even when under attack, Gandhi demanded his *ahimsa* practitioners retain their nonviolent nature and not harm any opponent. Ahimsa practitioners had to be willing to endure great harm without wavering from a nonviolent and non-hostile stance. Gandhi rightfully viewed *ahimsa* as a fearless act of ultimate courage.

WISDOM TRAILS: *Interconnected Categories*

Happiness, History, Health, The Future, Business, Peace, Work, Friendship, Compassion, Courage, Innovation, Nature

Trails to Other Chapters

- Thomas Jefferson proclaims *Happiness* of the general population to be the primary responsibility of government.
- Winston Churchill finds a profound lesson in the *History* of the world.
- John Locke connects government with the *Health* of people.
- Karl Marx views revolutions as the locomotives of *History*.
- Will and Ariel Durant find an ironic twist in the *History* of revolutions.
- John F. Kennedy warns not to allow *Fear* to inhibit our ability to negotiate. *(Business, War, Work)*
- Woodrow Wilson discusses the *History* of liberty.
- Malcolm X discusses the connection between freedom and *Peace*.
- Barbara Walters warns about the destructive power of politics in regards to *Friendship* and *Work*.
- Robert Solomon highlights the need for *Compassion* in the pursuit of justice.
- Mahatma Gandhi believes that nonviolent protests require *Courage* to succeed. Gandhi's principle of ahimsa also embraces the demonstration of *Compassion*.
- Alec Bogusky tells us progress in social justice requires *Innovation*.
- Amanda Nguyen highlights the interconnection of all justice movements and salutes the trailblazers who led them. *(History)*
- Ray Dalio links inventiveness and *Innovation* to societal progress.
- William Ophuls establishes civilization as the enemy of *Nature*.

CHAPTER 15

WAR & PEACE

War is harmful, not only to the conquered, but also to the conqueror.
—*William I, aka William the Conqueror (1028–1087)*

There never was a good war or a bad peace.
—*Benjamin Franklin (1706–1790)*
From letters written by Franklin in 1783

GREATMINDS THINK ALIKE: *War Is a Form of Failure*

War is a sign of defeat, a failure of politics.
—*Mikhail Gorbachev (1931–2022)*
Russian politician who became head of state and
general secretary of the Communist Party in the Soviet Union

All war is a symptom of man's failure as a thinking animal.
—*John Steinbeck (1902–1968)*
From his book *Once There Was A War*

Violence seldom accomplishes permanent and desired results.
Herein lies the futility of war.
—*Asa Philip Randolph (1889–1979)*
African American civil rights and labor leader

When the rich make war, it's the poor that die.
—*Jean-Paul Sartre (1905–1980)*
From *The Devil and the Good Lord*

The atomic bomb made the prospect of future war unendurable.
—*J. Robert Oppenheimer (1904–1967)*

In the contemporary, deeply interdependent world,
war is outdated and illogical.
—*14th Dalai Lama (1935)*
From *Beyond Religion: Ethics for a Whole World*

Peace is not absence of conflict,
but the ability to handle conflict by peaceful means.
—*Ronald Reagan (1911–2004)*
From his commencement address at Eureka College in 1982

To be prepared for war is the most effectual means to promote peace.
—*George Washington (1732–1799)*
Political leader, military general, statesman, founding father,
and first president of the United States (1789 to 1797)

Since wars begin in the minds of men, it is from the minds
of men that the defenses of peace must be constructed.
—*UNESCO*
United Nations Educational Scientific and Cultural Organization founded in 1945
to promote world peace through international cooperation

GREAT MINDS THINK ALIKE: *World Peace*

There can never be peace between nations
until there is true peace within the souls of men.
—*Black Elk (1863–1950)*

Without inner peace, it is impossible to have world peace.
—*Gesche Kelsang Gyatso (1931)*
Buddhist monk, meditation teacher, and author,
from *Transform Your Life: A Blissful Journey*

Peace is not an absence of war. It is a virtue, a state of mind,
a disposition for benevolence, confidence and justice.
—*Baruch Spinoza (1632–1677)*
Iconic Dutch philosopher

Surprise achieves superiority almost as strongly
as direct concentration of forces.
—*Carl von Clausewitz (1780–1831)*
Prussian general and military theorist

The danger of winning too many battles
is making too many jealous enemies.
—*Sun Tzu (544–496 BC)*
From multiple translations of *The Art of War*

Mankind must put an end to war, or war will put an end to mankind.
—*John F. Kennedy (1917–1963)*
From his 1961 speech at the United Nations

GREATE MINDS THINK ALIKE: *Military Leadership*

He who cannot obey, cannot command.
—*Benjamin Franklin (1706–1790)*
From *Poor Richard's Almanac*

He who wishes to be obeyed must know how to command.
—*Niccolo Machiavelli (1469–1527)*

He who has never learned to obey cannot be a good commander.
—*Aristotle (384–322 BC)*

He who is not a good servant will not be a good master.
—*Plato (429–347 BC)*
The above four quotes demonstrate the lineage of a concept that also applies
to leadership in non-military situations (see *Leadership* in Chapter 8)

If everyone is thinking alike, then somebody isn't thinking.
—*George S. Patton (1885–1945)*
U.S. Army general and tank commander in both WWI and WWII
who also competed in the pentathlon in the 1912 Olympics;
in the September 1933 Cavalry Journal, Patton added:
Wars may be fought with weapons, but they are won by men.
It is the spirit of the men who follow them and the men
who lead them that gains the victory.

Never interrupt your enemy when he is making a mistake.
—*Napoleon Bonaparte (1769–1821)*
Napoleon's comment is now an official mantra of the United States Army;
another piece of advice on war from Napoleon is
You must never fight too often with one enemy,
or you will teach him all your art of war.

Moderation in war is imbecility.
—*Thomas Babington Macaulay (1800–1859)*
English baron, historian, author, and politician who also
served as the U.S. Secretary of War

To command a group requires truthfulness.
—*Sun Tzu (544–496 BC)*
From multiple translations of *The Art of War*

<u>GREAT MINDS THINK ALIKE: *Military Strategy*</u>

Great strategy is better than great combat. It is in the formulation of strategy that victory is determined. Strategy comes before tactics. Strategy determines the allocation of resources. Tactics is the use of resources. Bad strategy supported by good tactics is a fast route to failure...to subdue an enemy without fighting is the supreme excellence.

—Sun Tzu (544–496 BC)
From multiple translations of *The Art of War*

Strength is defeated by strategy.

—Philippine proverb

Anyone can attack where people are weak, but a true master uses his enemy's strengths against him.

—Stephanie Storey (1975)
From *Oil and Marble*

Study the actions of illustrious men to see how they have borne themselves in war, examine the causes of their victories and defeats, so as to imitate the former and avoid the latter.

—Niccolo Machiavelli (1469–1527)
From his classic book *The Prince*

They can conquer who believe they can.

—Virgil (70–19 BC)
Great Minds Connect with William Hazlitt on page 286

The strongest response to terrorists is to carry on living our lives and our values as we have until now—self-confident and free, considerate and engaged.

—Angela Merkel (1954)

The strength of a wall is neither greater nor less than the courage of the men who defend it.

—Genghis Khan (1162–1227)

It is better to keep a conquered nation intact than to destroy it.

—Sun Tzu (544–496 BC)
From multiple translations of *The Art of War*

The supreme art of war is to subdue the enemy without fighting.
—*Sun Tzu (544–496 BC)*

As generals learn, even the best war plans rarely survive first contact with the enemy, but having planned is essential because it forces you to imagine different scenarios and prepare for the worst.
—*William Ophuls (1934)*
From his book *Apologies to the Grandchildren*

We are not hardwired for war. We learn it.
—*R. Brian Ferguson (1951)*
American professor of archaeology,
as quoted in Christopher Ryan's *Civilized To Death*

If you want to end a war, quit while your opponent is still confident and strong. You must leave him with self-respect if you don't want an enemy for life.
—*Herb Cohen (1938)*
As quoted in the book *The Adventures of Herbie Cohen;* another quote
by Herbie Cohen applies to both war and interpersonal relationships:
Appeasing aggression only incites more aggression.
Great Minds Connect with Albert Einstein on page 232

The story of the human race is war. Except for brief and precarious interludes, there has never been peace in the world, and before history began, murderous strife was universal and unending.
—*Winston Churchill (1874–1965)*
From the 1937 *The Collected Essays of Sir Winston Churchill*

The Way of the Warrior has been misunderstood. It is not a means to kill and destroy others. To smash, injure, or destroy is the worst thing a human being can do. The real Way of a Warrior is to prevent such slaughter—it is the Art of Peace, the power of love.
—*Morihei Ueshiba (1883–1969)*
Japanese martial artist who created aikido

Freedom cannot be secured or sustained without a framework of order to keep the peace. Order and freedom, sometimes described as opposites on the spectrum of experience, should instead be understood as interdependent.

–Henry Kissinger (1923–2023)

From his book *World Order*. In that book, Kissinger also stated:

In international affairs, a reputation for reliability is more important than demonstrations of tactical cleverness… history punishes strategic frivolity sooner or later.

Kissinger also noted that at the conclusion of wars,
a stable postwar order never comes about without

an ultimate reconciliation of victor and defeated.

This explains why the punitive Treaty of Versailles after WWI
was so ineffective and actually led to WWII. Kissinger concluded:

The only times in the history of the world that we have had any extended period of peace is when there has been balance of power.

In war, there are no unwounded soldiers.

—José Narosky (1930)
Argentinian journalist and author

World peace can be achieved when the power of love replaces the love of power.

—Sri Chinmoy (1931–2007)

Spiritual teacher, author, artist, poet, and musician born in India who began teaching meditation in New York in 1964, he eventually had thousands of followers worldwide

CONSOLIDATING CHAPTER 15
War & Peace

As it discusses war and peace, Chapter 15 highlights strategies of legendary military guru Sun Tzu, many of which align with strategies of Niccolo Machiavelli centuries later. It's surprising how seamlessly Sun Tzu's war strategies apply to sports, politics, business, and interpersonal relationships. This demonstrates the fact that strategy is essential for success in all these genres and life in general. In addition to being the title of a Tolstoy novel, war and peace are two monumentally important words in the history of human civilization. War is the great destroyer, while peace is the great protector and restorer. The Nobel Peace Center in Oslo, Norway, provides an international showcase for the Nobel Peace Prize. The ideals it represents form an intersection where culture and politics join to promote involvement, debate, and reflection around topics such as war, peace, and conflict resolution.

Although they usually end with peace treaties, wars seemingly never end in the hearts and minds of their combatants and descendants. A study of history reveals that many wars of the distant past are still being fought, as they linger in the minds of the vanquished and conquered. Like fireplace embers waiting for a future spark to combust them, ancestral grudges churn endlessly. Such hostilities perpetuate in the hearts of descendants, a reality apparent in the Middle East since the Crusades and in the United States since the Civil War. Strict punishments imposed by the Versailles Agreement fomented resentments that enabled the rise of Hitler and led to WWII. The Marshall Plan to rebuild Europe represented a learning of lessons from the Versailles Agreement. Likewise, General MacArthur's rebuilding of Japan after WWII represented evolutionary progress in the execution of post-war strategy.

As mentioned above, although wars are fought in different ways under different conditions by vastly differing populations, the resentments and animosities of ancestors continually simmer in their descendants. This unfortunate truth creates many innocent victims who have nothing to do with seminal conflicts that occurred hundreds, or even thousands, of years before. A recent example is the ongoing violence and hatred between Arab countries and Israel that sprouted from the creation of Israel on Arab land after World War II. This geopolitical unrest is very short-lived in comparison to hostilities between the Sunnis and Shiites since the death of Muhammad about 1,400 years ago. Times of peace often overlook escalating tensions between tribes and nations constantly on the brink of boiling over into violent confrontation and military conflict. Sri Chinmoy concludes Chapter 15 with a charming circular phrase citing the power of love as antidote for the love of power, thereby establishing love as a potential savior of humanity. Interestingly, the great military strategist Sun Tzu was against war, as he believed the greatest military accomplishment is victory without fighting. Realizing this type of victory seldom occurs, Sun Tzu proceeded to fill the rest of *The Art of War* with instructions about achieving military victory.

The more one reflects on quotes about war and peace, the more it becomes clear that sports competitions and political campaigns resemble war, and the achievement of lasting peace is unquestionably the greatest victory. The lingering question hovering over this chapter is:

Are times of peace merely interludes between wars, or are wars unfortunate, nasty events disrupting our innate desire for peace?

This leads to a more fundamental question:

Are humans more inclined to war or peace?

WISDOM TRAILS: *Interconnected Categories*

Politics, Science, Technology, The Future, Native American Wisdom, Fear, Spirituality, Social Justice, Business, Sports, Government, Courage, Innovation, Creativity, Observing Human Nature, Love, History

Trails to Other Chapters

- Mikhail Gorbachev views war as a failure of *Politics*.
- J. Robert Oppenheimer discusses the atomic bomb.
  (*Science, Technology, The Future*)
- Quotes in *World Peace* connect world peace with inner peace.
  (*Spirituality, Native American Wisdom*)
- Sun Tzu offers advice on commanding groups.
  (*Practical Advice, Business, Sports, Government*)
- Quotes in *Military Strategy* directly apply to *Sports, Politics,* and *Government*.
- Virgil believes *Faith* in one's ability is essential for victory.
  (*Success, Business, Sports*)
- Franklin Roosevelt presents an optimistic view of *The Future*. (*Faith*)
- Genghis Khan highlights the need for *Courage*.
- Plato, Aristotle, Machiavelli, and Ben Franklin provide insights about *Leadership*.
- Sun Tzu offers advice on how to govern conquered nations.
  (*Practical Advice, Government*)
- William Ophuls stresses the need for *Innovation* after initial plans have been exhausted.
  (*Business, Science, Technology, Sports, Politics, Government*)
- R. Brian Ferguson points out that warfare is not inherent in *Human Nature*.
- Herb Cohen's quote on aggression is applicable to *Business, Politics, Government* and all of *Human Nature*.
- Morihei Ueshiba surprisingly connects the way of the warrior with *Love*.
- Winston Churchill outlines the *History* of war.
- Sri Chinmoy tells us the achievement of world peace requires a replacement of the love of power with the power of *Love*.
- Henry Kissinger notes an important pattern in the *History* of peace treaties.

CHAPTER 16

HUMOR &
THE IMMORTAL
YOGI BERRA

The clearest sign of wisdom is continued cheerfulness.
—*Michel de Montaigne (1533–1592)*
Great Minds Connect with Sai Baba on page 303

Laughter is an instant vacation.
—*Milton Berle (1908–2002)*
American comedian, actor, radio, and television star whose
80-year career began in silent films

Nothing is worth more than laughter. It is strength
to laugh and to abandon oneself, to be light.
—*Frida Kahlo (1907–1954)*
Birth name: Magdalena Carmen Frida Kahlo y Calderón
Mexican painter who spent her life in considerable physical pain

The sound of laughter has always seemed to me
the most civilized music in the universe.
—*Peter Ustinov (1921–2004)*
English actor, filmmaker, and screenwriter who was a true Renaissance man;
a winner of multiple Academy Awards as a supporting actor, Emmy Awards,
and a Grammy Award, he also served as Goodwill Ambassador for UNICEF

The highest form of understandings we can achieve
are laughter and compassion
—*Richard P. Feynman (1918–1988)*

The Four Levels of Comedy are... Make your friends laugh,
make strangers laugh, get paid to make strangers laugh...
and make people talk like you because it's so much fun.
—*Jerry Seinfeld (1954)*
Seinfeld added:
Crankiness is at the essence of all comedy.

Humor is by far the most significant activity of the brain.
—*Edward de Bono (1933–2021)*

Humor is the soul's last line of defense.
—*Fredrik Backman (1981)*
Best-selling Swedish author, from *Anxious People*

Horse sense is what keeps horses from betting on people.
—*W.C. Fields (1880–1946)*
Birth name: William Claude Dukenfield
American vaudevillian, comedy juggler, writer, and actor
in both silent and early "talkie" films

They say they climb mountains because they are there.
That's the same reason why the rest of us go around them.
—*S. Omar Barker (1894–1985)*
American cowboy poet and rancher who authored
many books, including one titled *Cowboy Poetry*

People who drink to drown their sorrow
should be told that sorrow knows how to swim.
—*Ann Landers (1918–2002)*

I drink to make other people more interesting.
—*George Jean Nathan (1882–1958)*
American drama critic and magazine editor

True terror is to wake up one morning and discover
that your high-school class is running the country.
—*Kurt Vonnegut (1922–2007)*
Prolific American writer

I don't want to own anything that won't fit into my coffin.
—*Fred Allen (1894–1956)*
American comedian immortalized on the Hollywood Walk of Fame
for his radio show *Allen's Alley* that aired from 1932 to 1949

Don't accept your dog's admiration
as conclusive evidence that you are wonderful.
—Ann Landers (1918–2002)

The secret source of humor itself is not joy, but sorrow.
—Mark Twain (1835–1910)

Anything is possible if you don't know what you are talking about.
—Green's Law of Debate
A popular member of the *Murphy's Law* club

Nobody will ever win the battle of the sexes.
There's too much fraternizing with the enemy.
—Henry Kissinger (1923—2023)
Another humorous quote from Kissinger is:
The nice thing about being a celebrity is that
if you bore people, they think it's their fault.

All my best thoughts were stolen by the ancients.
—Ralph Waldo Emerson (1803–1882)

A bank is a place that will lend you money
if you can prove you don't need it.
—Bob Hope (1903–2003)
Birth name: Leslie Townes Hope
British-born American comedian, vaudevillian, movie star, singer, and author
who hosted the Academy Awards more times than anyone else

How long a minute is depends on
which side of the bathroom door you're on.
—Arthur Bloch (1948)

When a man sits with a pretty girl for an hour, it seems
like a minute. But let him sit on a hot stove for a minute,
and it seems longer than any hour. That's relativity!
—Albert Einstein (1879–1955)

__Age is a question of mind over matter.__
__If you don't mind, it doesn't matter.__
—Leroy "Satchel" Paige (1906—1982)
Although this phrase is most often attributed to Paige,
it was actually coined by Mark Twain, whose phrase was:
__Age is an issue of mind over matter.__
__If you don't mind, it doesn't matter.__

__Old age is always fifteen years older than I am.__
—Bernard Baruch (1870–1965)
Immensely wealthy Wall Street speculator, financier, and adviser to presidents
Woodrow Wilson and Franklin D. Roosevelt; this quote is known as
Baruch's Rule for Determining Old Age

__Music and laughter are medicine for the soul.__
—Marlo Morgan (1937)
From her novel *Mutant Message From Forever*

__If opportunity doesn't knock, build a door.__
—Milton Berle (1908-2002)

__If at first you don't succeed, destroy all evidence that you tried.__
—Fahnestock's Rule for Failure
This Murphy's Law phrase seems to be very popular, as it has been attributed to many, such
as comedian Steven Wright and romance novelist Jill Shalvis, who in her book *Head Over
Heels* has a character named Chloe Traeger utter the phrase. This phrase is also the title
of a book published by Crazy Old Broad Books, and was attributed to poet laureate
Billy Collins in the October 8, 2021 issue of *The Week* magazine.
Additional research unearthed the related quote by Steven Wright:
__If at first you don't succeed, then skydiving definitely isn't for you.__
—Steven Wright (1955)
American stand-up comedian, actor, and writer

__No matter how great the talent or effort, some things just take time:__
__you can't produce a baby in one month by getting nine women__
__pregnant.__
—Warren Buffett (1930)

It is better to be a failure at something you love
than a success at something you hate.
—*George Burns (1896–1996)*
Birth name: Nathan Birnbaum
American comedian, actor, singer, and writer whose career began
in vaudeville before he starred in radio, film, and television

Humor in native cultures is as natural as breathing.
Humor among tribal people is intimacy.
—*Anne Wilson Schaef (1934–2020)*
From her book *Native Wisdom for White Minds*

Knowledge is knowing a tomato is a fruit.
Wisdom is not putting it in a fruit salad.
—*Katonah Lewisboro Times* January 4, 2021
This quote was cited in an article as an example of a paraprosdokian. There's debate
about the origin of this phrase, with credit being given to two different individuals:
Miles Kington (1941-2008)
British journalist, musician, and broadcaster credited with
the invention of the fictional language Franglais, and
Brian O'Driscoll (1979)
Irish former professional rugby player
Readers are encouraged to research the word *paraprosdokian*
as an exercise in the wisdom of humor.

GREAT MINDS THINK ALIKE: *Where Are You Going?*

If you don't know where you are going,
how will you know when you get there?
—*Robin Sharma (1964)*
From his book *The Monk Who Sold His Ferrari*

If you don't know where you're going,
any road will take you there.
—*George Harrison (1943–2001)*
Lead guitarist of the Beatles, singer & songwriter

It takes a smart brunette to play a dumb blonde.
—*Marilyn Monroe (1926–1962)*
Birth name: Norma Jeane (Baker) Mortenson
Iconic movie star and sex symbol

***We must strive always to be useful,
with a pleasant degree of humor.***
—*Robert B. Thomas (1766–1846)*
American bookseller, bookbinder, and editor who published the first *Old Farmer's Almanac* in 1792; this periodical has been published annually ever since, making it the oldest continually published periodical in North America

***Give your brain as much attention as you do your hair
and you'll be a thousand times better off.***
—*Malcolm X (1925–1965)*
Birth name: Malcolm Little

***An economist is an expert who will know tomorrow why
the things he predicted yesterday didn't happen today.***
—*Lawrence J. Peter (1919–1990)*

When a thing is funny, search it carefully for a hidden truth.
—*George Bernard Shaw (1856–1950)*
From his 1922 play *Back to Methuselah*. According to the Bible, Methuselah, the grandfather of Noah, 969 years at his death, was the longest-living human

***When science discovers the center of the universe,
a lot of people will be disappointed to find they are not it.***
—*Bernard Baily (1916–1996)*
American comic book artist, editor, and publisher

Laughter is always good medicine.
—*Dr. Bernie S. Siegel (1932)*
From his book *365 Prescriptions For the Soul*

THE IMMORTAL YOGI BERRA
Lawrence Peter Berra (1925–2015)
Hall of Fame catcher for the New York Yankees during the 1950s glory days, he won more
World Series rings than any other player in baseball history. He also managed both the New
York Yankees and New York Mets. One of the most quoted athletes in history and
famous for uttering the following classic lines that now reside in New Jersey's
Yogi Berra Museum and Learning Center. These and other famous Yogi quotes
can also be found in *The Yogi Book*.

The future ain't what it used to be.

It got late early.

*Always go to other people's funerals.
Otherwise, they won't come to yours.*

Anyone who is popular is bound to be disliked.

Nobody goes there anymore because it's too crowded.

*Little league baseball is a very good thing 'cause it keeps
the parents off the streets and the kids out of the house.*

When you come to the fork in the road, take it.

*You've got to be very careful if you don't know
where you are going, because you might not get there.*

*You better cut that pizza into four pieces
because I'm not hungry enough to eat six.*

It was like déjà-vu all over again.

If the world were perfect, it wouldn't be.

CONSOLIDATING CHAPTER 16
Humorous Wisdom & The Immortal Yogi Berra

Great humor usually contains some element of wisdom and is one of the joys of existence, symbolizing a playful side of human nature. Comedians, cartoonists, and other humorists shine their lights on all aspects of society and human nature. No category is off-limits. The following quote epitomizes the jovial relationship between humor and wisdom:

> **The clearest sign of wisdom is continued cheerfulness.**
> —*Michel de Montaigne (1533–1592)*

Humor provides us with an ongoing commentary on every phase of human life. Although comedy is most frequently presented by entertainers, humor finds its way into every level of society as it bubbles up from creativity inherent in human nature. The concept of being able to laugh at ourselves and "make light" of difficult situations eases the pains of daily life. A vibrant sense of humor is a great asset to any personality; losing one's sense of humor is a great tragedy. In other words, having some semblance of a sense of humor is essential to happiness.

Making others smile is an accomplishment in itself. If you can manage to sprinkle in some insights and wisdom while inspiring a smile or laugh, you've done something special. Medical research has found that laughter significantly relaxes blood vessels, thereby improving blood flow, demonstrating humor's significant health value. Two notable quotes in this chapter are Anne Wilson Schaef's statement about the importance of humor in indigenous cultures, and George Bernard Shaw's comment that humor usually contains hidden truths. These two quotes tell us great comedy penetrates much deeper than the mere turning of a phrase.

You may be wondering, of all the great minds of history, of all the famous people to have blessed our planet with their wisdom during the past 5,000 years, *why is Yogi Berra the only person given a full page in Consolidated Wisdom?*

This is a valid question. While reviewing the more than 1,400 entries in this book, it became evident Yogi Berra's quirky phrases embody a uniquely endearing jovial wisdom. Although his sayings seem humorously simplistic, they depict intuitive wisdom and accurate insights into the human psyche. Yogi was always one of the most quoted people of his generation because his phrases were contagious. They went viral long before the internet was born. One method of evaluating quotes for this publication was how extensively their words and ideas have spread. The fact so many people have parroted Yogi Berra's phrases during the past half-century attests to his ability to feed humanity to itself. This is a form of genius, and the reason Yogi Berra was so loved. His nuggets of wisdom morphed into a social phenomenon that led to creation of the term "Yogi-isms." As a game show host for more than 30 years, the author of this book found, of all the brilliant quotes from the annals of history presented in his game shows, the most popular and best-remembered phrases were from Yogi Berra. Beyond their spread across all demographics of American society, Yogi-isms never fail to bring smiles to all who utter or hear them, whether for the first or hundredth time. Yogi had a unique ability to disguise his brilliance by expressing wisdom in a humble and humorous way. His witty sayings have brought great pleasure to millions, while also bestowing a sense of brotherhood on those who recite them to each other. It's this unique combination of homespun humor and wisdom that elevates Yogi Berra into the company of the great minds of history.

WISDOM TRAILS: *Interconnected Categories*
Wisdom, Work, The Arts, Compassion, Spirituality, Government, Science, Work, Success, Native American Wisdom, Health

Trails to Other Chapters
- Michel de Montaigne connects cheerfulness with *Wisdom*.
- Milton Berle says laughter is an instant vacation. (*Work*)
- Peter Ustinov views laughter as a form of music. (*The Arts*)
- Richard Feynman touts the value of laughter and *Compassion*.
- Fredrik Backman views humor as the soul's last line of defense. (*Spirituality*)
- Kurt Vonnegut humorously laments about who is running *Government*.
- Albert Einstein offers a humorous version of his theory of relativity. (*Science*)
- Marlo Morgan highlights the beneficial aspects of music and laughter. (*The Arts*)
- George Burns quips about failure, *Success,* and *Work*.
- Anne Wilson Schaef mentions the importance of humor in indigenous cultures. (*Native American Wisdom*)
- Dr. Bernie S. Siegel believes laughter is good medicine. (*Health*)
- Yogi Berra offers his classic quote about *The Future*.

CHAPTER 17

NATURE &
NATIVE AMERICAN
WISDOM

One touch of nature makes the whole world kin.
—John Muir (1838–1914)
Scottish American naturalist and environmentalist who fought for preservation
of the wilderness and became known as "father of the National Parks"

***One moment standing in the midst of nature with open heart
is a whole lifetime if one is in tune with nature.***
—Hazrat Inayat Khan (1882–1927)

***The fact that we can't see the beauty in something
doesn't suggest that it's not there.***
—Richard Carlson, PhD (1961–2006)
From his book *Don't Sweat The Small Stuff*

***In the realm of Nature there is nothing purposeless,
trivial or unnecessary.***
—Maimonides (1138–1204)

***Nature needs no home; it is home. We can have no deficit of nature;
we are nature, even when we are unaware of this nature.***
—David George Haskell (1969)
American & British (dual citizenship) biologist, from his book *The Song of Trees*

GREAT MINDS THINK ALIKE: *Treat Nature Well*

Nature, to be commanded, must be obeyed.
—Francis Bacon (1561–1626)
A scientific observer of natural phenomena

***Treat nature well, and nature will treat you well.
Hurt or destroy nature, and nature will soon destroy you.***
—Aldous Huxley (1894–1963)

***Begin to care for nature, and nature cares for you
in unsuspected ways.***
—Big Bill Neidjie (1913–2002)
Australian Aboriginal elder of the Gaagudju people known as *Kakadu Man*

Nothing is accomplished all at once, and it is one of my great maxims,
and one of the most completely verified that Nature makes no leaps,
a maxim which I have called the Law of Continuity.
—Gottfried Leibniz (1646–1716)

The greatest joy in nature is the absence of man.
—Bliss Carman (1861–1929)
Canadian poet laureate

If mankind were to disappear, the world would regenerate back to
the rich state of equilibrium that existed ten thousand years ago. If
insects were to vanish, the environment would collapse into chaos.
—Edward Osbourne (E.O.) Wilson (1929)
Pulitzer Prize-winning American biologist and writer known as the world's
leading authority of myrmecology, which is the study of ants

Nature does not hurry, yet everything is accomplished.
—Lao Tzu (571–unknown BC)

The laws of nature always insure that
when one door closes, another opens.
—Robin Sharma (1964)
From The Monk Who Sold His Ferrari
Great Minds Connect with Tom Stoppard on page 318

If you help others, you will be helped, perhaps tomorrow, perhaps
in one hundred years, but you will be helped. Nature must pay of the
debt. It is a mathematical law, and all life is mathematics.
—George I. Gurdjieff (1866–1949)
Armenian philosopher, mystic, author, composer, and spiritual teacher

The center of the universe is everywhere.
—Black Elk (1863–1950)

The moment one gives close attention to any thing,
even a blade of grass becomes a mysterious, awesome,
indescribably magnificent world in itself.
—Henry Miller (1891–1980)
From *Ions Noetic Sciences Review* September 9, 2001

Our connection to all things natural is spiritual.
—Diane Ackerman (1948)
From her book *Deep Play*

GREAT MINDS THINK ALIKE: *Hearing Trees Talk*

Did you know that trees talk? Well, they do. They
talk to each other, and they'll talk to you if you listen.
—Tatanga Mani (1870–1967)
aka Walking Buffalo and/or George McLean
Canadian Stoney-Nakoda tribal leader, philosopher, and statesman

Understanding that nature is a network
is the first step in hearing trees talk.
—David George Haskell (1969)
From his book *The Song of Trees*

The wilderness is not wild, and civilization is not civilized. We need
to return to the wholeness of nature and walk once again side by
side with it. That is where the real peace and order exist that must be
brought back into our lives if we are ever to be truly civilized.
—Dr. Bernie S. Siegel (1932)

Our old people taught us that the earth is always speaking to us, but
that we have to be silent to hear her...I can understand all the trees.
The wind. All the animals. The insects. I can tell what a color of the
sky means. Everything speaks to me...I know where the dead are
buried. They speak to me in some ancient tongue.
—Lakota elder Dan, as quoted in Kent Nerburn's *Neither Wolf Nor Dog;*
Dan the elder also said:
Words are like stones. Even if they are very beautiful, if you throw them out
without thinking, they can hurt someone...anger is only for the one
who speaks. It never opens the heart of the one who listens.

***When you lose the rhythm of the drumbeat of God,
you are lost from the peace and rhythm of life.***
—Cheyenne proverb
The Cheyenne tribe lived in parts of what are now Minnesota, Montana,
Oklahoma, Colorado, Wyoming, and South Dakota

A man's heart away from nature becomes hard.
—Standing Bear (1829–1908)
Indian name: Machúnuzhe
Ponca chief, lecturer, and civil rights leader on behalf of Native Americans

***Coexistence of nature with man cannot be forced.
It's more of a delicate patient dance with no guarantees.***
—John Chester (1971)
Emmy Award winning American filmmaker and director,
from the documentary film *The Biggest Little Farm*

***What is man in nature? A nothing in relation to infinity, all in relation
to nothing, a central point between nothing and all and infinitely
far from understanding either. He is equally incapable of seeing the
nothingness out of which he was drawn and the infinite in which
he is engulfed.***
—Blaise Pascal (1623–1662)

You can't make a rainbow without a little rain.
—Brandon McMillan (1977)
Dog trainer and star of the CBS TV show *Lucky Dog*

Take only what you need, and leave the land as you found it.
—Arapaho proverb
Before European migration forced them westward, the Arapaho lived in what are now
Manitoba, Canada and Minnesota, eventually migrating to the plains of Colorado and
Wyoming as close allies of the Cheyenne tribe. Modern Arapaho live in Wyoming on the
Wind River Reservation and in Oklahoma with the Southern Cheyenne.
Two other Arapaho proverbs are:
If we wonder often, the gift of knowledge will come.
Before eating, always take a little time to thank the food.

GREAT MINDS THINK ALIKE: *All Living Things*

All living organisms are but leaves on the same tree of life. The various functions of plants and animals and their specialized organs are manifestations of the same living matter.
—*Albert Szent-Gyorgyi (1893–1986)*
Hungarian biochemist who won the Nobel Prize for Physiology or Medicine in 1937,
as quoted in the book *Breath* by James Nestor
Great Minds Connect with Mudrooroo on page 40

All plants are our brothers and sisters. They talk to us and if we listen, we can hear them...When we show our respect for other living things, they respond with respect for us.
—*Two Arapaho proverbs*
As quoted in *Native American Wisdom: The Sacred in Everyday Life*

With all things and in all things, we are relatives.
—*Sioux proverb*
The Sioux nation is currently divided into three groups: the Lakota, Dakota,
and Nakota who mostly live in North and South Dakota

Over time, we as humans have developed a different attitude towards nature and we've forgotten about our inner power...we are so successful at becoming comfortable, that comfort has become the enemy of our success.
—*Wim Hof (1959)*
From his book *The Wim Hof Method: Activate Your Full Human Potential*; Hof's method
features the use of the hormetic stress theory that endorses the administration
of small doses of stress to stimulate beneficial physiological changes to revive
the body's dormant inner strength

GREAT MINDS THINK ALIKE: *The Power of the Circle*

Everything an Indian does is in a circle, and that is because the Power of the World always works in circles...when we were a strong and happy people, all our power came to us from the sacred hoop of the nation, and so long as the hoop was unbroken, the people flourished.
—*Black Elk (1863–1950)*
From the book *Black Elk Speaks*

Lakota warriors always gathered in circular formations because the circle was a symbol of the fundamental harmony of the universe.
—*Phil Jackson (1945)*
From his book *Eleven Rings*

Healing is a return to beauty.
—Navajo saying
The Navajo tribe originated in Canada, but over many centuries, migrated south. Currently, the Navajo Nation is the largest geographical American Indian reservation in the United States, occupying more than 27,000 square miles in New Mexico, Arizona, and Utah.

There is no fear where there is faith.
—Kiowa proverb as quoted in Native American Wisdom
Nomadic tribe of the great plains of the United States, now centered in Oklahoma; their original name was Kaigwa, which described the unusual way tribal members wore their hair

Be careful when speaking.
You create the world around you with your words.
—Navajo wisdom, from In Beauty May I Walk

Better to stumble with the toe than with the tongue.
—Swahili proverb

Listen! Or your tongue will make you deaf.
—Cherokee wisdom, from In Beauty May I Walk:
Words of Peace and Wisdom by Native Americans
With more than 300,000 members, the Cherokee comprise the largest of all Native American tribes in the United States. They practice what they call *gadugi,* which is collective community work toward a common goal

To the Indian people, tobacco is the Creator's gift. It comes from the earth and rises up to heaven. When the Creator sees it, he pays attention. So when tobacco is presented to someone, it's a sacred statement. It means that the Creator is being called upon to witness the interaction.
—Kent Nerburn (1946)
From his book *Neither Wolf Nor Dog* in which he informs us that tobacco serves as the gift of respect among traditional Indian people

In our Native American traditions we see spirit as the life force energy that is the connective tissue between any living thing and the Great Mystery, the Creator, God.
—Jamie Sams (1951)
From *Dancing the Dream,* in which Sams also wrote:
Anything that has ever happened in a location is still there.
Great Minds Connect with Ram Dass on page 69

GREAT MINDS THINK ALIKE: *The Boomerang Effect*

If we do bad medicine to others, we do bad medicine to ourselves.
—Don Coyhis (1943)
Wisconsin-born Mohican alcohol and addiction recovery counselor for Native Americans. Originally based in upstate New York and New England, the Mohicans eventually sold all their land and migrated to Wisconsin. Their tribal name was immortalized by the book and movie *Last of the Mohicans. Great Minds Connect* with Buddha on page 292

We did not weave the web of life— we are merely a strand in it. Whatever we do to the web, we do to ourselves.
—Chief Seattle (1786–1866)
Powerful Native American chief immortalized with the decision to name Seattle, Washington, after him

Dreams and prophecies lie at the heart of native spirituality, as the spirit is believed to travel to other realms, returning with guidance that fulfills the "secret desires of the soul."
—Kristen Marée Cleary
From her book *Native American Wisdom*

Always teach by story, because stories lodge deep in the heart.
—Red Lake Ojibwe elder
As quoted by Kent Nerburn in his book *Neither Wolf Nor Dog*
Great Minds Connect with Kobe Bryant on page 198

In the Navajo language, the word for balance and the word for beauty are the same.
—*The Sun* magazine

The Aboriginal people believe that a person's mind exists in every part of his body, in every single cell. Because of this, every thought we have, each emotion we experience, have a physical effect upon our body.

—Gary Holz (1950–2007)

Award-winning American physicist who founded an aerospace company before being crippled by multiple sclerosis. That tragedy led to his being healed by an Australian Aboriginal tribe. This quote is from his book about that healing journey titled *Secrets of Aboriginal Healing. Great Minds Connect* with *Health & The Mind* on page 304

When you say "I'm sorry," you are giving away your power. Never say "I'm sorry." Always say I "apologize."

—Rose, the Aboriginal healer, in Secrets of Aboriginal Healing

All their wisdom and knowledge came to them in dreams. They tested their dreams, and in that way learned their own strength.

—Ojibwa elder

The Ojibwa (also known as the Ojibwe or Chippewa) are part of a large tribal community that stretches from Southern Canada into the Midwestern United States; along with many indigenous tribes, they believe that dreams are an important window into the supernatural world

You already possess everything necessary to become great.

—Crow proverb

A Native American tribe of southern Montana. Before they became proficient horsemen, the Crow hunted buffalo on foot. One of their interesting hunting techniques was "buffalo jumping" where Crow warriors chased buffalo to the edge of specific cliffs, causing the buffalo to jump to their deaths.

Working together makes each man's task simpler.

—Cree saying

The Cree are one of the largest First Nations tribes of Canada who also once populated the northern parts of what are now North Dakota, Minnesota, and Montana. The Cree live mostly north and west of Lake Superior. In the United States, they share the Montana Rocky Boy Indian Reservation with the Chippewa.

***Peace is not merely the absence of war, but the constant effort
to maintain harmonious existence between all peoples, from
individual to individual, and between humans and other beings
of this planet.***

—*The 1979 Haudenosaunee Declaration*

Haudenosaunee Confederacy is a term used to describe the Six Nations (Mohawk, Oneida,
Onondaga, Cayuga, Seneca, and Tuscarora tribes) whose members still live in
New York State and parts of Canada. This quote is from *In Beauty I Walk*

CONSOLIDATING CHAPTER 17
Nature & Native American Wisdom

Chapter 17 winds its way through nature and the wisdom of indigenous cultures, demonstrating the intimate connection between those cultures and the natural world. Indigenous cultures focus their belief systems around the interconnectedness of all things, the power of dreams, and a deep respect for nature. Ann Wilson Schaef pinpoints the anchor for Native American traditions: *The wisdom of elders.* Elders in tribal societies provide historical perspective and identity to younger generations. They pass down wisdom of the ancients by distilling that wisdom into stories and rituals. In this manner, elders serve as backbones of their tribal societies, representing a tradition that contemporary Western civilizations would be wise to emulate.

Chapter 17 begins with a number of profound comments and observations about man's relationship with nature. George David Haskell echoes the words of Albert Szent-Gyorgyi by emphasizing how humans are part of nature, not some separate entity. On a more cynical note, Edward Osbourne Wilson asserts insects are more important to the ecosystems of Earth than humans. At the heart of Native American wisdom is an ability to decipher the intelligence inherent in nature, an ability that has allowed Native Americans to live in harmony with the natural world for many centuries. Although Chapter 17 features the primal connection of Native Americans to nature and their rich spiritual wisdom traditions, this chapter is not just about Native Americans; it's about all of the world's indigenous cultures and their intimate, respectful connection to the natural world. Indigenous cultures of the world center their existence around nature, dreams, and community. The Arapaho call plants their brothers and sisters and Jamie Sams reminds us dreaming has always been a powerful aspect of Native American wisdom traditions, with dreams often translated as actual events of the past and future. Similarly, Australian Aboriginals feature a practice they call "Dreamtime" that aligns with a quote from the book *Native American Wisdom* about dreams and prophecies dwelling at the heart of native spirituality.

Tatanga Mani's provocative statement about trees talking inspired additional research to confirm this phenomenon. This research revealed that the Waorani tribe of the Ecuadorian Amazon rain forest often hear trees scream when being cut. Further digging unearthed David George Haskell's quote, *"Understanding that nature is a network is the first step in hearing trees talk."* It was surprising to discover biologists, ecologists, foresters, and naturalists increasingly contend that trees speak, and we humans can learn to hear them if we listen properly. Haskell believes we need to recognize trees as masters of connection and communication that manage complex networks. His technical explanation of this phenomenon extends to the whole plant kingdom:

The proteins that we vertebrate animals use to create the electrical gradients that enliven our nerves are closely related to the proteins in plant cells. The signals in galvanized plant cells...perform a similar function as an animal's nerves, using pulses of electrical charge to communicate from one part of the plant to another. Plants have no brain to coordinate these signals, so plant thinking is diffuse, located in the connections among every cell.

Concurring with this concept, Israeli American writer, artist, and lawyer Ephrat Livni wrote an article about trees while serving as senior editor at *Quartz*. Her article began with:

I'm in a redwood forest in Santa Cruz, California, taking dictation for the trees outside my cabin. They speak constantly, even if quietly, communicating above and underground using sound, scents, signals, and vibes. They're naturally networking, connected with everything that exists.

Canadian/British Columbian ecologist Suzanne Simard presented a TED Talk titled *How Trees Talk to Each Other,* in which she said:

Underground, there is this other world, a world of infinite biological pathways that connect trees and allow them to communicate and allow the forest to behave as though it's a single organism. It might remind you of a sort of intelligence.

German forester and author Peter Wohlleben came to a similar conclusion while managing an ancient birch forest in Germany. He believes trees, like humans, have family lives in addition to relationships with other species. This belief led Wohlleben to write a book titled *The Hidden Life of Trees*.

One of the most fascinating experiments about trees communicating is on YouTube, where *Strange World* connected a lie detector to a tree. In the video, the tree hooked up to the lie detector witnesses a man chopping down and destroying a nearby tree. One at a time, different men are brought in to stand in front of the surviving tree. The tree produces no reaction on the lie detector machine until the man who murdered the nearby tree enters the room. As soon as the murderer approaches, the lie detector machine goes wild, demonstrating the surviving tree's significant emotional response.

WISDOM TRAILS: *Interconnected Categories*

*Practical Advice, History, Spirituality, Peace, Harmony, Health, Dreams,
Education, Fear, Faith, Wisdom, Work, War*

(Please note: Chapters 17 and 18 are so intimately connected
that they can essentially be viewed as one expansive chapter.)

Trails to Other Chapters

- Quotes in *Treat Nature Well* offer advice on how to treat nature.
- Edward Wilson believes planet Earth was in equilibrium ten thousand years ago. (*History, Science*)
- Diane Ackerman finds a *Spiritual* connection between humans and nature. *(Observing Human Nature)*
- Dr. Bernie S. Siegel says civilizations need to return to the wholeness of nature if they desire real *Peace.*
- A Cheyenne proverb discusses the rhythm of life. *(Peace)*
- Standing Bear finds connections between nature and our hearts. (*Compassion*)
- Wim Hof believes the desire to become comfortable has warped our attitude toward nature, and has become the enemy of our overall *Success.*
- Black Elk discusses the power of the circle. *(Harmony)*
- The Navajo believe healing is a return to beauty. (*Health*)
- Cherokee wisdom commands us to listen better. *(Practical Advice)*
- Jamie Sams discusses *The Great Mystery. (Spirituality)*
- Kristen Marie Cleary informs us that *Dreams* and prophecies are at the heart of native *Spirituality.*
- A Red Lake Ojibwe elder gives advice on teaching. (*Education*).
- Gary Holz explains the Aboriginal concept of the mind, emotions, and *Health.*
- A Kiowa tribe proverb establishes *Faith* as the antidote for *Fear.*
- Aboriginal healer Rose tells why we should never say we are sorry. (*Practical Advice*)
- The Ojibwa believe wisdom and knowledge come from *Dreams.*
- A Cree saying highlights the power of togetherness in *Work.*
- The 1979 *Haudenosaunee Declaration* provides a unique definition of *Peace.*

CHAPTER 18

SPIRITUALITY, FAITH & PHILOSOPHY

Our lifetime offers us unlimited opportunities for spiritual growth
until the end...the path of spirituality is a path of lifelong learning.
—M. Scott Peck (1936–2005)
From *The Road Less Traveled: A New Psychology of Love, Traditional Values*
and Spiritual Growth

The spiritual is not something that descends from above,
rather it is an illumination that is to be discovered within.
—Ajit Mookerjee (1915–1990)
Scholar on the texts of sacred texts of India, as quoted in *The Tao of Abundance*

It is only because of problems that we grow mentally and spiritually.
It is in the whole process of meeting and solving problems that life
has meaning.
—M. Scott Peck (1936–2005)
From *The Road Less Traveled: A New Psychology of Love,*
Traditional Values and Spiritual Growth

The basic teaching of spiritual practice is not to wait,
but to live now the way you'll wish you had lived
when you come to the end of your life.
—Jack Kornfield (1945)
American Buddhist monk, spiritual teacher, and author

The history of man is that of his voyage toward the unknown,
in the search for the realization of his immortal self, or his soul.
—Rabindranath Tagore (1861–1941)
From *Wisdom: 365 Thoughts from Indian Masters*

If there is at least one person you've helped in life,
then your life has been worthwhile.
—Lawrence Abel, aka L. Sydney Abel
British author of poetry and psychological fiction

Art, literature, myth, cult, philosophy and ascetic disciplines are all instruments to help the individual put his limited horizons into spheres of ever-expanding realization...The agony of breaking through personal limitations is the agony of spiritual growth.
—Joseph Campbell (1904–1987)
Professor of literature, renowned mythology expert, and author,
from his book *The Hero With a Thousand Faces*

Myth is an arrangement of the past, whether real or imagined, in patterns that reinforce a culture's deepest values and aspirations...Myths are the maps by which cultures navigate through time.
—Ronald Wright (1948)
From his book *A Short History of Progress*

Learning, growth, healing and higher states of consciousness are not possible without chaos. When we experience chaos in life, it means that something is trying to change. The change from an old pattern to a new one always involves chaos.
—John Beaulieu (1950)
American naturopathic doctor, composer, pianist, and renowned practitioner of sound healing, who created a technique called biosonic repatterning, from *Human Tuning*

Great leaps in level of consciousness are always preceded by surrender of the illusion that "I know."
—David R. Hawkins, MD (1927–2012)
From *Power vs. Force*. Great Minds Connect with Yuan Wu on page 122

We must not wish for the disappearance of our troubles, but for the grace to transform them.
—Simone Weil (1909–1943)

By spiritual training I mean education of the heart.
—Mohandas (Mahatma) Gandhi (1869–1948)
Great Minds Connect with Aristotle on page 213

Every major religion of the world has similar ideas of love, the same goal of benefiting humanity through spiritual practice, and the same desire to make their followers into better human beings. The time has come to find a way of thinking about spirituality and ethics that is beyond religion.
—14th Dalai Lama (1935)
From *Beyond Religion: Ethics for a Whole World*

GREAT MINDS THINK ALIKE: *The Power of Silence*

In silence the teachings are heard.
In stillness the world is transformed.
—Lao Tzu (571–unknown BC)

There is nothing in all creation so like God as stillness.
—Meister Eckhart (1260–1328)
German theologian, philosopher, and mystic

The purpose of life is a life of purpose.
—Robin Sharma (1964)
From *The Monk Who Sold His Ferrari*

True prayer is learning to love and to include all mankind in one affection.
—Mary Baker Eddy (1821–1910)
American religious leader who founded Christian Science

Prayer is good, but while calling on the gods, a man should himself lend a hand.
—Hippocrates (460–370 BC)
Physician of ancient Greece known as the "father of Western medicine"

Prayer is you telephoning God. Intuition is God telephoning you.
—Florence Scovel Shinn (1871–1940)
American artist and book illustrator who became a spiritual teacher and writer

You cannot believe in God until you believe in yourself.
—Swami Vivekananda (1863–1902)
Birth name: Narendranath Datta
Hindu monk from India who introduced Hinduism and yoga to the Western world

Don't put people down. Instead, put them on your prayer list.
—*Daystar.com and positiveprayers.com*

When I let go of what I am, I become what I might be.
—*Lao Tzu (571–unknown BC)*

GREAT MINDS THINK ALIKE: *The Value of Experience*

I hear and I forget. I see and I remember.
I do and I understand.
—*Confucius (551-479 BC)*

To know and not yet to do, is not yet to know.
—*Lao Tzu (571–unknown BC)*

There are many truths of which the full meaning cannot
be realized until personal experience has brought it home.
—*John Stuart Mills (1806–1873)*
British philosopher, political economist, and civil servant
who was a proponent of utilitarianism

There is no substitute for learning from experience...
no teacher is greater than one's own experience.
—*Timothy Gallwey (1938)*
From *The Inner Game of Tennis*

A spiritual retreat is medicine for soul starvation. Through silence,
solitary practice, and a simple living, we begin to fill the empty
reservoir. This creates space within for the feelings of forgiveness,
compassion, and loving kindness that are so often blocked.
—*David A. Cooper (1939)*
Author, lecturer, teacher, and meditation facilitator,
from *Silence, Simplicity and Solitude*

What we are today comes from our thoughts of yesterday and our
present thoughts build our life of tomorrow. Our life is the creation
of our mind. If a man speaks or acts with a pure mind, joy follows
him as his own shadow.
—*Buddha (563–483 BC)*
From the *Dhammapada*

Ritual, mythology and metaphysics are but guides to the brink of a transcendent illumination, the final step of which must be taken by each individual in his own silent experience. Mythology is psychology misread as biography, history and cosmology...its understated function is to serve as a powerful picture language for the communication of traditional wisdom.
—Joseph Campbell (1904–1987)
From *The Hero With a Thousand Faces*

The regular practice of seems to be able to alter the trajectory of age-related changes.
—Richard Davidson, PhD (1951)
Psychologist, psychiatrist, and founder of The Center for Healthy Minds

Meditation in movement is a hundred, a thousand, a million times superior to meditation at rest.
—Zen proverb

GREAT MINDS THINK ALIKE: *Interconnectedness*

Every aspect of our lives is connected to every other aspect of our lives.
—Sharon Salzberg (1952)
From her book *Lovingkindness*

Our spirituality is a oneness and an interconnectedness with all that lives and breathes, even all that does not live or breathe.
—Mudrooroo (1938–2019)
Birth name: Colin Thomas Johnson
Australian novelist, poet, and playwright who focused on aboriginal subjects and characters. Mudrooroo translates as "paperbark," a type of Australian tree. The above quote was sourced from *mindofnature.wordpress.com.*
Great Minds Connect with Albert Szent-Gyorgy and the Sioux proverb on page 265

Everything is interrelated. There is a direct relationship between the macrocosm and the microcosm. When we influence one, we influence the other. We heal the planet, we heal ourselves... We heal ourselves and we heal the planet.
—Jonathan Goldman (1949)
American musician, author, teacher, and pioneer in the field of sound healing, from *The Seven Secrets of Sound Healing*

The universe is like a safe to which there is a combination,
but the combination is locked up in the safe.
—*Peter De Vries (1910–1993)*
Former U.S. Marine who became a prolific author of novels,
as quoted in *The Sun* magazine April 2006

The same one Consciousness is present in all forms—all people,
all things, all situations, all universes, all dimensions. There is
no difference in the basic substratum of anything, anywhere.
Everything that exists is nothing but a momentary appearance
of the universal energy within the field of time and space.
—*Lee Lyon*
Renowned meditation teacher, author, and founder of the Foundation for Integrative
Meditation, from his book *112 Meditations From the Book of Divine Wisdom*

Mending is a good metaphor for daily spiritual life. We are each
part of the great woven fabric of the world community. When a
couple in their mud brick house in Africa maintains a just and joyful
relationship, the world is a little bit better because of them.
—*Mavis & Merle Fossum*
Co-founders of the Family Therapy Institute in Minnesota from their book
The More We Find in Each Other. Great Minds Connect with the reference to
the couple in Africa and is an example of the Butterfly Effect discussed on page 40

Living artfully might require taking time to buy things with soul
for the home. Good linens, a special rug, or a simple teapot can be a
source of enrichment not only in our own life, but also in the lives of
our children and grandchildren. We can't discover the soul in a thing
without first taking time to observe it and be with it for a while.
—*Thomas Moore (1940)*
American psychotherapist, monk, and writer of spiritual books, from *Care of the Soul*

Solitude is the furnace of transformation.
—*Henri Jozef Machiel Nouwen (1932–1996)*
Internationally acclaimed Dutch Catholic priest, college professor, writer, and spiritual
guide whose 39 books have sold more than 7 million copies worldwide,
from his book *The Way of the Heart: The Spirituality of the Desert Fathers and Mothers*

GREAT MINDS THINK ALIKE: *The Nonexistence of Time*

Time by itself does not exist; but from things themselves there results a sense of what has already taken place, what is now going on and what is to ensue. It must not be claimed that anyone can sense time by itself apart from the movement of things.
—Lucretius (c.99–c.55 BC)
Full name: Titus Lucretius Carus
Roman philosopher, poet, and author of *On the Nature of Things*.
Great Minds Connect with Julian Barbour & Deepak Chopra
on page 28 and Yoko Ono on page 100

Time is a human construct. Only the eternal present exists.
—Dan Millman (1946)
From his book *The Hidden School*

Time is a created thing. To say "I don't have time is like saying "I don't want to."
—Lao Tzu (571–unknown BC)

Life is an unfoldment, and the further we travel the more truth we can comprehend.
—Hypatia of Alexandria (355–415)
Philosopher, astronomer, and first female mathematician in recorded history;
a bold feminist of ancient times who was brutally murdered

GREAT MINDS THINK ALIKE: *Fullness from Emptiness*

We too should make ourselves empty, that the great soul of the universe may fill us with its breath.
—Lawrence Binyon (1869–1943)
English dramatist, art scholar, and poet

If your mind is empty, it is ready for anything, open to everything. In the beginner's mind there are infinite possibilities, in the expert's mind there are few.
—Shunryu Suzuki-Roshi (1904–1971)
Japanese Zen monk instrumental in popularizing Zen Buddhism
in the United States, from *Zen Mind, Beginner's Mind*

The soul should always stand ajar, ready to welcome the ecstatic experience.
—Emily Dickinson (1830–1886)
Iconic American poet

Hospitality means we take people into the space that is our lives, our minds, our hearts and our work. It is the first step toward dismantling the barriers of the world. Hospitality is the way we turn a prejudiced world around, one heart at a time.
—Joan D. Chittister (1936)
American Benedictine nun, theologian, author, and speaker,
from *Wisdom Distilled from The Daily*

There is no end to beauty for the person who is aware. Even cracks in the sidewalk contain geometric patterns of amazing beauty. If we take pictures of them and blow up the photographs, we realize we walk on beauty every day, even when things around us seem ugly.
—Matthew Fox (1940)
Theologian, Episcopal priest, and author of 37 books on spirituality and contemporary
culture that have been translated into 70 languages, from *Creation Spirituality*

Idleness is the enemy of the soul.
—Anselm of Canterbury (1033–1109)
aka Saint Anselm
Italian Benedictine monk, abbot, and philosopher

Magic is a sudden opening of our minds to the wonder of existence... that we do not have to be confined by limited views our family, society, or our habitual thoughts impose on us. Life contains many dimensions, depths, textures, and meanings extending far beyond our familiar beliefs and concepts.
—John Welwood (1943–2019)
American clinical psychologist, psychotherapist, teacher, and author integrating
Western psychology and Eastern wisdom, from *Ordinary Magic*

I hope you will go out and let stories happen to you, that you will work them, water them with your blood, tears and laughter until they bloom, until you yourself burst into bloom
—Clarissa Pinkola Estes (1945)
Jungian psychoanalyst, post-trauma recovery specialist,
poet, and author, from *Women Who Run with the Wolves*

The purpose of a prophet is to be wrong. What a prophet does is give a wake-up call. If he is successful, we hear the call, and the prophecy does not come to be.
—Bob Frissell (1943)
Prolific American author, speaker, teacher, and spiritualist

The clues to your life path are not lost. They are often scattered and hidden right under your nose.
—Barbara Sher (1943)
American author, speaker, and career & lifestyle coach, from her book *Wishcraft*

For a long time it seemed that life was about to begin— real life. But there was always some obstacle in the way...something to be gotten through first, some unfinished business...then life would begin. At last it dawned on me that these obstacles were my life.
—Alfred D'Souza (1945)
Prominent Catholic bishop in India, from *Seven Choices*

The greatest good you can do for another is not just to share your riches, but to reveal to him his own.
—Benjamin Disraeli (1804–1881)
Great Minds Connect with Warren Bennis on page 148

The more you listen to the voice within you, the better you will hear what is sounding outside.
—Dag Hammarskjold (1905–1961)
Swedish economist, diplomat, and the second secretary general of the United Nations

It is not good to be praised; it is better to be criticized. It is not good to have comfort; it is better to have discomfort. If you have comfort, you exhaust the merit accumulated in past times. Experiencing problems is the blessing of the guru. Each problem gives an opportunity to develop the mind.
—Lama Zopa Rinpoche (1946)
Nepali Lama who founded the Kopan Monastery and Foundation for the Preservation of the Mahayana Tradition, from *Transforming Problems into Happiness*

If you are losing your leisure, look out!
You may be losing your soul.
—*Logan Pearsall Smith (1865–1946)*
American essayist and author who lived his adult life in Great Britain

Strength does not come from physical capacity.
It comes from an indomitable will.
—*Mohandas (Mahatma) Gandhi (1869–1948)*
Great Minds Connect with Confucius on page 133

There is an Indian proverb that says everyone is a house with four
rooms: physical, mental, emotional, and spiritual, and unless we get
into every room every day, even if only to keep it aired, we are not
a complete person.
—*Rumer Godden (1907–1998)*
English author of more than 60 books who lived
many years in India, from *A House with Four Rooms*

All suffering is caused by a single illusion: You believe
you live in the world when in truth, the world lives in you.
—*Wisdom of India*

Everything exists on the planet for a reason. There are no freaks,
misfits or accidents. There are only misunderstandings and
mysteries not yet revealed to mortal man.
—*Marlo Morgan (1937)*
From *Mutant Message Down Under*

There is nothing in my life that isn't spiritual. Spiritual laws
transcend national laws. They link us together as planetary citizens
who need each other…spirituality gives us security in changing times.
—*Anne Wilson Schaef (1934–2020)*
From *Native Wisdom for White Minds*

Spiritual growth is now replacing survival as the central objective of the human experience...Finding and healing the cause of emotional pain is the core of spiritual growth...emotional awareness is preventative medicine.
—*Gary Zukav (1942)*
From *The Heart of the Soul* that he co-authored with his wife, Linda Francis

Death is by no means separate from life. We all interact with death every day, tasting it as we might a wine, feeling its keen edge even in trifling losses and disappointments, holding it by the hand, as a dancer might a partner, in every separation. We pump the soul into every mystery from within, from inside our own experience.
—*Eugene Kennedy (1928–2015)*
Psychologist, award-winning writer, public intellectual, syndicated columnist, and professor emeritus of Loyola University Chicago, from *On Being a Friend*

The threat of death usually makes people a lot more aware of their lives.
—*Paulo Coelho (1947)*
From his book *The Alchemist*

Remembering that you are going to die is the best way I know to avoid the trap of thinking you have something to lose...stay hungry, stay foolish. Have the courage to follow your heart and intuition. They somehow already know what you truly want to become.
—*Steve Jobs (1955–2011)*
From his 2005 commencement speech at Stanford University

Both science and mysticism describe a force that connects everything together and gives us the power to influence how matter behaves, and reality itself, simply through the way we perceive the world around us.
—*Gregg Braden (1954)*
American author and teacher of spiritual technology, spiritual consciousness, and quantum healing, from *The Divine Matrix: Bridging Time, Space, Miracles and Belief*

GREAT MINDS THINK ALIKE: *Change Is a Rebirth*

The secret of change is to focus all your energy,
not on fighting the old, but on building the new.
—Socrates (470–399 BC)

In every crisis there is a message. Crises are nature's way of forcing
change— breaking down old structures, shaking loose negative
habits so that something new and better can take their place.
—Susan L. Taylor (1946)
African American writer, author, and magazine editor

Only birth can conquer death...the birth not
of the old thing again, but of something new.
—Joseph Campbell (1904–1987)
From *The Hero With a Thousand Faces.*
In *A Joseph Campbell Companion: Reflections on the Art of Living,* Campbell added
We must be willing to get rid of the life we've planned,
to have the life that is waiting for us. The old skin
has to be shed before a new one can come.

The most beautiful thing we can experience is the mysterious.
It is the source of all true art and science. The important thing
is not to stop questioning. One cannot help but be in awe
when contemplating the mysteries of eternity, of life,
of the marvelous structure of reality.
—Albert Einstein (1879–1955)

GREAT MINDS THINK ALIKE: *River of Change*

Change is like a river.
Nothing is the same, even for an instant.
—Wu Wei
A Taoist concept arising from Confucianism,
from the book *I Ching Wisdom Volumes I and II*

No man ever steps in the same river twice, for
it's not the same river, and he's not the same man.
—Heraclitus (535–475 BC)

You encourage people by seeing the good in them.
—Nelson Mandela (1918–2013)

***Faith removes limitations. Our only limitations are those
we set up in our own minds. Desire backed by faith
knows no such word as impossible.***
—Napoleon Hill (1883–1970)
From his book *Think and Grow Rich*. *Great Minds Connect* with Gerald A. Michaelson
and *Great Minds Think Alike: Impossible Is Possible* on page 56. This quote also applies to
the subject of *Extreme Desire* discussed in Chapter 12.

When fear knocks, let faith answer the door.
—Robin Roberts (1960)
ESPN sportscaster for 15 years who became anchor of ABC's *Good Morning America*,
from her speech when receiving the *Arthur Ashe Courage Award* as a cancer survivor

***Faith is to believe what you do not see; the
reward of this faith is to see what you believe.***
—Saint Augustine/Augustine of Hippo (354–430)
Birth name: Aurelias Augustinus Hipponensis
Roman philosopher and theologian who lived in Numidia, now known as Algeria

***To sacrifice what you are, and to live without belief,
is a fate more terrible than dying.***
—Joan of Arc (1412–1431)
Burned at the stake when 19 years old but later found innocent of all charges by the Pope,
Joan of Arc became an iconic martyr and was declared a national symbol of France
by Napoleon Bonaparte; she has since been declared a saint

***If you think you can win, you can win.
Faith is necessary for victory***.
—William Hazlitt (1778–1830)
British art critic, painter, and philosopher considered one of the great critics
and essayists in the history of the English language
Great Minds Connect with Virgil on page 245

As far as possible, join faith to reason.
—Boethius (477–524)

What is faith worth if it is not translated into action?
—*Mohandas (Mahatma) Gandhi (1869–1948)*

Perfect faith is something that produces perfect peace of mind, but perfect peace of mind is something that practically nobody possesses. Therefore, practically nobody possesses perfect faith.
—*Aldous Huxley (1894–1963)*
From his Utopian novel *Island,* written shortly before his death

Respect all religions. When someone else believes what his creator is, we can stand and pray together.
—*Horace Axtell (1924–2015)*
Nez Percé tribal historian, storyteller, drum maker, and singer

GREAT MINDS THINK ALIKE: *Philosophy & Wisdom*

Philosophy is nothing else...than the love of wisdom.
—*Marcus Tullius Cicero (106–43 BC)*

Philosophy...is not quite wisdom, but only the love (philo) of wisdom (sophia)...philosophy has become essentially the history of ideas.
—*Luc Ferry (1951)*
From *A Brief History of Thought*

It's easy to build a philosophy. It doesn't have to run.
—*Charles F. Kettering (1876–1958)*

A philosophical outlook will help you no matter what you are doing. Philosophy helps you in terms of acknowledging some sense of perspective in your life and in the world around you.
—*Alex Trebek (1940–2020)*
From *Alex Trebek: The Answer Is...*

Most mothers are instinctive philosophers.
—*Harriet Beecher Stowe (1811–1896)*

The primary task of philosophy is to perceive what is intrinsic about the world; what is most real, most important and most meaningful.
—Luc Ferry (1951)
From his book *A Brief History of Thought*

Philosophy is at once the most sublime and the most trivial of human pursuits.
—William James (1842–1910)

To truly know oneself, one must assert oneself.
—Albert Camus (1913–1960)
French philosopher, author, and journalist who contributed to the rise of philosophy known as absurdism

Life has no meaning a priori ...it is up to you to give it a meaning, and value is nothing but the meaning that you choose.
—Jean-Paul Sartre (1905–1980),
From *Existentialism is Humanism*

Life can only be understood backwards, but it must be lived forwards.
—Soren Kierkegaard (1813–1855)
Danish theologian, poet, social critic, and religious author widely considered to be the first existentialist philosopher

Each and every day is a canvas waiting to be painted.
—Craig Sagar (1951–2016)
Flamboyant American sports reporter who heroically battled cancer

Whoever wishes to become a philosopher must learn not to be frightened by absurdities.
—Bertrand Russell (1872–1970)

They are never alone who are accompanied by noble thoughts.
—*Philip Sydney (1554–1586)*
Prominent English poet, courtier, scholar, and soldier

God, grant me the serenity to accept the things I cannot change, courage to change the things I can, and the wisdom to know the difference.
—*Reinhold Niebuhr (1892–1971)*
American theologian, writer, lecturer, and political philosopher who coined this famous Serenity Prayer that has since been adopted by Alcoholics Anonymous

Our generally accepted notion of the history of philosophy is founded on a completely false assumption, mainly that abstract and metaphysical thought begins where it first appears in our extant records.
—*Joseph Campbell (1904–1987)*
From his book *The Hero With a Thousand Faces*

There is no enemy for one who keeps the radiant light of the sun in his heart.
—*Sanskrit wisdom phrase translated by Rick Jarow (1952-2024)*

Nothing great is ever achieved without people making frightening leaps of faith...the basic law of prosperity is that to receive, you must first provide something of great value.
—*Tom Butler-Bowdon (1967)*
From his book *50 Prosperity Classics*

Beauty is eternity gazing at itself in a mirror. But you are eternity and you are the mirror.
—*Kahlil Gibran (1883–1931)*
From his classic book *The Prophet*

***Great tranquility of heart is his
who cares for neither praise nor blame.***
—*Thomas Kempis (1360–1471)*
German Dutch canon regular (a type of priest) and author

Heart power is stronger than horsepower.
—*Henry J. Heinz (1844–1919)*

Bless what you want.
—*T. Harv Eker (1983)*
From his book *Secrets of the Millionaire Mind.*
Eker encourages the use of this phrase to set the universe in motion to give you what you ask for. Eker mentions this phrase as an example of the Huna Philosophy. *Huna* is Hawaiian for secret. It's also an abbreviated name for the Kahunas of Hawaii, who are the keepers of secrets. Further investigation of this exotic sounding term revealed it was coined by American novelist and New Age author Max Freedom Long (1890–1971) who lived in Hawaii for many years. Long began writing about the Huna Philosophy in 1936, but Hawaiian scholars dispute its Hawaiian roots; it appears that Huna is actually a New Age creation derived from numerous other spiritual traditions, including those of Polynesia.

***The great lesson from the true mystics, from the Zen monks…is that
the sacred is in the ordinary, that it is to be found in one's daily life,
in one's neighbors, friends, and family, in one's back yard.***
—*Abraham Maslow (1908–1970)*
From *Religions, Values and Peak Experiences*

***I give people what they want in the hope they will
begin to want what I want to give them.***
—*Sai Baba (1838–1918)*
Spiritual master from India considered by many to be a saint

***The only true sign of spiritual progress
is an increasing ability to serve.***
—*Thomas Ashley-Farrand (1940–2010)*
American scholar, teacher, and author who was one of the foremost authorities
in the Western world on the subject of Sanskrit mantras. Another one of
Thomas Ashley-Farrand's favorite quotes was:
To clean the bottom of the pond, you must first stir up the mud.
Both of the above quotes are from his book *True Stories of Spiritual Power*

GREAT MINDS THINK ALIKE: *The Magical Power of Belief*

The force of your belief represents a transmitter to the universe that enters the minds of other people and even inanimate objects. The more powerful your broadcast, the more likely the world will pick it up and react accordingly.
—Claude M. Bristol (1891–1951)
World War I soldier, journalist, reporter, and author, from his book *The Magic of Belief*

Belief is the thermostat that regulates what we accomplish in life… belief in success is the one basic, absolutely essential ingredient of successful people. The size of your success is determined by the size of your belief.
—David J. Schwartz (1927–1987)
From his book *The Magic of Thinking Big*

*If you cannot find peace within yourself,
you will never find it anywhere else.*
—Marvin Gaye (1939–1984)
African American singer/songwriter known as the "prince of Motown"

Not all those who wander are lost.
—J.R.R. Tolkien (1892–1973)
English writer and philologist who penned *The Hobbit* and *The Lord of the Rings*

*The best way to find yourself is
to lose yourself in the service of others.*
—Mahatma Gandhi (1869–1948)

Ruin is a gift. Ruin is the road to transformation.
—Elizabeth Gilbert (1969)

*For transformation to take place, we have to practice mindfulness
all day long, not just on our meditation cushion.*
—Thich Nhat Hanh (1926–2022)

The law of giving is very simple: If you want joy, give joy.
If love is what you seek, offer love. If you crave material affluence,
help others become prosperous.
—Deepak Chopra (1946)
From *The Seven Spiritual Laws of Success*

Throughout history, the wisest men and women have known that
their highest good came from surrender—not as in losing a battle, but
as in letting go of their personal limitations and aligning totally with
an intelligence greater than themselves.
—Marci Shimoff (1958)
From her book *Happy For No Reason*

If there is light in the soul, there will be beauty in the person.
If there is beauty in the person, there will be harmony in the house.
If there is harmony in the house, there will be order in the nation.
If there is order in the nation, there will be peace in the world.
—Chinese proverb
This proverb exemplifies the *Butterfly Effect* that is discussed on page 40
and earlier in this chapter

Whatever you do to others, you do to yourself.
—Buddha (563–483 BC)
Great Minds Connect with *The Boomerang Effect* on page 267

Everything becomes spiritual in its deepest sense...such is the power
of mindful selfless generosity. At the deepest level, there is no giver,
no gift...only the universe rearranging itself.
—Jon Kabat-Zinn (1944)
American professor emeritus of medicine, mindfulness expert, and author, from his book
Wherever You Go There You Are: Mindfulness Meditation in Everyday Life

Philosophies should only be judged
by the success and failures they produce.
–Ray Dalio (1949)
Dalio made this statement in his book *The Changing World Order*
while summing up the beliefs of Karl Marx.

Personal growth and spirituality never exist within an economic vacuum. The spirituality of the future will be one that is woven together with a work ethic that supports justice, sustainability, and abundance, integrating our personal processes with the social and economic structures of the world.
—Rick Jarow (1952–2024)
From his book *Alchemy of Abundance*

There is intelligence in everything that exists in the universe, and we're all linked by a kind of universal mind.
—Claude M. Bristol (1891–1951)
This quote parallels Carl Jung's concept of the collective unconscious that is also discussed by Napoleon Hill in his book *Think and Grow Rich*. The concepts of universal intelligence and the interconnectedness of all things are intrinsic to the spiritual teachings of all indigenous cultures. *Great Minds Connect* with Shakti Gawain on page 18 and Mudrooroo earlier in this chapter.

GREAT MINDS THINK ALIKE: *What Is Spirituality?*

By "spiritual" I don't mean religious. I mean the act of self-discovery that happens when you step beyond your routine way of seeing the world.
—Phil Jackson (1945)
From his book *Eleven Rings*

All spiritual teachings attempt to lead ultimately to the same thing: an understanding of the mysteries of the universe, and the role we each play in it.
—Elaine St. James (1943)
From her book *Inner Simplicity*

CONSOLIDATING CHAPTER 18
Spirituality, Faith & Philosophy

Spirituality is a fundamental aspect of human nature. Forming a circular connection, spirituality is the soul of human nature and human nature is the interpreter of spirituality. Chapter 18 provides a panoramic assortment of quotes about spirituality and its connections to faith and philosophy. From the mundane to the ethereal, from 3,000 years ago to modern times, this chapter covers a lot of ground. Lao Tzu and Confucius tell us experience is the path to knowing, while Lao Tzu teams up with Meister Eckhart to tout the power of silence. We hear about hospitality's ability to dismantle barriers and potentially save the world, and we are warned not to lose our leisure if we want to retain our souls; leading us to David Cooper praising the benefits of spiritual retreats. Phrases in this chapter ask profound questions while providing equally profound suggestions and options. These intense discussions of spirituality often usher in more questions than answers. While it's difficult to reach any specific conclusions, Chapter 18 contains the profound lesson that respecting each other's spiritual beliefs is vitally important. There are many different ways to absorb and demonstrate spirituality, so it becomes clear the biggest mistake would be to believe anyone has an exclusively correct answer to the great mysteries of existence.

Numerous spiritual traditions assert we are all interconnected, which means even those who don't agree with this concept are still connected to it in some way. Denial of reality does not necessarily negate its reality, just as denying a truth does not cause the truth to become false. It's also true that perception can create reality...so in the end, spirituality leaves us in the middle of what Native Americans call *The Great Mystery*...but hopefully now armed with enough information, inner peace, and strength to create more fulfilling lives. This is the benefit of combining spirituality with faith to form a cohesive philosophy.

Spirituality is also about living artfully as opposed to creating works of art. It adds texture and meaning to any activity it touches. Spirituality nurtures self-awareness and illuminates the path to living with grace. Every category in this book has a connection to spirituality. Fittingly, this chapter begins with Ann Wilson Schaef finding spirituality in every aspect of life, M. Scott Peck describing spirituality as a path of lifelong learning, and Gary Zukav insisting spiritual growth is necessary for the survival of our species. Zukav also believes emotional awareness is preventative medicine. Mahatma Gandhi defines spirituality as education of the heart, and Sharon Salzberg tells us every aspect of our lives is connected to all other aspects. Mudrooroo expands on that concept by finding interconnectedness between non-living things as well living things. This theory of interconnectedness aligns with spiritual beliefs of indigenous cultures worldwide, demonstrating how Chapters

17 and 18 are so intimately connected that they can essentially be viewed as one chapter. A major component of spirituality is faith. Although faith manifests itself in a variety of ways through multiple belief systems, faith is a universal aspect of all world cultures. Napoleon Hill tells us faith removes our limitations, while William Hazlitt finds faith to be necessary for victory in any significant endeavor. Taking a broader view of faith, the Dalai Lama has embarked on a search for forms of spirituality and ethics that extend beyond religion. Tom Butler-Bowdon has the final thought on faith in saying the path to greatness always requires a leap of faith.

The third section of Chapter 18 delves into the realm of philosophy. Spiritual beliefs are essentially philosophies in that both spirituality and philosophy seek to understand human nature and comprehend humanity's place in the universe...the source of our individual and collective identities. Deepak Chopra defines philosophy as an attempt to understand and articulate our relationship to the planet and universe. Epicurus describes philosophy as "medicine for the soul." These two men's perspectives depict the core connection of philosophy with spirituality. Our philosophies form our worldview...our belief systems. On a more practical level, philosophies are systems of thought; integrated cerebral systems providing guidance for making decisions and establishing lifestyles. On the macro level, philosophies guide governmental decisions and political agendas. In the world of sports, they determine styles of play for both individual athletes and teams.

Even those who reject the subject of philosophy have their own specific belief systems, as any group of beliefs inadvertently forms a philosophy even if those beliefs are not formally expressed. Whether or not they are stated, personal philosophies shape everyone's identity. On the subject of finding identity, Albert Camus believes we learn who we really are when we exert ourselves. Alex Trebek believes a philosophical outlook helps any pursuit. Seeing both sides of this proverbial coin, William James believes philosophy is both sublime and trivial at the same time. Steve Jobs recounts the philosophy of life he formed after receiving a prognosis of premature death, a prognosis he surprisingly found inspirational. Facing impending death urged him to live life fully in every moment. His advice was "stay hungry, foolish, and follow your heart." Jobs's point of view connects with Socrates and Joseph Campbell, who both saw change as a form of rebirth, as it's often necessary to shed the old to create something new.

Other notable quotes in Chapter 18 are Craig Sagar visualizing every day as a fresh canvas ready to be painted, Henry J. Heinz promoting heart power over horsepower, John Beaulieu embracing chaos as a catalyst for higher consciousness, and Emily Dickinson advising us to always keep our souls open to the possibility of an ecstatic experience. Mahatma Gandhi reminds us strength comes from willpower more than physical prowess, and Lama Zopa Rinpoche views problems as *blessings of the guru,* explaining how problems present great opportunities to develop our minds, since hardship often teaches us lessons we need to learn. This unleashes the potential for our problems to become our greatest assets. Though it's challenging to become genuinely grateful for difficulties and problems, that is the essence of spiritually based gratitude. To that end, T. Harv Eker advises us to bless what we want, thereby combining faith with gratitude. Not to be outdone, Lucretius and Dan Millman claim that time does not exist...connecting us back to Chapter 1.

WISDOM TRAILS: *Interconnected Categories*

Education, History, The Arts, Education, Love, Health, Social Justice, Compassion, The Future, Sports, Business, Politics, Science, Fear, War, Sports, Wisdom, Courage, Friendship, Success, Peace, Harmony

Trails to Other Chapters

- M. Scott Peck views spirituality as part of lifelong learning. (*Spirituality*)
- Mahatma Gandhi views spiritual training as education of the heart. (*Compassion*)
- Rabindranath Tagore connects spirituality to the *History* of humans.
- Joseph Campbell connects *The Arts*, literature, and spiritual growth.
- Ronald Wright connects myth to *History*.
- John Beaulieu discusses the role of chaos in consciousness. (*Health, Education*)
- The 14th Dalai Lama discusses *Love*, spirituality, and religion.
- Mary Baker Eddy includes *Love* as an essential element of prayer.
- Timothy Gallwey praises the value of experience in learning. (*Education*)
- Buddha discusses the past and *The Future*.
- David A. Cooper adds *Compassion* and loving kindness as aspects that are rekindled in spiritual retreats.
- Mavis and Merle Fossum connect daily spiritual life to *Health*.
- Thomas Moore discusses how to turn our lives into works of *Art*.
- Lucretius and Dan Millman claim that time does not exist; this claim has an interesting relationship with *History* and *The Future*.
- John Chittister seeks to improve the world by warming the hearts of others with hospitality. (*Compassion*)
- Matthew Fox connects spirituality with beauty and *The Arts*.
- Mahatma Gandhi's statement that strength comes from indomitable will is applicable to *Work, Business, Sports, Politics,* and *War*.
- Gary Zukav believes spiritual growth and emotional awareness serve as preventive medicine. (*Health*)

- Albert Einstein identifies the mysterious as the source of all *Art* and *Science.*
- Gregg Braden connects mysticism with *Science.*
- Robin Roberts uses faith to combat *Fear.*
- William Hazlitt's insistence that faith is necessary for victory connects with *Sports, Politics, Business,* and *War.*
- Aldous Huxley reasons that faith and *Peace* of mind are never perfect.
- Cicero and Luc Ferry agree that philosophy is the *Love* of wisdom.
- Alex Trebek touts the importance of employing a philosophy in all endeavors.
  (*Science, Work, Business, The Arts, Sports, Politics, Government, War*)
- Craig Sagar's philosophy views every day as a potential work of *Art.*
- Bertrand Russell warns philosophers not to *Fear* the absurd.
- Reinhold Neibuhr's Serenity Prayer directly applies to *Courage, Wisdom, Business, Health,* and *Work.*
- Joseph Campbell discusses the *History* of philosophy.
- Jonathan Goldman believes healing ourselves helps heal our planet. *(Health)*
- Mudrooroo embodies indigenous people's belief in the interconnectedness of all things. *(Native American Wisdom)*
- Tom Butler-Bowdon combines the *Law of Prosperity* with faith to overcome *Fear* and achieve *Success.*
- Abraham Maslow informs us the sacred can be found in *Friendship.*
- Henry J. Heinz believes in the power of the heart. (*Love, Compassion*)
- T. Harv Eker recommends blessing what we want to achieve *Success.*
- Claude M. Bristol and David J. Schwartz highlight the connection between faith and *Success.*
- Marvin Gaye stresses the need for inner *Peace.*
- Deepak Chopra advises us to give love if we desire to receive *Love.*
- Marci Shimoff says *History* demonstrates that surrender leads to the highest good being achieved.
- A Chinese proverb connects spirituality and beauty with *Harmony* and *Peace* in the world.
- Ray Dalio's statement about philosophy applies directly to *Success.*
- Rick Jarow connects spirituality with *Work* and *Social Justice.*

CHAPTER 19

FENG SHUI, HEALTH & HARMONY

Architecture is frozen music.
—Johann Wolfgang von Goethe (1749–1832)
Goethe's phrase inspired the creation of this feng shui chapter. Architecture, when conceived as frozen music, creates and transforms energy vibrations that, when thawed out, powerfully affect our existence. This is the essence of feng shui—a science and art form that seeks to optimize the energy inside and around all architecture, thereby aligning with the forces of nature. Literally translated, *feng shui* means wind and water.

We shape our buildings; thereafter, they shape us.
—Winston Churchill (1874–1965)
As quoted in *Feng Shui Journal* by Teresa Polanco

Feng shui is one of the Five Arts of Chinese Metaphysics, classified as physiognomy, which is defined as the observation of appearances through formulas and calculations.
—Guo Po (276–324)
Chinese historian, Taoist mystic, and editor of ancient texts who was the first person in history to define feng shui, in *The Book of Burial*

Feng shui is the science of arranging the living space using correct orientations that reflect the patterns of chi energy in the environment...when a home is oriented to harmonize with surrounding landforms, good feng shui is welcomed, and health, wealth and prosperity ensue. Feng shui science is based on the I Ching's trigrams, the Five Elements and the theory of yin and yang.
—Lillian Too (1946)
From *Total Feng Shui*

Feng shui is environmental acupuncture...The environmental art of feng shui creates harmony in the buildings we have created and the people who inhabit them. Among the scientific disciplines that have influenced feng shui are Bioenergetics, Ergonomics, Architecture, Environmental Engineering, and especially Biological Construction or Bau-Biologie.
—Juan M. Alvarez
Senior member of the American Institute of Industrial Engineers and internationally recognized authority on feng shui, from *Feng Shui: The Harmony of Life*

Feng shui is a way of creating harmony between humans and our environment to enhance our well-being.
—Belinda Henwood
Feng shui expert and author, from *Feng Shui: How to Create Harmony and Balance in Your Living and Working Environment*

Give yourself good feng shui by ensuring that your living, working and leisure conditions are favorable to your health and well-being.
—Dr. Charles Windridge
Author of *Tong Sing: The Chinese Book of Wisdom*, which is based on the ancient Chinese Almanac

In essence, tidying ought to be the act of restoring balance among people, their possessions, and the house they live in...the question of what you want to own is actually the question of how you want to live your life...keep only those things that speak to your heart...that spark joy. To truly cherish the things that are important to you, you must first discard those that have outlived their purpose...when we reduce what we own and essentially "detox" our house, it has a detox effect on our bodies as well.
—Marie Kondo (1984)
Japanese organizing consultant, author, and television show host whose books have sold millions of copies, from *The Life-Changing Magic of Tidying Up*. Tidying, as practiced by Kondo, is a specific protocol for decluttering.

You must create a space for the good that you desire.
—Bob Proctor (1934)
Canadian self-help author and speaker who created this phrase known as *The Vacuum Law of Prosperity*, advising us to rid ourselves of old ideas so new ones can enter and flourish; a concept that aligns with the clutter clearing advice of feng shui

It's uncanny how often people find a correlation between the way their homes are designed and their ongoing problems...one of the most powerful actions you can take is to live with what you love... the more you practice living with what you love, the more exciting and affirmational your life will become.
—Terah Kathryn Collins

GREAT MINDS THINK ALIKE: *Clearing Space*

New things cannot come where there is no room.
—Marlo Morgan (1937)

Every aspect of your life is anchored energetically in your living space. Clutter clearing is one of the most powerful transformative aspects of feng shui. Clearing space will allow new opportunities to blossom.
—Karen Kingston

When you declutter, identify what you are making room for. Knowing what brings joy will help keep the clutter out for good.
—Courtney Carver (1969)
Self-help author, speaker, and blogger, from bemorewithless.com

When you have the courage to push out of your life the things you do not want, it makes space for the things you want to come rushing in.
—From *Feng Shui Wisdom* (no author credited)

When I let go of something that I don't need, what I do need manifests in my life.
—Terah Kathryn Collins
Internationally recognized feng shui consultant, speaker, teacher, and author from *Feng Shui: Room By Room*

At least once a year, if not more often, clear out old newspapers, unwanted clothes, and other objects whose energy has become stale. You may not realize it, but stale energy has a significant negative effect on your immune system.
—Lillian Too (1946)
From *Total Feng Shui*
Great Minds Connect with Dee Hock on page 159

Cleansing or purification is the first step in prosperity. Without releasing mentally, emotionally, and in our visible world, there can be no permanent satisfying prosperity. Along with cleaning out the closets, clean up and clear out your life. The skeletons in the closet have got to go if you wish to be truly prosperous.
—Catherine Ponder (1927)
From her book *Open Your Mind to Prosperity*

If you want a change in your life, move 27 things in your house.
—Chinese proverb

Space is vibrational. Rearranging space rearranges energy.
—Rick Jarow (1952-2024)
From *The Ultimate Anti Career Guide*;
this quote embodies the rationale for clutter-clearing

*A home is not dead but living, and like all living things
must obey the laws of nature by constantly changing.*
—Carl Larsson (1855–1919)
Celebrated Swedish painter, and illustrator, as quoted in *The Feng Shui Journal*

*A house can be a simple shelter, but a home
is the physical manifestation of one's inner life.*
—Diane Ackerman (1948)
From her book *Deep Play*

*When positioning your bed, ensure that your feet do not point
directly toward the door. This may cause sleepless nights.*
—Rosalind Simmons
British author, palmist, and tarot card expert,
from *Feng Shui: The Art of Living*

*Avoid placing mattresses directly on the floor.
Air and energy must circulate beneath you.*
—Peter Pauper Press
From *Feng Shui for the Home*

*Don't forget to look under the bed. Storing junk there
can cause marital difficulties as well as bad health.*
—Belinda Henwood
From her book *Feng Shui*

*Avoid using dried flowers in your home, as they represent dead
energy...Refrain from hanging items on the backs of doors. Doing this
increases the weight of the door and adds more struggle to your life.*
—Rosalind Simmons
From *Feng Shui: The Art of Living*

When furnishing your home, remember sharp corners and angles create disruptive energy while rounder objects create harmony.
—From *Feng Shui Wisdom* (no author credited)

The secret of perfect health lies in keeping the mind always cheerful— never worried, hurried or borne down by fear, thought or anxiety.
—Sai Baba (1838–1918)
Great Minds Connect with Michel de Montaigne on page 251

When you really listen to yourself, you can heal yourself.
—Ceanne Derohan
Author of spirituality books, as quoted in *Vein of Gold* by Julia Cameron

If I had to limit my advice on healthier living to just one tip, it would be simply to learn how to breathe better.
—Dr. Andrew Weil (1942)
Famous American doctor and author who is a leading spokesperson for the fields of alternative and integrative medicine, from his book *Breathing: The Master Key to Self-Healing*

The measure of mental health is flexibility. The essence of illness is the freezing of behavior into unalterable patterns.
—C. Alexander Simpkins, PhD (1949) and Annellen Simpkins (1962)
Eclectic American psychologists specializing in meditation, neuroscience, and hypnosis who have written numerous books together, from *Simple Zen: A Guide to Living Moment to Moment*

Thought alone can completely change the body.
—Candace Pert, PhD (1946–2013)
Internationally recognized American neuroscientist and pharmacologist; this reflects the essence of psychoneuroimmunology

The secret of health for both mind and body is not to mourn for the past, worry about the future, or anticipate troubles, but to live in the present moment wisely and earnestly.
—Paramahansa Yogananda (1893–1952)

GREATMINDS THINK ALIKE: *Health & the Mind*

Emotional awareness is preventative medicine.

—*Gary Zukav (1942)*

From *The Heart of the Soul,* which he co-authored with his wife, Linda Francis

Emotion affects the body's biochemistry. Optimistic purposeful stubborn people tend to live longest. Longevity has more to do with lifestyle choices you make than your genes.

—*Art Linkletter (1912–2010)*

Legendary Canadian-born American radio and television show host, from his book *How To Make The Rest of Your Life The Best of Your Life*; this is the essence underlying the concept of psychoneuroimmunology

Thinking sick may make you sick.

—*David S. Kidder and Noah D. Oppenheim (1978)*

Kidder is an investor, author, and speaker; Oppenheim is an American television producer and author. This statement that exemplifies psychoneuroimmunology, was made during a discussion of the placebo effect in their book *Intellectual Devotional.*

Half the beds in our hospitals are filled with people who worried themselves into them.

—*Dr. Charles Mayo (1865–1939)*

American surgeon who co-founded the Mayo Clinic with his older brother William and five of their colleagues, as quoted in *The Tao of Abundance*

Recovery from any disease is dependent on willingness to explore new ways of looking at one's self and life.

—*David R. Hawkins MD (1927–2012)*

From *Power vs. Force*

Health and longevity studies show that when people live with a sense of purpose, no matter how big or small, they live longer and healthier lives.

—*Marci Shimoff (1958)*

From her book *Happy For No Reason*

Those who are at peace with themselves and their immediate surroundings have far fewer serious illnesses than those who are not...People who can see nature from their hospital rooms or have scenes of the outdoors instead of abstract painting in their room heal faster and experience less pain...The treatment that cures you may not be what really cures you. It may be your belief in it.

—*Dr. Bernie S. Siegel (1932)*

From his books *365 Prescriptions For The Soul* and *Love, Medicine & Miracles*

There are no limits to the prosperity, happiness,
and peace of mind you can achieve simply by using
the power of the subconscious mind.
—*Joseph Murphy (1898–1981)*
This phrase is actually the title of a best-selling book by Joseph Murphy,
an Irish author and New Thought minister

Illness almost always has a spiritual component.
—*Anne Wilson Schaef (1934–2020)*
From her book *Native Wisdom for White Minds*

The physician should not treat the disease but the patient
who is suffering from it...no disease that can be treated
by diet should be treated by any other means.
—*Maimonides (1138–1204)*
Spanish-born Jewish philosopher, physician, and Torah scholar; the second half of this two-
part quote appears in *Ancient Remedies* by Dr. Josh Axe. Maimonides' best-known quote is:
Give a man a fish and you feed him for a day;
teach a man to fish and you feed him for a lifetime.

Each patient carries his own doctor inside him. They come to us not
knowing this truth. We are at our best when we give the doctor who
resides within each patient a chance to go to work.
—*Albert Schweitzer (1875–1965)*
Nobel Peace Prize-winning Alsatian physician, theologian, organist,
writer, humanitarian, and philosopher

Medicine to produce health must examine disease; and music,
to create harmony must investigate discord.
—*Plutarch (46–120)*

Sound will be the medicine of the future.
—*Edgar Cayce (1877–1945)*
American clairvoyant and spiritual teacher who founded
the Association for Research and Enlightenment

Neurons that fire together, wire together.
Mental states become traits.
—Rick Hanson, PhD
From his book *Hardwiring Happiness*

Pleasing yourself with special treats from time to time is vital
to a healthy, satisfying life. We need to surround ourselves
with little rewards that have meaning to us. Small indulgences
can brighten and enliven our lives.
—David Sobel (1949)
Education writer and author, from *Healthy Pleasures*

All the tragedy in the world, in the individual and in the multitude,
comes from lack of harmony, and harmony is best given by producing
it in one's own life. The vibrations of mind are much stronger than
those of words. The earnest feelings of one heart can pierce the heart
of another; they speak in silence, spreading out into the sphere so that
the very atmosphere of a person's presence proclaims his thoughts
and emotions. The vibrations of the soul are far reaching.
They run like an electric current from soul to soul.
—Hazrat Inayat Khan (1882–1927)

All life is vibration. You combine with what you vibrate to.
If you are vibrating to injustice and resentment,
you will meet them on your pathway at every step.
—Florence Scovel Shinn (1871–1940)
As quoted in *The Feng Shui Journal*

Love produces harmony and harmony creates beauty. Therefore, the
chief motto in life is: Love, harmony and beauty. By love, harmony
and beauty you must turn the whole of life into a single vision of
divine glory.
—Hazrat Inayat Khan (1882–1927)
From *The Mysticism of Sound and Music*

From differences results the most beautiful harmony.
—Heraclitus (535-475 BC)

Everything in the universe is in a state of vibration, thereby producing a sound or frequency. Consciousness can be encoded upon vibration, truly affecting how the sound resonates.
Thus: Frequency + Intention= Healing
Vocalization + Visualization= Manifestation
Vibration+ Belief= Outcome
—Jonathan Goldman (1949)

Any effect you can produce in the human organism through a pharmacological intervention can also be produced, at least some of the time, purely by the mind. We should be investigating that mind mechanism with all our ability so that we can take greater advantage of it to treat disease and stimulate healing.
—Dr. Andrew Weil (1942)
As quoted in The Sun January 2011 issue

GREAT MINDS THINK ALIKE: *Good Health*

The groundwork for all happiness is good health.
—Leigh Hunt (1784–1859)
Birth name: James Henry Leigh Hunt
English essayist, editor, and poet

The greatest wealth is health.
—Virgil (70–19 BC)

Always focus on wellness as opposed to illness...placing your attention on what you want as opposed to what you don't want.
—Rose, an Aboriginal healer,
as quoted in Gary Holz's Secrets of Aboriginal Healing. Rose continued:
When my people talk about healing, we include not only the body, but also the mind, emotions, and spirit...When you have problems in your body, it's actually your body sending you a message to change your actions.

CONSOLIDATING CHAPTER 19
Feng Shui, Health & Harmony

By connecting vibration, thought, and health, Chapter 19 provides enlightening strategies for harmonizing your daily lifestyle with your environment. Essentially, feng shui practice seeks to balance energy, and all energy is vibrational. Therefore, feng shui, health, and harmony are closely related, as all deal with energy and vibration. You may wonder, *why include feng shui in a book about wisdom?*

The answer is: Because feng shui's concepts and advice represent specialized wisdom offering major potential benefits to everyday life. Another logical question is: *If feng shui offers advice, why isn't it part of the Practical Advice chapter?*

This issue was contemplated during the organization of *Consolidated Wisdom*. Although feng shui represents a type of practical advice, feng shui was given its own chapter because its advice is so specialized. Additionally, feng shui is an unknown subject to many that requires special clarification.

The next logical question is: *So what is feng shui?*

Also known as Chinese geomancy, the practice of feng shui originated in China approximately 3,000 years ago. The term *feng shui* literally translates as *wind and water* in English. Feng shui texts discuss architecture in terms of invisible forces known as *qi* (pronounced *chi*) that bind together the universe, our planet, and humanity. Historically, feng shui has been used to advantageously orient homes, businesses, and large tombs, as well as governmental and public structures. Feng shui is practiced to generate prosperity, good fortune, good health, and overall happiness. Containing elements of both art and science, feng shui helps us align ourselves with the energetic forces of nature to create more prosperous and fulfilling lives.

If you're still confused, here is another way of stating what feng shui is: The art and science of arranging your environment to enhance health, wealth, and happiness to maximize your chances for prosperity and improve your quality of life. Good feng shui calms the nervous system and teaches us how to harness the powerful forces of nature so they positively impact our existence. By working with the power of nature, which is vibrantly alive and contains hidden forces, feng shui provides specific methods for humans to harmonize with the natural world.

On a macro level, this scientifically based practice governs the positioning and shape of architecture plus all the contents of architectural structures, in addition to the arrangement of plants, gardens, and walkways. On the micro level, feng shui is about organizing your personal space to maximize relationships, health, and prosperity, while minimizing the afflictions of life. It is about unblocking obstacles and allowing positive energy to flow both around you and through you. Feng shui advice applies to the positioning of rooms in a house, location of doors and windows, arrangement of furniture, and even the colors of paint on walls. Using a specialized map called a *bagua*, feng shui practitioners prescribe remedies to overcome energetic shortfalls existing in any given location.

The most commonly known Western application of feng shui is clearing out clutter. Feng shui practitioner and clutter-clearing expert Marie Kondo recommends the first step toward getting rid of clutter is organizing it and limiting the number of places it exists, thereby creating as many clutter-free zones as possible. Kondo's method establishes one centralized place where all clutter is deposited before being evaluated for disposal. The concept of removing clutter from a home is linked to lingering negative emotions; a type of internal clutter needing to be cleared to make room for forward progress. In psychological terms, *clutter* equates to *blockages*.

Rearranging space rearranges vibrations, causing everything in a space to resonate differently. This causes physical and psychological rebalancing. In feng shui theory, moving furniture represents the activation of a shift in other aspects of your life. Clearing space unblocks energy (*chi*), which shifts other dimensions of your awareness. Once you figure out what has been blocking you in a room and what it represents, you can access and resolve the underlying issue(s) you need to resolve. Clearing clutter also frees up the parts of your mind holding onto those items, epitomizing the phrase "less is more." Essentially, less stuff means more space, and more space helps energy flow more freely. Decluttering your mind becomes *cerebral feng shui* that can enhance creative thinking.

Feng shui also warns us to avoid *sha energy,* which is translated as "killer energy." This type of bad energy can be created by the sharpness of natural or man-made structures pointing to your front door or windows. Feng shui calls such entities "poison arrows." Sha energy can also exist within a building. Feng shui practitioners have very specific methods for detecting and prescribing cures for these situations. In Japan, feng shui experts are consulted before the construction of large buildings to ensure no sha energy will afflict the occupants of the new structure. The power of feng shui protocols should not be overlooked, as bad feng shui can be detrimental to your health and personal relationships, as well as your wallet.

Chapter 19 offers a few specific feng shui remedies. In *The Feng Shui Journal,* Teresa Polanco offers some simple suggestions to enhance prosperity, such as always keeping your toilet seat down when not in use, fixing leaky faucets, and using all burners on your stove equally. An additional recommendation is to place a fish tank in the finance area of your home or office, as moving water in a prosperity area improves cash flow. Another interesting feng shui guideline is that the ratio of windows to doors in any home or building should be at least 3 to 1. There are also numerous species of plants that provide good feng shui.

After the quotes on feng shui, Chapter 19 shifts direction to health and harmony. Harmony is equated with resonance, which is a soothing and beneficial type of vibrational relationship. Numerous quotes about health connect our emotional state with our overall health. A contemporary term used to describe the direct connection between our minds and bodies is *psychoneuroimmunology*. This term focuses on the power of thought in determining our health, especially when recovering from illness or trauma. The need for balance, or homeostasis, is described as a vibrational issue by a number of contributors, aligning with Edgar Cayce's claim about sonic protocols emerging as major medical treatment methods in the near future.

WISDOM TRAILS: *Interconnected Categories*
The Arts, Science, Health, Happiness, Work, Courage, Love, Nature, Fear, History, The Future, Peace, Happiness, Spirituality, Native American Wisdom

Trails to Other Chapters
- Goethe equates architecture to an eclectic form of music. (*The Arts*)
- Lillian Too informs us that feng shui is based on *Science*.
- Juan Alvarez considers feng shui to be an *Art* form.
- Dr. Charles Windridge emphasizes the connection of feng shui to *Work*.
- Marie Kondo advises us to only keep things that bring us *Happiness,* which will be good for our *Health.*
- *Feng Shui Wisdom* advises us to have the *Courage* to get rid of things we no longer need.
- Terah Kathryn Collins advises us to live with what we *Love.*
- Carl Larsson applies the laws of *Nature* to our home living conditions.
- Sai Baba connects the elimination of *Fear* and anxiety with improved health.
- Paramahansa Yogananda advises us not to worry about *The Future.*
- Dr. Bernie Siegel informs us that people who are at *Peace* with themselves and their surroundings enjoy better health.
- Joseph Murphy believes the subconscious mind provides unlimited potential for *Success and Happiness.*
- Anne Wilson Schaef states that illness always has a *Spiritual* component.
- Plutarch believes music creates harmony and promotes good health. (*The Arts*)
- Edgar Cayce predicts sound will establish itself as a major field of medicine in *The Future.*
- Florence Scovel Shinn warns against vibrating to injustice. (*Social Justice*)
- Hazrat Inayat Khan connects beauty, harmony, and *Love.*
- Leigh Hunt proclaims that good health is the foundation for all *Happiness.*
- Aboriginal healer Rose offers *Practical Advice* on healing, and connects it with *Spirituality.*

CHAPTER 20

PRACTICAL ADVICE

A list of "do's" and "don'ts" for a better life

Never be afraid to sit awhile and think.
—*Lorraine Hansberry (1930–1965)*
African American playwright, poet, and civil rights activist who wrote *A Raisin in the Sun*,
the first Broadway play written by an African American woman

Everyone knows good advice except those who need it.
—*German proverb*

Many receive advice, but only the wise profit from it.
—*Harper Lee (1926–2016)*
Pulitzer Prize-winning American novelist who wrote the classic *To Kill a Mockingbird*

Learn from the mistakes of others. You can't live long enough to make them all yourself.
—*Eleanor Roosevelt (1884–1962)*

Find the most believable people possible who disagree with you, and try to understand their reasoning.
—*Ray Dalio (1949)*
In his book *Principles: Life and Work*, Dalio calls for *radical transparency* in
business culture where the goal of all disagreements and dissent is finding the truth.
Great Minds Connect with Norman Vincent Peale and Frank A. Clark on page 96 and
John Wooden on page 141

Be yourself. Everyone else is already taken.
—*Oscar Wilde (1854–1900)*

Make each day your masterpiece.
—*John Wooden (1910–2010)*
From *WOODEN: A Lifetime of Observations and Reflections On and Off the Court*

You must be the change you wish to see in the world.
—*Mohandas (Mahatma) Gandhi (1869–1948)*

GREAT MINDS THINK ALIKE: *Stay Ahead of Change*

It's time to start moving ahead of the winds of change
instead of being blown by them.
—*William C. "Bill" Sullivan (1912–1977)*
Director of the FBI's domestic intelligence unit, as quoted
in the book *Enemies: A History of the FBI*

Change before you have to.
Control your own destiny, or someone else will.
—*Jack Welch (1935–2020)*

Go as far as you can see. When you get there,
you'll be able to see farther.
—*J.P. Morgan (1837–1913)*

Never argue with a fool, because from a distance,
people can't tell who is who.
—*Michael Smith (1979)*
Sports journalist, *ESPN* host and commentator, while hosting an *ESPN* show

Life needs to be more than just solving problems
every day. You need to wake up, be excited about
the future and be inspired.
—*Elon Musk (1971)*

Somebody should tell us right at the start of our lives, that
we are dying. Then we might live to the limit every minute
of every day. Whatever you want to do, do it now!
There are only so many tomorrows.
—*Michael Landon (1936–1991)*
American television star, soon after receiving a terminal cancer diagnosis

Aim for the moon. If you miss, you may hit a star.
—*William Clement Stone (1902–2002)*
Businessman, philanthropist, and self-help author

Be moderate in order to taste the joys of life in abundance.
—*Epicurus (341–270 BC)*

***Divide each difficulty into as many parts
as is feasible and necessary to resolve it.***
—*Rene Descartes (1596–1650)*
This aligns with the concept of manifesting miracles by breaking the
difficult or impossible into manageable pieces

Never get so busy making a living that you forget to make a life.
—*Dolly Parton (1946)*
American country music star singer, songwriter, producer, actress, and philanthropist
who created *Dollywood. Great Minds Connect* with Maya Angelou on page 132

If you cannot do great things, do small things in a great way.
—*Napoleon Hill (1883–1970)*
From his book *Think and Grow Rich*

***When you are laboring for others, let it be with
the same zeal as if it were for yourself.***
—*Confucius (551–479 BC)*

***You have to motivate yourself with challenges.
That's how you know you're still alive.***
—*Jerry Seinfeld (1954)*
American comedian, actor, and comedy writer famous for his television show *Seinfeld*

***Treat people as if they were what they ought to be, and
you help them become what they are capable of becoming.***
—*Johann Wolfgang von Goethe (1749–1832)*

When you focus on the goodness in your life, you create more of it.
—*Oprah Winfrey (1954)*

Treat yourself as if you already are what you'd like to be.
—*Dr. Wayne Dyer (1940–2015)*
From *10 Secrets for Success and Inner Peace*

GREAT MINDS THINK ALIKE: *Beware of Perfect*

Never let perfect get in the way of better.
—Roger Goodell (1959)
American businessman and National Football League Commissioner

Done is better than perfect.
—Sheryl Sandberg (1969)
American billionaire technology executive, philanthropist, and writer
who made this phrase a Facebook motto while she was its CEO

If thine enemy be hungry, give him bread to eat;
and if he be thirsty, give him water to drink.
—King James Bible
Proverbs 25:21

Don't let uncertainty talk you into pursuing
a backup plan instead of your purpose.
—Bob Goff (1959)
Writer, international speaker, and adjunct professor

Choose in marriage only a woman
you would choose as a friend if she were a man.
—Joseph Joubert (1754–1824)
French essayist and moralist

It does not matter how slowly you go, as long as you do not stop.
—Confucius (551-479 BC)

Slow is smooth, and smooth is fast.
—U.S. Navy Seal training motto
later adopted by Jeff Bezos' aerospace company Blue Origin

If you obey all the rules, you miss all the fun.
—Katharine Hepburn (1907–2003)
American actress who won the Oscar for Best Actress four times

GREAT MINDS THINK ALIKE: *Water Wisdom*

Dig the well before you are thirsty.
—*Chinese proverb*

When the well is dry, we know the worth of water.
—*Benjamin Franklin (1706–1790)*

We can no more afford to spend major time on minor things
than we can to spend minor time on major things.
—*Jim Rohn (1930–2009)*
This is an essential aspect of time management

Adapt what is useful, reject what is useless,
and add what is specifically your own.
—*Bruce Lee (1940–1973)*

GREAT MINDS THINK ALIKE: *Your Personal History*

Don't use your energy to feed your history.
Use energy to feed your destiny.
—*Joel Osteen (1963)*
From one of his weekly televised sermons

Breathe. Let go. Remind yourself that this very moment
is the only one you know you have for sure. Step out
of the history that is holding you back and step into
the new story you are willing to create.
—*Oprah Winfrey (1954)*

Don't let what you cannot do interfere with what you can do.
—*John Wooden (1910–2010)*
From *WOODEN: A Lifetime of Observations and Reflection On and Off the Court*

Don't be afraid of enemies who attack you.
Be afraid of the friends who flatter you.
—*Dale Carnegie (1885–1965)*
From *How To Win Friends & Influence People*

Be kind to unkind people. They need it the most.
—*A Yogi Teabag*
Courtesy of the East West Tea Company

It's one of the greatest gifts you can give yourself, to forgive.
Forgive everybody.
—*Maya Angelou (1928–2014)*
Great Minds Connect with Robert Muller on page 77

Promise only what you can deliver,
then deliver more than you promised.
—*Tony Robbins (1960)*

If you want children to keep their feet on the ground,
put some responsibility on their shoulders.
—*Abigail Van Buren, aka Dear Abby (1918–2013)*
Dear Abby was the most widely read syndicated advice column in the world,
appearing in 1,400 newspapers with 110 million readers

Trust only those who stand to lose as much as you
when things go wrong.
—*Bralek's Rule for Success*

Trust in God, but always tie down your camel.
—*Arabic proverb*

No matter how far you have traveled
on the wrong road, turn back.
—*Turkish proverb*

Never underestimate the big importance of small things
—*Matt Haig (1975)*
British journalist and author, from his very eclectic book *The Midnight Library*

Never go to a doctor whose office plants have died.
—Erma Bombeck (1927–1996)
Popular American humorist, author, and syndicated newspaper columnist.
Although this is a humorous anecdote, there is underlying logic to it as well. If a doctor
cannot keep his plants healthy, it may be a red flag about his medical practice.

Enjoy the process more than you covet the goal.
—Mihaly Csikszentmihalyi (1934–2021)
Hungarian American psychologist and college professor,
from *Flow: The Psychology of Optimal Experience*
Great Minds Connect with Homer on page 85

Look on every exit as being an entrance to somewhere else.
—Tom Stoppard (1937)
Prolific Czech-born British playwright and screenwriter, from *Rosencrantz and
Guildenstern Are Dead. Great Minds Connect* with Robin Sharma page 262

You cannot make yourself feel something you do not feel,
but you can make yourself do right in spite of your feelings.
—Pearl S. Buck (1892–1973)
Pulitzer Prize-winning American author

<u>GREAT MINDS THINK ALIKE:</u> *The Hazards of Anger*

If you are patient in one moment of anger,
you will escape a hundred days of sorrow...
Make no promises when you are seized by joy.
Write no letters when you are seized by anger.
—A merging of two Chinese proverbs

Speak when you are angry and you will make
the best speech you will ever regret
—Ambrose Bierce (1842–1913)
Controversial American journalist, short story writer, poet, and Civil War veteran who
mysteriously disappeared in December of 1913 and was never seen again; his disappearance
remains a mystery to this day and has been the source of many exotic theories

Don't be afraid of losing people. Be afraid of losing
yourself while trying not to lose someone else.
—Navee

Do not think the knowledge you presently possess is changeless, absolute truth. Avoid being narrow-minded and bound to present views...be open to receive others' viewpoints.
—Thich Nhat Hanh (1926–2022)
From his book *Be Still and Know*

Your goodwill toward others returns to yourself in the end.
—Japanese proverb

Instead of wondering when your next vacation is, maybe you should set up a life you don't need to escape from.
—Seth Godin (1960)
American author and former dot com executive

Let your acquaintances fill the empire, but your close friends be few.
—Chinese proverb

Whatever your income, always live below your means.
—Thomas J. Stanley (1944–2015)
American writer and business theorist who specialized in writing about the wealthy in America, from *The Millionaire Next Door*

Give so much time to improving yourself that you have no time to criticize others.
—John Wooden (1910–2010)
From *WOODEN: A Lifetime of Observations and Reflections On and Off the Court*

Undertake the easy as though it were difficult and the difficult as though it were easy so as not to grow overconfident or discouraged.
—Baltasar Gracian (1601–1658)
Spanish Jesuit and baroque philosopher who published a number of his works under a pen name, from *The Art of Worldly Wisdom*

There is nothing noble in being superior to some other man.
The true nobility is in being superior to your previous self.
—*Ernest Hemingway (1899–1961)*
Although this quote is currently attributed to Hemingway, it apparently was used by a
number of others before it was posthumously credited to Hemingway in a 1963 Playboy
article that many do not believe he actually wrote. The source of this quote may
be from a Hindu proverb, the ancient Roman sage Seneca, someone named Khryter,
or W. L. Sheldon who used this quote in a lecture in 1897, two years before Hemingway
was born.

GREAT MINDS THINK ALIKE: *Occam's Razor*

The explanation requiring the fewest assumptions is most likely
to be correct. All things being equal, the simplest solution tends to
be the best one. Entities are not to be multiplied without necessity.
—*William of Ockham (1285–1347)*
These three quotes paraphrase *Occam's Razor*, which features a misspelling of its author's
name, William of Ockham, who was an English Franciscan friar, philosopher, and
theologian. Also known as the *principle of parsimony*, there is some debate as to the true
origin of this concept, since quotes regarding the power of simplicity have been attributed
to numerous historical icons including Aristotle and Ptolemy.

What Franciscan friar William of Ockam really wanted to emphasize
is that you shouldn't complicate, that you shouldn't "stack" a theory if
a simpler explanation was at the read. Pare it down. Prune the excess.
—*Harlan Coben (1962)*
American novelist whose books have sold more than 75 million copies.
Great Minds Connect with *Great Minds Think Alike: Simplicity* on page 166
and Isaac Newton on page 86

It's not what happens to you, but how you react to it that matters.
—*Epictetus (55–13 BC)*

In dwelling, live close to the ground. In thinking, keep to
the simple. In conflict, be fair and generous. In governing,
don't try to control. In work, do what you enjoy.
In family life, be completely present.
—*Lao Tzu (571–unknown BC)*
From *Tao Te Ching*

In all things that you do, consider the end.
—Solon (638–558 BC)
Solon also advised:
Learn to obey before you command.
Great Minds Connect with *Great Minds Think Alike: Military Leadership* on page 244

Get comfortable with being uncomfortable.
—Jared Isaacman (1983)
American billionaire businessman, pilot, and commercial astronaut who owns a private
air force of fighter jets, as quoted in the August 23, 2021 issue of *Time*; Isaacman served as
commander of SpaceX's Inspiration4, the world's first private space flight for humans

***It is better to sleep on things beforehand
than lie awake about them afterwards.***
—Baltasar Gracian (1601–1658)

Be ashamed to die until you have won one victory for humanity.
—Horace Mann (1796–1859)
Educator and state senator instrumental in the establishment
of public education in the United States

Don't die with your music still in you.
—Dr. Wayne Dyer (1940–2015)
From *10 Secrets for Success and Inner Peace*

***Walk with those seeking the truth.
Run from those who think they've found it.***
—Deepak Chopra (1946)

The best way out is always through.
—Robert Frost (1874–1963)
American poet laureate and four-time winner of the Pulitzer Prize

Make a list of ten things you're grateful for in your life...
and read it each morning for the next thirty days.
—T. Harv Eker (1954)
From his book *Secrets of the Millionaire Mind*

Don't be afraid to give up the good to go for the great.
—John D. Rockefeller Sr. (1839–1937)

Follow your heart, and not the crowd.
—Carmine Gallo (1965)
From his book *The Innovation Secrets of Steve Jobs*

The primary purpose of life is to enjoy it.
—David J. Schwartz (1927–1987)
From *The Magic of Thinking Big*

If you don't go actively looking for surprises at work and in life,
surprises will sooner or later sneak up on you. Being on the hunt for
them is the best way to see the unseen before it's too late.
—Hal Gregersen (1958)
From his book *Questions Are the Answer*

Every time you are tempted to react in the same old way, ask if you
want to be a prisoner of the past, or a pioneer of the future.
—Deepak Chopra (1946)

Be calm in your love for yourself. It will enable you
to see others more clearly and with more compassion.
Don't seek to change others; change yourself.
—Wim Hof (1959)
From his book *The Wim Hof Method*, in which he urges people
to be led by curiosity and love instead of fear

Keep your eyes on the stars, but remember
to keep your feet on the ground.
—Theodore Roosevelt (1858–1919)
Another classic Teddy Roosevelt quote is:
Nobody cares how much you know until they know how much you care.

When you make a mistake, admit it, correct it,
and learn from it—immediately.
—*Stephen Covey (1932–2012)*

The real fast track path to getting everything, anything, and more
than everything you want is putting others ahead of what you want,
and focusing on their needs, their wants, their desires, and
fulfilling them.
—*Jay Abraham (1949)*

If you don't like something, change it.
If you can't change it, change your attitude.
—*Maya Angelou (1928–2014)*

If you want your life to change, change your mind.
—*Chris Attwood*
From the book he co-authored with Janet Attwood, *The Passion Test*

It is the greatest of all mistakes to do nothing
because you can only do little— do what you can.
—*Sydney Smith (1771–1845)*
English writer, cleric, and philosopher

If you have to ask how much it costs, you can't afford it.
—*J.P. Morgan (1837–1913)*

We should never underestimate the ingenuity
of our ancient ancestors.
—*William Shatner (1931)*
Canadian actor best known for playing Captain James T. Kirk in the original *Star Trek*,
as quoted on his History Channel show *The UnXplained*

Make the world a better place because you have lived in it.
—*Edgar Cayce (1877–1945)*
A profound universal mantra!

Don't overlook small and seemingly insignificant negative actions.
The smallest of sparks can burn down a mountain.
—*Tibetan proverb*
From *The Wisdom of the Tibetan Lamas* by Timothy Freke

GREAT MINDS THINK ALIKE: *It's Never Too Late*

It's never too late to become what you might have been.
—*George Eliot (1819–1880)*
Birth name: Mary Ann Evans
English novelist, poet, translator, and a major writer of the Victorian period, Evans wrote
under a male pen name because she felt female writers were not taken seriously.

You're never out of options...there's always something to be done.
—*Herb Cohen (1938)*
As quoted in *The Adventures of Herbie Cohen: World's Greatest Negotiator*

Do not feel lonely, the entire universe is inside you.
—*Rumi (1207–1273)*

CONSOLIDATING CHAPTER 20
Practical Advice

As with *Human Nature*, the contents of *Practical Advice* can be selectively sprinkled over all other categories of this book. The best kind of wisdom is wisdom with practical applications to everyday life...in other words, wisdom that works. Helping you connect and synchronize your thoughts with enlightened action is the ultimate goal of *Consolidated Wisdom*. There's a major difference between possessing wisdom and acting wisely. After scrutinizing all the previous chapters to absorb diverse insights of so many brilliant ancestral and contemporary thinkers, this chapter urges us to consider infusing our lives with the myriad of ideas those thinkers have offered.

 Practical Advice is wisdom's call to action. It's where wisdom joins forces with common sense to provide specific guidance for a myriad of activities. The implementation of wisdom at appropriate times is a skill independent of the actual wisdom itself. Developing this skill can serve as a major key to fulfillment in your life. The plethora of advice in Chapter 20 can be organized to help create your own personal code of behavior, preparing you for any situation or challenge you may face. The best guidance about all this advice is to pick and choose the suggestions applicable to your current life situation.

WISDOM TRAILS: *Interconnected Categories*
Wisdom, Science, Business, Work, Sports, Politics, Government, The Arts, The Future, Happiness, History, Friendship, Compassion, Health, Humor, Science, Leadership, Spirituality, Love

Trails to Other Chapters
- Harper Lee explains that it requires *Wisdom* to benefit from good advice.
- Ray Dalio's advice emphasizes the value of constructive dissent. *(Science, Technology, Work, Business, Sports, Politics, Government)*
- Elon Musk advises us to be excited about *The Future*.
- Epicurus singles out moderation as essential to *Happiness*.
- Roger Goodell's advice about perfectionism applies to *Work, Sports, Business, Government*, and *The Arts*.
- The King James Bible provides a lesson in *Compassion*.
- Bob Goff's advice about backup plans applies to *Work, Business, Politics, Sports, Government*, and *The Arts*.
- Joel Osteen and Oprah Winfrey advise us to transcend our personal *History*.
- Dale Carnegie advises us about *Friendship*.
- A Yogi teabag advises us about *Compassion*.

- Tony Robbins' advice on delivering more than we promise applies to *Business, Work, Politics, Sports,* and *Government* as well as interpersonal relationships.
- *Bralek's Rule for Success* is directed at *Business* and *Work.*
- Erma Bombeck provides humorous advice on choosing doctors. *(Humor, Health).*
- Thich Nhat Hanh advice about being open-minded applies to *Business, Science, Sports, Work,* and *Politics.*
- A Chinese proverb offers advice on *Friendship.*
- Occam's Razor applies to *Science, Creativity, Work, Business, The Arts, Politics, Government,* and *War.*
- Lao Tzu offers advice on *Government* and *Work.*
- Solon tells us the prerequisite for *Leadership.*
- Wayne Dyer's advice about not dying "with your music still in you" refers to much more than just music. It applies to *Love, Friendship, Work, Business, The Arts, Sports,* and *Spirituality.*
- John D. Rockefeller's recommendation to always strive for greatness applies to *Science, Technology, Work, Business, Sports, The Arts,* and *Politics.*
- David J. Schwartz believes pursuing *Happiness* is the main purpose of life.
- Hal Gregersen advises us to be ready for surprises in life and *Work.*
- Deepak Chopra encourages us to become pioneers of *The Future.*
- Wim Hof gives profound advice on *Love.*
- Jay Abraham offers strong advice on how to achieve *Success.*
- William Shatner advises us on how to view our ancient ancestors. *(History)*

CHAPTER 21

WISDOM MEDITATIONS

This chapter is based on the concept you are the CEO of your own life. The following meditations are designed to enhance your perspective on any situation or challenge. Brainstorming has become a popular method for teams to achieve creative solutions to their challenges, as companies of all sizes utilize teambuilding sessions to spark creative ideas and envision future action plans. However, many of us are not on a team. This necessitates a protocol for individuals to expand their thinking parameters in creative ways. One such protocol is *autobrainstorming,* a self-mentoring meditation that enables you to create a personal board of directors in your own mind by tapping into your inner wisdom. It takes a bit of preparation and practice to master this method, but once comfortable with it, you'll find this process creates insights from new connections within your mind as it brings your issues to a personal conference table populated by a group of handpicked advisors...your opportunity to receive insights from a diverse team of brilliant minds.

> **Keep listening for the voice. Guides surround you and are speaking to you. When you hear a voice, do not be afraid to question it to be sure it is guiding you on your true quest. Remember, you are the director of the movies of your mind.**
> —*Dr. Bernie S. Siegel (1932)*

Autobrainstorming is based on the practice of *doubling,* a very effective method utilized in the field of psychodrama. When doubling in psychodrama sessions, participants stand behind a protagonist and offer their perceptions of the protagonist's inner thoughts based on the protagonist's previous statements. When you speak for your mentors during an autobrainstorm session, you'll be doubling for those mentors based on their quotes and your research into their lives. The goal of this exercise is to stimulate your inner wisdom by providing new perspectives for your thinking process.

> **Meditation is one of the most powerful tools we have for self-expansion and inner growth. Through meditation we can reach levels of mental clarity that we cannot achieve through any other means. Meditation is a major pathway to the soul.**
> —*Elaine St. James (1943)*

Please note that *Wisdom Meditations* require some advanced preparation. To assist you in visualizing this process, suggested locations and mentors are provided. If you prefer different locations or mentors, feel free to change them. Then select additional mentors from your chosen chapter. To receive maximum benefit from these meditations, it's recommended you not only read all the quotes in this book by each chosen mentor, but also briefly research their lives. Write down the name of each mentor on separate pieces of paper. If you have specific questions in mind before starting a meditation, write them on a separate page headlined by your Central Question.

It's best to complete the following two *Warm-Up Meditations* before you begin the autobrainstorm process. Then review the list of chapter meditations and choose the one that best applies to your situation. Only practice one chapter meditation on any given day, as it's important to allow your mind time to digest any new connections and insights you generate.

To begin the following meditations, get comfortable in a chair, close your eyes and take a few deep breaths. Exhale each breath slowly, and with your eyes closed...begin. Both Warm-Up Meditations can be done on the same day, but it's recommended you relax for at least an hour between them.

First Warm-Up Meditation: *Life Assessment*

Find a quiet place, either in nature or in your home. Sit down with a pen and paper next to you. Take a deep breath. Close your eyes and relax into a series of slow and peaceful breaths. In this meditation, imagine yourself like Leonardo da Vinci on a hill observing the location of his next great project (see his quote this chapter in the *Creativity & Innovation Autobrainstorm* on page 335), but you are floating on a cloud, looking down at yourself in your current life. Study yourself. See yourself in all your daily activities, and note how you feel about the way you spend your time and who you spend it with.

How close is your current life to what you really desire?

When you've completed this meditative study of your life, open your eyes and write the story of your life as it is now. This warm-up should include how you feel about yourself, your surroundings, your relationships, your dreams and your life's work. This will be your baseline starting point.

Second Warm-Up Meditation: *Live Your Dream*

Once again, find a place of sanctuary to begin your meditation. Prepare exactly as you did for the first meditation: Sit down with a pen and paper next to you, close your eyes, and relax into a series of slow deep breaths.

This time, imagine the life of your dreams. Contemplate how to convert your life into a work of art. Project yourself into the work you dream of and picture yourself spending time under ideal conditions with people you treasure. If you've always dreamed of owning a house on a lake, visualize that house in your mind. Do this for every aspect of your life—whether dreaming up new relationships or idealizing the ones you are in. If you have children, picture your ideal relationships with them as they mature. Do this for your career as well. When you've concluded your meditation, slowly open your eyes and take a deep breath. Then write the story of your future life based on visualizations from this meditation.

You now have two life stories: The first is the life you've been living, and the second is the life you aspire to live. This should help clarify what you need to work on to build the life you truly desire. The goal of these two warm-up meditations is to assist you in building a bridge to your dreams.

How to create an autobrainstorm session

1. *Choose a Central Question*: Identify your main issue and write it down as clearly and succinctly as possible; 10 words or fewer is preferable. A Central Question is the most concise question you can ask, that if answered wisely, will help move you forward in pursuit of your goal. Central Questions seek to clarify intentions, challenges, and goals in a manner that inspires productive discussion, thereby leading you to understand issues and unearth your best options. It's important to identify your Central Question to determine your choice of mentors.

2. *Choose and Research Mentors and Location*: The setting and mentors suggested for each category's meditations are exactly that: *suggestions*. Feel free to reimagine each setting and replace suggested mentors to tailor all meditations to your state of mind. Choose up to six of your favorite quotes from the subject you've decided to focus on. Copy those quotes verbatim, including the author's name. These are the people who will sit at your board meeting...your mentors. Take some time to briefly research the career and life of each mentor, and find pictures of them so you can visualize everyone you interact with during each meditation.

If six mentors feel like too many to keep track of, feel free to eliminate one or two quotes and their authors.

A point of guidance is to choose as diverse a cast of characters as possible, because a diversity of perspectives expands peripheral vision. If the advantage provided by diversity isn't automatically clear to you, please read the final quote in Chapter 9, which explains the *Medici Effect* about creating diverse intersections of ideas. For assistance in creating better questions, refer to *The Art of the Question* on page 161.

Options

1. If you do not wish to use the suggested location, choose a new one.

2. If you do not wish to use the suggested mentors, choose your own. You will serve as the host and moderator of your meeting.

3. Before beginning your session, write down up to four follow-up questions to ask about your Central Question.

4. *Questionstorming.* This is a major option: An alternative protocol combining autobrainstorm's cerebral role-playing with the Socratic method. In autobrainstorm sessions, you seek answers. In questionstorming, your mentors respond to your questions with their own probing questions intended to nudge you into deeper contemplation about your Central Question. This autobrainstorm hybrid makes use of what's known as *question thinking*, designed to provide greater understanding

of issues. Having mentors respond to your questions with questions instead of answers often gets to the root of problems and challenges faster. Questionstorming provides expanded ways of looking at your situation... new perspectives to help you grasp the "why" of problems and formulate better solutions. Since the goal of wisdom meditations is to ignite new ideas in your mind, don't rush to conjure up immediate answers...just carry around a pen and paper or use a notes app on your smartphone. Be patient in waiting for insights to arise and confident that your unconscious mind cannot help but work on unresolved questions. It may take hours, days, or even a few weeks, but new information will cross your mind at some point. Your assignment is to listen intently to your inner voices.

Alternate Writing Meditation

If you aren't comfortable meditating with your eyes closed, know that all meditation exercises can provide comparable results through writing. It will take longer, as writing about all imagined interactions with your mentors takes more time. It's suggested you have at least 10 sheets of paper ready for this exercise. Follow all guidelines for autobrainstorm meditations, except do not close your eyes.

Please note: This written exercise works best as a questionstorming session with you as host and moderator.

1. Find a quiet, well-lit place with a comfortable chair and table.

2. Write down up to six quotes from the chapter of your choice and research their authors. These are your mentors. Each mentor should have a separate page. Locate pictures of your mentors to visualize them in your mind.

3. Get settled in your chair and take a few deep, relaxed breaths.

4. Write down one or more challenges you are dealing with, then choose one of them to be your Central Question.

5. Choose a location for your session and find a picture to help you visualize it.

6. Focus on your mentors one at a time (as opposed to a conversation among them all); imagine you are conducting interviews. Based on their quotes and your research, write down the questions you think each mentor would ask you in response to your Central Question. Write each question on its own page with the mentor's name at the top. If you have more than one pressing issue, another exercise can be done for each major issue, but *do not attempt to use more than one Central Question in any exercise.*

7. When you have written down all the questions from your mentors, take a few deep breaths then read all of their questions. Take as long as you wish before responding. If you feel like taking a break to walk around, that is

fine. It's often beneficial to let the thoughts swirl in your mind for a while. The next part of this exercise is your payoff.

8. It's time to write answers to each question. Study them first and then write from your heart. Be brutally honest. There is no time limit on this, so be as thorough as possible. If necessary, take extra time to consider each answer. If new questions arise from this process, write them down as well.

9. When you have answered every question, study your answers and look for patterns and clues as to what you need to do and what changes you should consider making. If this process reveals a new or revised Central Question, repeat this exercise on another day using that new question.

Coaching Tip: How to choose a mentor

It's important you feel a special connection to mentors based on their quotes, history, and demeanor. Choose mentors of different backgrounds and demographics so you receive a diversity of potential viewpoints. Also, be aware that different Central Questions may necessitate summoning different combinations of mentors, so do not get locked into the exact same lineup of mentors for all Central Questions.

Here are some guidelines for choosing mentors:
- The mentor's quotes resonate with you on a deep level.
- The mentor lives or lived in a way you aspire to live.
- The mentor radiates a special goodness and integrity.
- The mentor represents a principle you feel strongly about.
- The mentor has prevailed over difficulties and hardships by displaying determination, perseverance, or another quality you admire.
- The mentor seems to be like you in some way. You sense you could enjoy being friends with this person; they would understand your challenges, problems, and desires.

Sample Meditation Setups

The following are two sample wisdom meditation setups. The categories for these sample setups are *Questionstorming for Happiness* (quotes are from Chapter 7), and *Autobrainstorming for Creativity & Innovation* (quotes are from Chapter 9). Please note that although these sample meditations each contain numerous mentors, you can simplify the process: While it's important to complete multiple setups, you can invite each mentor to separate meditations instead of having multiple mentors in a single meditation. This one-at-a-time protocol of multiple short meditations can be spread out over a few days. For instance, if you have six quotes and six mentors, you can repeat this meditation with one mentor per meditation for six days, two mentors per meditation for three days, or three mentors per meditation for two days. This revised procedure can be applied to all meditations. If you choose this option, utilize the same Central Question in each meditation.

It's important to experience a diversity of inputs, but they do not have to be experienced all at once. There's no need to stress your memory or struggle to simultaneously voice more mentors than is comfortable for you. Some people thrive on the chaos created by overwhelming input, and others find it counterproductive. There's no right or wrong in this...only what's best for you.

SAMPLE SETUP: *Happiness Questionstorming Meditation*

1) Craft Your Central Question
(The wording of your Central Question is very important)

Here are a few choices. Choose <u>one</u> of the following:
- *How can I become happier?*
- *Why aren't I happy?*
- *How do I know if I'm happy?*
- *What is happiness?*
- *What in my life needs to change so I can become happier?*

2) Choose Phrases, Mentors and Location

The noblest art is that of making others happy.
—*P.T. Barnum*

Perfect happiness is the absence of striving for happiness.
—*Chuang Tzu, aka Zhuang Zhou*

I make myself rich by making my wants few.
—*Henry David Thoreau*

**Great trouble comes from not knowing what is enough.
Great conflict arises from wanting too much. When we know when
enough is enough, there will always be enough.**
—*Lao Tzu*

**It is not how much we have, but how much we love,
that makes happiness.**
—*Charles Spurgeon*

**The walls we build around us to keep out the sadness
also keep out the joy.**
—*Jim Rohn*

Based on this lineup of mentors, let's place the meeting at Disneyland in Anaheim, California, since it proclaims itself to be "happiest place on earth."

3) You now have your basic setup ready
LOCATION: Disneyland
MENTORS: Lao Tzu, Charles Spurgeon, Jim Rohn, Henry David Thoreau, Zhuang Zhou, and P.T. Barnum

The following is an example of a first round of questionstorming. Please note that the first question mentors ask is based on one of their quotes from this book. After the first round, allow the questions and conversation to flow spontaneously.

Happiness Questionstorming Session

P.T. Barnum asks, *"Who have you made happy recently?"* Zhuang Zhou inquires, *"How hard have you been trying to be happy?"* Charles Spurgeon follows up by asking, *"Do you truly love anyone or anything?"* Since Spurgeon is a preacher, he may use a religious term as well.

Henry David Thoreau wants to know, *"What do you want that you don't already have?"* He suspects you are making yourself unhappy by wanting too much. This inspires Lao Tzu to ask, *"How do you know when you have enough?"* Jim Rohn has been patiently listening, waiting for the right time to ask, *"What have you been missing out on because of fear?"*

The above is an example of how to begin digging into the heart of your happiness issue. Allow your mentors to ask as many follow-up questions as they wish. As soon as they stop asking questions, it's time to ask your follow-up questions. When the room falls silent, ask your mentors if they have any final words. When they have all finished talking, thank them and conclude the meditation.

<u>SAMPLE SETUP: *Autobrainstorming for Creativity & Innovation*</u>

1) Craft Your Central Question

Choose <u>one</u> of the following:
- *How can I become more creative and innovative?*
- *Why am I not more creative?*
- *What's the difference between creativity and innovation?*
- *Should I focus on my practical creativity, artistic creativity, or both?*

2) Choose Phrases, Mentors and Location

Creativity is not just for artists. It's for businesspeople looking for a new way to close a sale; it's for engineers trying to solve a problem; it's for parents who want their children to see the world in more than one way. In order to be creative, you have to know how to prepare to be creative. Discipline morphs into habit. The routine is just as important as the lightning bolt of inspiration. Creativity is a habit and the best creativity is a result of good habits.
(Two *Twyla Tharp* quotes from Chapter 9 have been combined)

Great ideas and great successes all begin with a passionate vision, and it's just as important for individuals as it is for corporations.
—Carmine Gallo

Men of lofty genius sometimes accomplish the most when they work the least, for their minds are occupied with their ideas and the perfection of their conceptions to which they afterwards give form.
—Leonardo da Vinci

Your mind is like a parachute. If it isn't open, it doesn't work.
—Buzz Aldrin

If you want more and better answers to your creative challenges, start by asking more and better questions.
—Bryan Mattimore

Be curious, not judgmental.
—Walt Whitman

You can only improvise if you're well prepared.
—Alex Trebek

3) You now have your basic setup ready

LOCATION: The Florence Cathedral in Florence, Italy (formerly the Cattedrale di Santa Maria del Fiore)
MENTORS: Walt Whitman, Alex Trebek, Bryan Mattimore, Carmine Gallo, Leonardo da Vinci, and Twyla Tharp...plus special guest Buzz Aldrin

The following is a sample first round of brainstorming statements. Please note that the first statement by each mentor is based on one of their quotes from this book. After the first round, allow the conversation to flow spontaneously.

Creativity & Innovation Autobrainstorm Session

Twyla Tharp starts the meeting by stating, "*Creativity is for everyone...not just artists.*" Bryan Mattimore immediately adds, "*Asking good questions can lead you to become more creative.*" Carmine Gallo urges, "*Find something you have great passion for,*" which prompts Twyla Tharp to advise, "*Dedicated practice is the key to bringing creative ideas to life.*"

Alex Trebek supports Twyla Tharp's comment on practice, emphasizing that improvisation and innovation require serious preparation. Leonardo da Vinci has been listening intently and is now a bit agitated. He rises out of his chair, blurting out, "*There is virtue in studying your challenge from every angle before you start working on a project. Do not simply dive into work with blind passion.*" Leonardo reminds everyone of his explanation to the friar who questioned his gestation period of extended observation. Walt Whitman thanks Leonardo for being a voice of reason, pointing out that curiosity is the key to creative growth, but Whitman also warns, "*Avoid being judgmental early in any creative process.*" Buzz Aldrin then reminds you, "*Always keep your mind open in search of new insights.*"

Setup Example Notes

For each meditation, visualize your mentors seated at a large oval table at a location of your choice. As host, picture yourself standing so you face three mentors on each side of the curved table. After you pose your Central Question, focus your gaze on each mentor, one at a time. Base their responses on your knowledge of them. Your goal is to imagine a lively discussion about issues meaningful to you. Do not consciously attempt to put words into anyone's mouth. Rather, allow the voices to emerge organically and see how your mentors interact both with you and with each other. Perhaps they either support or disagree with each other if they are not speaking directly to you. Let their voices rise from your inner voice.

Don't panic if there is a silence. Use that time to display patience and ponder. Feel free to ask follow-up questions whenever your mentors fall silent. Silences often carry important information. For instance, when a mentor falls silent or does not respond, it may be a signal to eliminate that mentor from your session. Although you have been instructed to begin with six mentors, one or two mentors usually move to the forefront and continue a conversation in your mind well beyond the actual meditation. It's not unusual for one mentor to become an ongoing guide in your unconscious mind for an extended period of time.

Each session concludes when you've finished asking questions and your mentors are done speaking. To close a session, thank your mentors, take a deep breath, exhale, and slowly open your eyes...then write down any thoughts that come to mind. After completing a meditation, you can expand the process by choosing another topic for meditation on another day. If none of the chapter meditation scenarios strongly attract you, proceed to the *Consolidation Meditation.*

Consolidation Meditation

This meditation encourages you to choose quotes from all categories instead of just one. Choose six favorite mentors and their quotes from *Consolidated Wisdom*. At this point, a good question to ask yourself is: *Who are my heroes?*

If you have heroes who are not quoted in this book, feel free to invite them to meet you at a location of your choice, and imagine them sitting around an oval conference table with you as host. Conjure up an exceptional location that makes your spirits soar, such as a pristine beach at an exclusive Caribbean resort or the peak of a majestic mountain. Reach into your imagination to suspend all restrictions of time and space so you can transport this special group into a magical world that inspires miraculous change and transformational insights. Then choose the challenge you want to request advice about, and compose your Central Question.

Close your eyes and slowly take a few deep breaths.

Begin an *Autobrainstorm* or *Questionstorming* session by projecting yourself into the minds of your mentors, listening to the questions they would ask or advice you believe they would offer. When the session concludes, take a deep breath, open your eyes...and write down all your thoughts.

Chapter 1 Sample Setup: *Wisdom, History & the Future*
Suggested Location: A large white tent on the desert sands of Giza at the foot of the Sphinx
Suggested Special Mentors: Confucius and Socrates

Chapter 2 Sample Setup: *Science & Technology*
Suggested Location: The New York Planetarium
Suggested Special Mentor: Neil deGrasse Tyson

Chapter 3 Sample Setup: *Dreams, Miracles & Luck*
Suggested Location: Walt Disney Imagineering Research & Development headquarters in Glendale, CA
Suggested Special Mentor: Walt Disney

Chapter 4 Sample Setup: *Love, Friendship & Compassion*
Suggested Location: The United Nations in New York City
Suggested Special Mentor: The 14th Dalai Lama

Chapter 5 Sample Setup: *Observing Human Nature*
Suggested Location: Institute of the Noetic Sciences conference center in Petaluma, CA
Suggested Special Mentors: George Bernard Shaw and Carl Jung

Chapter 6 Sample Setup: *Courage, Fear & Doubt*
Suggested Location: The new World Trade Center in New York City
Suggested Special Mentors: Winston Churchill and Mark Twain

Chapter 7 Sample Setup: *Happiness, Success & Work*
Suggested Location: P.T. Barnum Museum in Bridgeport, CT
Suggested Special Mentor: P.T. Barnum

Chapter 8 Sample Setup: *Business & Leadership*
Suggested Location: The New York Stock Exchange
Suggested Special Mentors: Napoleon Hill and Warren Buffett

Chapter 9 Sample Setup: *Creativity, Innovation & Curiosity*
Suggested Location: The Florence Cathedral in Italy (formerly Cattedrale di Santa Maria del Fiore), where Brunelleschi's dome epitomizes Renaissance creativity and innovation
Suggested Special Mentors: Twyla Tharp and Leonardo da Vinci

Chapter 10 Sample Setup: *The Arts & Literature*
Suggested Location: The Louvre Museum in Paris, France
Suggested Special Mentor: Michelangelo

Chapter 11 Sample Setup: *The Power of Play*
Suggested Location: The Strong National Museum of Play in Rochester, NY
Suggested Special Mentor: Albert Einstein

Chapter 12 Sample Setup: *The Lessons of Sports & Extreme Desire*
Suggested Location: U.S. Olympic Training Center in Colorado Springs, CO
Suggested Special Mentors: Vince Lombardi, Muhammad Ali, and Pat Riley

Chapter 13 Sample Setup: *Education*
Suggested Location: Princeton Institute for Advanced Study
Suggested Special Mentors: Aristotle and Maria Montessori

Chapter 14 Sample Setup: *Government, Politics & Social Justice*
Suggested Location: The White House
Suggested Special Mentors: George Washington and Martin Luther King Jr.

Chapter 15 Sample Setup: *War & Peace*
Suggested Location: The Nobel Peace Center in Oslo, Norway
Suggested Special Mentors: Sun Tzu and Ben Franklin

Chapter 16 Sample Setup: *Humor & The Immortal Yogi Berra*
Suggested Location: The Yogi Berra Museum in Montclair, New Jersey
Suggested Special Mentors: Jerry Seinfeld and Yogi Berra

Chapter 17 Sample Setup: *Nature & Native American Wisdom*
Suggested Location: Yellowstone National Park in Wyoming
or the National Museum of the American Indian in NYC
Suggested Special Mentor: Black Elk

Chapter 18 Sample Setup: *Spirituality, Faith & Philosophy*
Suggested Location: The Parthenon on the Acropolis in Athens, Greece, on
a crystal-clear sunny day with warm breezes blowing between the massive
columns
Suggested Special Mentor: Mahatma Gandhi

Chapter 19 Sample Setup: *Feng Shui, Health & Harmony*
Suggested Location: The Feng Shui Museum in the ancient city of
Langzhong, China...by special permission of the Chinese government
Suggested Special Mentor: Marie Kondo

Chapter 20 Sample Setup: *Practical Advice*
Suggested Location: Under a tent at the ruins of the Oracle at Delphi on
Mount Parnassus in Greece
Suggested Special Mentor: Oprah Winfrey

Final Notes

Please bear in mind that there's no time limit on these meditations; they should be as long as is comfortable for you. The only advice on time is not to rush. With that said, most autobrainstorm meditations last between 10 and 20 minutes, followed by open-ended note-taking to codify your thoughts. Relaxation is a vital part of productive meditations, so make sure to find a peaceful, comfortable place to practice, and remember to breathe deeply and fully. It's also important to understand that autobrainstorming functions as a catalyst to activate your unconscious mind, since your unconscious mind will continue to work on the questions you've cogitated long after your meditations end. Many autobrainstormers experience epiphanies days or even weeks after a meditation, so do not despair if you don't receive immediate results from a session. Have faith that a productive process is taking place in your mind.

Autobrainstorm techniques can also be extended into group teambuilding exercises. As teambuilders, these exercises transform into role-playing *ideation* sessions, with each team member being assigned a specific person to portray based on quotes from *Consolidated Wisdom*. Two members of the group are not assigned character roles but will serve as secretary and host for all ensuing sessions. Participants are given a specific amount of break time (half hour or full hour) to research their role assignments, and are encouraged to use cell phones and computers for online research. When the group reconvenes, a *role-playing brainstorm session* is moderated by the chosen host, and the secretary records all statements made by each participant on an easel or flip chart. The number of rounds—three is suggested—should be set in advance. This means each team member will be required to make at least three statements or ask three different questions. After these rounds, your group can decide whether to conclude the conversation or perform one additional round. When the role-playing has run its course, the host concludes this phase of the exercise. It should be noted that this exercise is most effective as a *questionstorming* session.

In the second phase, group members shed their assigned roles (except for secretary and host) to discuss the questions and statements made in phase one. The secretary reads each statement to launch the discussion. From this point, the meeting becomes a more traditional brainstorm session led by the host. The ideal number of participants for these sessions is eight—a host, secretary and six role players. The session facilitator may choose whether the host should assume a role, as it's possible for a host to also serve as a role-player. If so, seven is the optimal number of participants. While groups of six also work well, groups should never exceed eight; they should be divided into smaller groups working independently. Having the host also portray a character adds playfulness to this exercise. An even more playful way of conducting this exercise is to separate it into three phases: preparation, idea, and decision-making, with the final decision-making phase commencing after a group dinner. In this scenario, wine can be served during dinner to maximize social interaction.

CHAPTER 22

FINAL CONSOLIDATION

Wisdom is everywhere just waiting for us to pluck it from the ether. We are surrounded by wisdom on a daily basis, but too often it goes unseen and unheard. If we allow wisdom to take hold, it flows like a river, connecting all the tributaries of our lives with its sagacious power. This truth highlights the profound interconnections inherent in human nature. After studying all the phrases in *Consolidated Wisdom*, an intriguing question arises:

Is there an overall message we can extract from all the wisdom presented, some compressed epiphany that encapsulates this collection of wisdom?

Although no singular conclusion or panacea can be derived from the myriad of quotes, there's an underlying optimism created by the presence of so much diverse wisdom. One way of viewing that optimism is the following:

If the events of daily life are weighing you down...if the constant political bickering you observe has caused you to lose faith in government...if tragic events occurring around the world upset you...if your life is not where you would like it to be...do not despair, because there are brilliant minds on every continent generating wisdom and good will on a daily basis. Take comfort in knowing the bright light of wisdom is always available to you. Wisdom's journey is eternal, and the time to begin is always now.

Another lingering question is: *What is wisdom?*

Before attempting to answer this provocative question, here are definitions of wisdom from some well-known sources.

- Wikipedia defines wisdom as: The ability to contemplate and act productively using knowledge, experience, understanding, common sense, and insight.
- Merriam-Webster dictionary defines wisdom as: An ability to discern inner qualities and relationships...insight, good sense, accumulated philosophical or scientific learning...a wise attitude or course of action. The teachings of the ancient wise men.
- Gotquestions.org defines wisdom as: The ability to discern or judge what is true, right, or lasting.
- Oxford Languages (Google's dictionary) defines wisdom as: The quality of having experience, knowledge, and good judgment... the soundness of an action or decision with regard to the application of experience, knowledge, and good judgment. The body of knowledge and principles that develops within a specified society or period.

Decades of research and endless hours of pondering have led to *Consolidated Wisdom's* definition of wisdom:

- The insightful application of various combinations of information, understanding, and positive emotion that provide greater clarity about any subject or situation. Wisdom is one of the human mind's greatest and most treasured attributes.

A number of quotes in this book attempt to define wisdom, including Lao Tzu's *"knowing others is wisdom,"* Aristotle's *"knowing yourself is the beginning of all wisdom,"* Samuel Taylor Coleridge's *"common sense in an uncommon degree is what the world calls wisdom,"* and Lin Yutang's *"the wisdom of life consists in the elimination of nonessentials."* Peter Abelard adds, *"the beginning of wisdom is found in doubting,"* and William James states *"the art of being wise is the art of knowing what to overlook."* Two eclectic analyses of wisdom come from M. Scott Peck's *"the capacity to embrace paradox, to perceive the validity of opposites, is a major key to wisdom,"* and Takuan Sōhō, who describes immovable wisdom as *"having complete fluidity around an unmoving center so your mind is clear and ready to direct its attention wherever it may be needed."* In the final analysis, wisdom appears to be an ethereal entity defying description, yet somehow we all manage to recognize it when we read it, hear it, or witness it in action.

Consolidated Wisdom depicts wisdom in a variety of forms that feature keen observation, insightful understanding, and expansive vision. Wisdom is an accurate analyst of the human psyche and an excellent predictor of behavior, as well as a reflection of the times from which it unfolds. When summoned, wisdom serves as a valuable advisor for politicians, business executives, athletes, military leaders, parents, and romantics. Wisdom expands peripheral vision by supplementing our powers of observation. It also improves our decision-making abilities while deepening an understanding of ourselves and others. In a nutshell, wisdom represents the human mind operating at its clearest and highest level. In so doing, wisdom follows the trajectory of human evolution, pointing out the brilliance and shortcomings of our species throughout recorded history.

Stepping back to take an aerial view of all the wisdom phrases in this book, an interesting phenomenon emerges: the multi-dimensionality of numerous categories. The duality of doubt is discussed in Chapter 6, as is the duality of extreme desire in Chapter 12, but those are not the only dualities. Chapter 9 touches on the potential of creativity to be used for destructive purposes, and Chapter 2 highlights the dark side of technological progress in contrast to the marvelous technologies currently assisting all levels of modern societies. Looking back to Chapter 6, it's clear there's also a duality to fear, with the primal emotion of fear being to warn and protect humans from danger. However, fear can also become a great inhibitor capable of paralyzing its victims. Courage also has a dual nature. While courage is a commendable character trait, if not combined with some degree of caution, courage can become reckless.

The most profound duality pulses through Mother Nature herself, as nature gives life and also takes it away. Hurricanes, volcanoes, earthquakes, floods, tsunamis, and other natural disasters kill randomly without conscience. Additionally, the animal kingdom often serves as a ruthless killing field…yet nature is also a source of unmatched sustenance, beauty, and wonder. Chapters 16 and 18 focus on the duality of peace, pointing out the difference between inner peace and outer peace, which expands into a "triangularity" featuring inner peace, interpersonal peace, and peace between nations. Interestingly enough, war is connected to this triangularity in that war represents a destruction of peace on all three levels. Even wisdom itself demonstrates a dual nature, as wisdom in one arena of life does not guarantee wisdom in any other. Many of us are very wise in one aspect of our lives but clueless in some other aspect, a reality that unintentionally exposes the duality of success.

Of all the categories in *Consolidated Wisdom,* love is unquestionably the most multidimensional. An initial study of love notes the triangularity created by love, hate, and indifference. Chapter 4 contains phrases arguing that indifference is actually more damaging than hate. While there's no quantitative method to declare a winner between those two treacherous states of mind, the power of indifference is established merely by the existence of such an argument.

Love itself is a supremely complex concept. There is romantic love, platonic love, love of children, love of pets, love of nature, love of possessions, as well as the very important love of self. Love can be exalting but it can also become wildly destructive, especially when weaponized. Love can be the most sincere emotion but can also be faked by individuals with ulterior motives. At its purest level, love is unconditional, but then again, many withhold their love for a variety of reasons. Love is virtually impossible to fully define, yet humans have spent millennia attempting to accurately describe it.

All the dualities of this book need to be corralled during any attempt to round up the many dimensions of love. Fear, courage, extreme desire, doubt, friendship, creativity, and even elements of war and peace come into play, thereby establishing love as the most profound entity in the lexicon of human existence. In terms of wisdom, love is where even the wise can be transformed into fools. The presence of love expands human potential, and loss of a loved one can break even the most powerful. Love serves as its own measure of success, being considered by many as the greatest human achievement. The emotion of love penetrates the core of human existence. For those fortunate enough to experience true love, it's imperative to acquire enough wisdom to nurture and maintain it. That's the overriding message inherent in this dissertation on dualities:

The solution to the challenges of all dualities is wisdom.

The infinite dimensions of wisdom offer us valuable methods, paths, and behaviors to activate whenever dualities create turbulence in our lives. The more wisdom we acquire, the better prepared we will be for all such challenges.

To reach its full potential, wisdom requires appropriate responses...more specifically, enlightened action, since the ultimate purpose of acquiring wisdom is to live happier and more fulfilling lives. While it's not necessary to agree with all quotes in this book, it's helpful to be aware of the cornucopia of thoughts they represent...the vast expanse of human cogitation. Please remember that words of wisdom need not be regarded as absolutes. They are meant to serve as nuggets of guidance aimed at enhancing our ability to prosper by providing a more accurate and pragmatic worldview.

Although wisdom phrases are tangible entities, wisdom is primarily a process with four foundational phases. Those four basic phases are *creation, acquisition, comprehension,* and *application.* Newly acquired wisdom must be digested and merged with other knowledge and beliefs to synthesize a more profound understanding. Much like soup, wisdom concepts must simmer so all ingredients have time to gel. It then behooves us to apply our enhanced perspectives to everyday challenges. It should be noted that there is a fifth phase of this process: *dissemination*—the spreading of wisdom through conversation, the written word, oral traditions and social media.

Wisdom traditions empower us to weave together stories that form personalized wisdom narratives. Embracing a mixture of wisdom concepts enables us to create our own unique tapestries of beliefs that evolve into codes of behavior. When viewed as a collective entity, wisdom phrases demonstrate the profound interconnectedness of all disciplines, implying that wisdom categories are as closely related as the proverbial six degrees of separation. Their intricate relationships flow from one subject to another, connecting every avenue of life whether those connections be direct or indirect, readily apparent or hidden from sight. This realization confirms wisdom's important contribution to the human condition. No matter what your field of interest, no matter what your stage of life, no matter what continent you live on or your social status...wisdom beckons to you with the promise of a better life.

Consolidated Wisdom's mission is based on the belief that acquisition and possession of wisdom is just the first step. Ideally, wisdom traditions are assimilated, contemplated, and then applied. Wisdom's true value becomes realized when we put it into action...when we act wisely. What a wonderful way to start building a better world!

ALPHABETICAL INDEX

GREAT MINDS SUBJECT INDEX

WISDOM TIMELINE

Fu Hsi (29th Century BC)
Akhenaten (14th century BC)
Homer (unknown between 1250-850 BC)
King Solomon (990–931 BC)
Solon (638–558 BC)
Lao Tzu (571–unknown BC)
Xenophanes (c.570–475 BC)
Buddha (563–483 BC)
Simonides (556–468 BC)
Confucius (551–479 BC)
Sun Tzu (545–496 BC)
Heraclitus (535–475 BC)
Socrates (470–399 BC)
Thucydides (460–400 BC)
Democritus (c.460–c.370 BC)
Hippocrates (460–370 BC)
Aristophanes (446–386 BC)
Plato (429–347 BC)
Aristotle (384–322 BC)
Demosthenes (384–322 BC)
Meng Ke (372–289 BC)
Zhuang Zhou (369–286 BC)
Epicurus (341–270 BC)
Patanjali (2nd century BC)
Marcus Tullius Cicero (106–43 BC)
Julius Caesar (100–44 BC)
Lucretius (c.99–c.55 BC)
Publilius Syrus (85–40 BC)
Virgil (70–19 BC)
Epictetus (55–13 BC)
Ovid (43 BC–17 AD)
Lucius Annaeus Seneca (4 BC–65 AD)
Tacitus (56–120)
Plutarch (46–120)
Marcus Aurelius (121–180)
Guo Po (276–324)
Saint Augustine (354–430)
Hypatia (355–415)
Boethius (477–524)
Muhammad (c.570–632)
Shantideva (685–763)
Charlemagne (748–814)
Solomon ibn Gabirol (1022–1070)
William the Conqueror (1028–1087)
Anselm of Canterbury (1033–1109)
Yuan-Wu (1063–1135)

Peter Abelard (1079–1142)
Hildegard (1098–1179)
Maimonides (1138–1204)
Prince William Marshal (1146–1219)
Genghis Khan (1162–1227)
St. Francis of Assisi (1181–1226)
Rumi (1207-1273)
St. Thomas Aquinas (1225–1274)
Meister Eckhart (1260–1328)
William of Ockham (1285–1347)
Thomas Kempis (1360–1471)
Joan of Arc (1412–1431)
Mehmed II (1432–1481)
Kabir (1440–1518)
Leonardo da Vinci (1452–1519)
Niccolo Machiavelli (1469–1527)
Nicolaus Copernicus (1473–1543)
Michelangelo (1475–1564)
Michel de Montaigne (1533–1592)
Mary Stuart: Queen of Scots (1542–1587)
John Lyly (1553–1606)
Philip Sydney (1554–1586)
Francis Bacon (1561–1626)
William Shakespeare (1564–1616)
Galileo Galilei (1564–1642)
Takuan Sōhō (1573–1645)
Thomas Hobbes (1588–1679)
Baltasar Gracian (1601–1658)
Thomas Fuller (1608–1661)
John Milton (1608–1674)
Francois de la Rochefoucauld (1613–1680)
Blaise Pascal (1623–1662)
John Ray (1627–1705)
Baruch Spinoza (1632–1677)
John Locke (1632–1704)
Isaac Newton (1643–1727)
William Penn (1644–1718)
Jean de La Bruyere (1646–1696)
Gottfried Leibniz (1646–1716)
Emanuel Swedenborg (1688–1772)
Voltaire (1694–1778)
Benjamin Franklin (1706–1790)
Samuel Johnson (1709–1784)
Jean-Jacques Rousseau (1712–1778)
Frederick the Great (1712–1786)
Emanuel Kant (1724–1804)

Edmund Burke (1729–1797)
George Washington (1732–1799)
Pierre Beaumarchais (1732–1799)
John Adams (1735–1826)
Thomas Paine (1737–1809)
Georg Christoph Lichtenberg (1742–1799)
Thomas Jefferson (1743–1826)
Jean-Paul Marat (1743–1793)
Abigail Adams (1744–1818)
Johann Wolfgang von Goethe (1749–1832)
James Madison (1751–1839)
Joseph Joubert (1754–1824)
Marie Antoinette (1755–1793)
Alexander Hamilton (1757–1804)
Jean Paul Richter (1763–1825)
Robert B. Thomas (1766–1866)
Andrew Jackson (1767–1845)
John Quincy Adams (1767–1848)
Napoleon Bonaparte (1769–1821)
Samuel Taylor Coleridge (1772–1834)
William Hazlitt (1778–1830)
Carl von Clausewitz (1780–1831)
Ludwig Borne (1786–1837)
Chief Seattle (1786–1866)
Cornelius Vanderbilt (1794–1877)
Horace Mann (1796–1859)
Thomas Babbington Macauley (1800–1859)
Victor Hugo (1802–1885)
Ralph Waldo Emerson (1803–1882)
Benjamin Disraeli (1804–1881)
Alexis de Tocqueville (1805–1859)
John Stuart Mills (1806–1873)
Henry Wadsworth Longfellow (1807–1882)
Abraham Lincoln (1809–1865)
Alfred Lord Tennyson (1809–1892)
Oliver Wendell Holmes Sr. (1809–1894)
Robert Schumann (1810–1856)
P.T. Barnum (1810–1891)
Harriet Beecher Stowe (1811–1896)
Charles Dickens (1812–1870)
Soren Kierkegaard (1813–1855)
Richard Wagner (1813–1883)
Charlotte Bronte (1816–1855)
Henry David Thoreau (1817–1862)
Karl Marx (1818–1883)
Josh Billings (1818–1885)
George Eliot (1819–1880)
Walt Whitman (1819–1892)
James Russell Lowell (1819–1892)
Susan B. Anthony (1820–1906)
Gustave Flaubert (1821–1880)
Mary Baker Eddy (1821–1910)
Harriet Tubman (1822–1913)
Louis Pasteur (1822–1895)

George Macdonald 1825–1904)
Thomas Huxley (1825–1895)
Standing Bear (1829–1908)
Marie von Ebner-Eschenbach (1830–1916)
Emily Dickinson (1830–1886)
Horatio Alger (1832–1899)
Edward Burnett Tylor (1832–1917)
Robert Ingersoll (1833–1899)
Charles Spurgeon (1834–1892)
Mark Twain (1835–1910)
Andrew Carnegie (1835–1919)
Booker T. Washington (1836–1915)
Grover Cleveland (1837–1908)
J.P. Morgan (1837–1913)
Washington Roebling (1837–1926)
John Muir (1838-1914)
Sai Baba (1838–1918)
Henry Adams (1838–1918)
Charles Sanders Peirce (1839–1914)
John D. Rockefeller (1839–1937)
Auguste Rodin (1840–1917)
Pierre-August Renoir (1841–1919)
Oliver Wendell Holmes Jr. (1841–1935)
William James (1842–1910)
Ambrose Bierce (1842–1913)
Russell Cromwell (1843–1925)
Friedrich Nietzsche (1844–1900)
Henry J. Heinz (1844–1919)
Thomas Alva Edison (1847–1931)
Kate Sheppard (1848–1934)
Edgar Watson Howe (1853–1937)
Vincent van Gogh (1853–1890)
Oscar Wilde (1854–1900)
Carl Larsson (1855–1919)
George Bernard Shaw (1856–1950)
Woodrow Wilson (1856–1924)
Sigmund Freud (1856–1939)
Nikola Tesla (1856–1943)
Clarence Darrow (1857–1938)
Joseph Conrad (1857–1924)
Milton Hershey (1857–1945)
Eleonora Duse (1858–1924)
Theodore Roosevelt (1858–1919)
Max Planck (1858–1947)
Frank A. Clark (1860–1935)
James M. Barrie (1860–1937)
William K. Kellogg (1860–1951)
Rudolph Steiner (1861–1925)
Bliss Carman (1861–1929)
Rabindranath Tagore (1861–1941)
Julia Huxley (1862–1908)
John Jay Chapman (1862–1933)
Swami Vivekananda (1863–1902)
George Santayana (1863–1952)

Black Elk (1863–1950)
John Huston Finley (1863–1940)
Henry Ford (1863–1947)
James Allen (1864–1912)
Jesse C. Hart (1864–1933)
George Washington Carver (1864–1943)
William Butler Yeats (1865–1939)
Dr. Charles Mayo (1865–1939)
Logan Pearsall Smith (1865–1946)
Bernard Berenson (1865–1959)
George I. Gurdjieff (1866–1949)
Marie Curie (1867–1934)
Frank Lloyd Wright (1867–1959)
Lawrence Binyon (1869–1943)
Mohandas (Mahatma) Gandhi (1869–1948)
Henri Matisse (1869–1954)
Maria Montessori (1870–1952)
Bertrand Baruch (1870–1965)
D.T. Suzuki (1870–1966)
Tatanga Mani (1970–1967)
Bernard Russell (1872–1970)
Ellen Glasgow (1873–1945)
Hugo von Hofmannsthal (1874–1929)
Florence Scovel Shinn (1871–1940)
Marcel Proust (1871–1922)
Paul Valery (1871–1945)
Bertrand Russell (1872–1970)
Sir Winston Churchill (1874–1965)
Albert Schweitzer (1875–1965)
Carl Jung (1875–1961)
Charles F. Kettering (1876–1958)
Edgar Cayce (1877–1945)
Herman Hesse (1877–1962)
William John (W.J.) Cameron (1879–1953)
Albert Einstein (1879–1955)
Sam Goldwyn (1879–1974)
W.C. Fields (1880–1946)
Daniel Vare (1880–1956)
Hans Hoffman (1880–1966)
Helen Keller (1880–1968)
Pablo Picasso (1881–1973)
Cecille B. DeMille (1881–1959)
Hazrat Inayat Khan (1882–1927)
Jean Giraudoux (1882–1944)
George Jean Nathan (1882–1958)
Franklin D. Roosevelt (1882–1945)
Robert Goddard (1882–1945)
Igor Stravinsky (1882–1971)
Kahlil Gibran(1883–1931)
Morihei Ueshiba (1883–1969)
Napoleon Hill (1883–1970)
Harry S. Truman (1884–1972)
Eleanor Roosevelt (1884–1962)
George S. Patton (1885–1945)

Will Durant (1885–1981)
George Mallory (1886–1924)
Paul Tillich (1886–1965)
Bruce Fairchild Barton (1886–1967)
Marcus Garvey (1887–1940)
Conrad Hilton (1887–1979)
Arthur Rubinstein (1887–1982)
Georgia O'Keeffe (1887–1986)
Richard E. Byrd (1888–1957)
T.S. Eliot (1888–1965)
Dale Carnegie (1888–1965)
Alex F. Osborn (1888–1966)
Charlie Chaplin (1889–1977)
Asa Philip Randolph (1889–1979)
Christopher Morley (1890–1957)
Gene Fowler (1890–1960)
Claude M. Bristol (1891–1951)
George Yeomans Pocock (1891–1976)
Alma Thomas (1891–1978)
Henry Miller (1891–1980)
Reinhold Niebuhr (1892–1971)
Pearl S. Buck (1892–1973)
J.R.R. Tolkien (1892–1973)
James B. Conant (1893–1978)
Dorothea Brande (1893–1948)
Paramahansa Yogananda (1893–1952)
Albert Szent-Gyorgyi (1893–1986)
S. Omar Barker (1894–1985)
Fred Allen (1894–1956)
Aldous Huxley (1894–1963)
Martha Graham (1894–1991)
Babe Ruth (1895–1948)
R. Buckminster Fuller (1895–1983)
Lin Yutang (1895–1976)
George Burns (1896–1996)
Amelia Earhart (1897–1937)
C.S. Lewis (1898–1963)
Ben Shahn (1898–1969)
Ariel Durant (1898–1981)
Joseph Murphy (1898–1981)
Norman Vincent Peale (1898–1993)
Ernest Hemingway (1899–1961)
Elizabeth Bowen (1899–1973)
Antoine de Saint-Exupery (1900–1944)
Erich Fromm (1900–1980)
Admiral Hyman Rickover (1900–1986)
Walt Disney (1901–1966)
André Malraux (1901–1976)
Linus Pauling (1901–1994)
Enrico Fermi (1901–1954)
John Steinbeck (1902–1968)
Ray Kroc (1902–1984)
William Clement Stone (1902–2002)
Christmas Humphreys (1901–1983)

Eric Hoffer (1902–1983)
Norman Maclean (1902–1990)
Karl Popper (1902–1994)
Boris Marshalov (1902–1967)
William Clement Stone (1902–2002)
George Orwell (1903–1950)
Bob Hope (1903–2003)
Anais Nin (1903–1977)
Clare Boothe Luce (1903–1987)
Arshile Gorky (1904–1948)
J. Robert Oppenheimer (1904–1967)
Joan Crawford (1904—1977)
Joseph Campbell (1904–1987)
Doctor Seuss (1904–1991)
Shunryu Suzuki-Roshi (1904–1971)
Salvador Dalí (1904–1989)
Dag Hammarskjold (1905–1961)
C.P. Snow (1905–1980)
Jean-Paul Sartre (1905–1980)
Viktor Frankl (1905–1997)
Satchel Paige (1906—1982)
Hannah Arendt (1906–1975)
Frida Kahlo (1907–1954)
William Barkley (1907–1978)
Rumer Godden (1907–1998)
Cus D'Amato (1908–1985)
Dr. Raymond Lindquist (1907–2001)
Katherine Hepburn (1907–2003)
Abraham Maslow (1908–1970)
Arthur Goldberg (1908–1990)
Milton Berle (1908–2002)
Simone Weil (1909–1943)
Edwin Land (1909–1991)
C. Northcote Parkinson (1909–1993)
Eugene Ionesco (1909–1994)
Peter F. Drucker (1909–2005)
David Niven (1910–1983)
Peter De Vries (1910–1993)
Mother Teresa (1910–1997)
John Wooden (1910–2010)
Babe Didrikson (1911–1956)
Marshall McLuhan (1911–1980)
Lucille Ball (1911–1989)
Ronald Reagan (1911–2004)
Naguib Mahfouz (1911–2006)
William C. Sullivan (1912–1977)
John W. Gardner (1912–2002)
Julia Child (1912–2004)
Art Linkletter (1912–2012)
Albert Camus (1913–1960)
Robertson Davies (1913–1995)
Vince Lombardi (1913–1970)
Big Bill Neidjie (1913–2002)
Rosa Parks (1913–2005)

Billie Holiday (1915–1959)
Ajit Mookerjee (1915–1990)
Mark Goodson (1915–1992)
Abba Eban (1915–2002)
Bernard Baily (1916–1996)
Robert S. McNamara (1916–2009)
Walter Cronkite (1916–2009)
John F. Kennedy (1917–1963)
Robert B. Woodward (1917–1979)
Indira Gandhi (1917–1984)
David Bohm (1917–1992)
Edward Lorenz (1917–2008)
Richard P. Feynman (1918–1988)
George Allen (1918–1990)
Leonard Bernstein (1918–1990)
Ann Landers (1918–2002)
Paul Harvey (1918–2009)
Nelson Mandela (1918–2013)
Jackie Robinson (1919–1972)
Liberace (1919–1987)
Lawrence J. Peter (1919–1990)
Iris Murdoch (1919–1999)
Isaac Asimov (1920–1992)
William Arthur Ward (1921–1994)
Charles E. Fritz (1921–2000)
Dorothy Maclean (1920–2020)
Hugh Downs (1921–2020)
Peter Ustinov (1921–2004)
Kurt Vonnegut (1922–2007)
Charles Weingartner (1922–2007)
Arnold Palmer (1923–2016)
Robert Muller (1923–2010)
Henry Kissinger (1923–2023)
Leo Buscaglia (1924–1998)
Tom Landry (1924–2000)
Thomas Berger (1924–2014)
Horace Axtell (1924–2015)
Lee Iacocca (1924–2019)
Malcolm X (1925–1965)
Joe Karbo (1925–1980)
Gore Vidal (1925–2012)
Margaret Thatcher (1925–2013)
Warren Bennis (1925–2014)
Lawrence Peter Berra (1925–2015)
Bertha Calloway (1925–2017)
Jiro Ono (1925)
Joe D. Batten (1925)
Marilyn Monroe (1926–1962)
Angela Lansbury (1926–2022)
Thich Nhat Hanh (1926–2022)
Zig Ziglar (1926–2012)
Robert H. Schuller (1926–2015)
Louise Hay (1926–2017)
Joe Paterno (1926–2012)

Harper Lee (1926–2016)

David J. Schwartz (1927–1987)

Erma Bombeck (1927–1996)

Jerry Hicks (1927–2011)

David R. Hawkins MD (1927–2012)

Gabriel Marquez (1927–2014)

Tommy Lasorda (1927–2020)

Catherine Ponder (1927)

Eugene Kennedy (1928–2015)

Jeanne Moreau (1928–2017)

Maya Angelou (1928–2014)

Robert U. Akeret (1928–2016)

Elie Wiesel (1928–2016)

Luciano De Crescenzo (1928)

Martin Luther King Jr. (1929–1968)

Audrey Hepburn (1929–1993)

Jacqueline Kennedy Onassis (1929–1994)

Charles D. Aring, MD (1929–1998)

Gerald A. Michaelson (1929–2004)

Bo Schembechler (1929–2006)

Dee Hock (1929–2022)

Edward Osborne (E.O.) Wilson (1929–2021)

Barbara Walters (1929–2022)

José Narosky (1930)

Lorraine Hansberry (1930–1965)

George Steinbrenner III (1930–2010)

Jim Rohn (1930–2009)

Buzz Aldrin (1930)

Michael Murphy (1930)

Irving H. Buchen (1930)

Warren Buffett (1930)

Sri Chinmoy (1931–2007)

Neil Postman (1931–2003)

Roon Arledge (1931–2002)

Dr. Wil Rose (1931–2011)

Leonard Nimoy (1931–2015)

E.L. Doctorow (1931–2015)

Ram Dass (1931–2019)

Maxine Singer (1931)

Gesche Kelsang Gyatso (1931)

William Shatner (1931)

Mikhail Gorbachev (1931–2022)

Henri Nouwen (1932–1996)

Stephen Covey (1932–2012)

Dr. Bernie S. Siegel (1932)

Clive Davis (1932)

Ruth Bader Ginsburg (1933–2020)

Edward de Bono (1933–2021)

Denis Waitley (1933)

Yoko Ono (1933)

Cormac McCarthy (1933)

Anne Wilson Schaef (1934–2020)

Mihaly Csikszentmihalyi (1934–2021)

Bobby Unser (1934–2021)

Gloria Steinem (1934)

William Ophuls (1934)

Bill Moyers (1934)

Carl Sagan (1934–1996)

Gene Cernan (1934–2017)

Bill Russell (1934–2022)

Joseph Jaworski (1934)

Eldridge Cleaver (1935–1998)

Luciano Pavarotti (1935–2007)

Mary Oliver (1935–2019)

Jack Welch (1935–2020)

14th Dalai Lama (1935)

Sylvia Earle (1935)

Harville Hendrix, PhD (1935)

Richard Saul Wurman (1935)

Michael Landon (1936–1991)

M. Scott Peck (1936–2005)

John Madden (1936–2021)

David Suzuki (1936)

Michael Gerber (1936)

Joan D. Chittister (1936)

Thomas K. Mattingly II (1936)

Colin Powell (1937–2,021)

Michael Grosso (1937)

Tom Stoppard (1937)

Jared Diamond (1937)

Marlo Morgan (1937)

Robert Fulghum (1937)

Lou Holtz (1937)

Julian Barbour (1937)

David Viscott (1938–1996)

Linda Weltner (1938)

Herb Cohen (1938)

Jerry West (1938)

Yvon Chouinard (1938)

Laurel Thatcher Ulrich (1938)

Timothy Gallwey (1938)

Marvin Gaye (1939–1984)

John Updike (1939–2002)

David Frost (1939–2013)

David A. Cooper (1939)

John Cleese (1939)

Bruce Lee (1940–1973)

John Lennon (1940–1980)

Kay Gardner (1940–2002)

Thomas Ashley-Farrand (1940–2010)

Wangari Maathal (1940–2011)

Dr. Wayne Dyer (1940–2015)

Alex Trebek (1940–2020)

H. Jackson Brown Jr. (1940)

Thomas Moore (1940)

Jack Nicklaus (1940)

Matthew Fox (1940)

Muhammad Yunus (1940)

Michael Michalko (1940)

Alan Curtis Kay (1940)

Twyla Tharp (1941)
Miles Kington (1941–2008)
Robert C. Solomon (1942–2007)
Muhammad Ali (1942–2016)
Frank Delaney (1942–2017)
Roger Staubach (1942)
Dr. Andrew Weil (1942)
Gary Zukav (1942)
Arthur Ashe (1943–1993)
George Harrison (1943–2001)
John Welwood (1943–2019)
Bob Frissell (1943)
O. Fred Donaldson (1943)
Barbara Sher (1943)
Billy Jean King (1943)
Les Brown (1943)
Doris Kearns Goodwin (1943)
David Geffen (1943)
Don Coyhis (1943)
Elaine St. James (1943)
Jack Canfield (1944)
Steve Chandler (1944)
China Galland (1944)
George Lucas (1944)
Jon Kabat-Zinn (1944)
Bob Marley (1945–1981)
Charles Case (1945–2016)
Jack Kornfield (1945)
Curtis R. Carlson (1945)
Pat Riley (1945)
Alfred D'Souza (1945)
Clarissa Pinkola Estes (1945)
Phil Jackson (1945)
Marilyn vos Savant (1946)
Jim Valvano (1946–1993)
Candace Pert, PhD (1946–2013)
Ahmed Zewail (1946–2016)
Kent Nerburn (1946)
Dennis Deaton (1946)
Lama Zopa Rinpoche (1946)
Robert Kegan (1946)
Dolly Parton (1946)
Deepak Chopra (1946)
Dan Millman (1946)
Steven Spielberg (1946)
Lillian Too (1946)
Susan L. Taylor (1946)
Octavia Butler (1947–2006)
Tom Clancy (1947–2013)
Paulo Coelho (1947)
Roger Jahnke (1947)
A.G. Lafley (1947)
Stephen M. Millett (1947)
Stephen King (1947)
Arnold Schwarzenegger (1947)

Shakti Gawain (1948–2018)
Robert Gass (1948)
Arthur Bloch (1948)
Julia Cameron (1948)
Diane Ackerman (1948)
Esther Hicks (1948)
Ronald Wright (1948)
Ray Kurzweil (1948)
Eckhart Tolle (1948)
Susan Linn (1948)
C. Alexander Simpkins (1949)
Ray Dalio (1949)
Jay Abraham (1949)
Barbara Corcoran (1949)
Jonathan Goldman (1949)
Bruce Springsteen (1949)
Gary Holz (1950–2007)
Sir Ken Robinson (1950–2020)
Julius Erving (1950)
Bobby McFerrin (1950)
Stephen Nachmanovitch (1950)
Alan Cohen (1950)
Arianna Huffington (1950)
Richard Branson (1950)
John Beaulieu (1950)
Graham Hancock (1950)
Sally Ride (1951–2012)
Craig Sagar (1951–2016)
Richard Davidson (1951)
David Kelley (1951)
Luc Ferry (1951)
Jamie Sams (1951)
Robert Iger (1951)
John Mellencamp (1951)
R. Brian Ferguson (1951)
Pat Summit (1952–2016)
John D. Barrow (1952–2020)
Rick Jarow (1952-2024)
Jim Tressel (1952)
Walter Isaacson (1952)
Michael J. Gelb (1952)
Sharon Salzberg (1952)
Benazir Bhutto (1953)
Clayton Christensen (1952)
Howard Schultz (1953)
William Ury (1953)
Jeffrey Hollander (1954)
Angela Merkel (1954)
John Hagelin, PhD (1954)
Jerry Seinfeld (1954)
T. Harv Eker (1954)
Mario Testino (1954)
Anne Lamott (1954)
Chris Evert (1954)
Gregg Braden (1954)

Oprah Winfrey (1954)
Bill Gates (1955)
Steve Jobs (1955–2011)
Frank Sonnenberg (1955)
Stephen Wright (1955)
Margaret Hefferman(1955)
Bryan Mattimore (1955)
Anne Geddes (1956)
Dr. Mae Jemison (1956)
Nancy Lopez (1957)
Michael Jackson (1958–2009)
Mark Cuban (1958)
Tina Seelig (1958)
Neil deGrasse Tyson (1958)
Marci Shimoff (1958)
Hal Gregersen (1958)
Roger Goodell (1959)
Donna Brazile (1959)
Suzy Welch (1959)
Wim Hof (1959)
John McEnroe (1959)
Jeff Dyer (1959)
Bob Goff (1959)
Yoshikazu Ono (1959)
Randy Pausch (1960–2008)
Seth Godin (1960)
Robin Roberts (1960)
Barb Krantz Taylor (1960)
Bertice Berry (1960)
Tony Robbins (1960)
Reed Hastings (1960)
Suzanne Simard (1960)
Richard Carlson (1961–2006)
Wayne Gretzky (1961)
Rebecca Solnit (1961)
Barack Obama (1961)
David Brooks (1961)
Vik Muniz (1961)
Adam L. Penenberg (1962)
Christopher Ryan (1962)
Harlan Coben (1962)
Michael Jordan (1963)
Malcolm Gladwell (1963)
Alex Bogusky (1963)
Joel Osteen (1963)
Rick Rubin (1963)
Jean-Claude van Rijckeghem (1963)
Jeff Bezos (1964)
Dan Brown (1964)
Mark Benioff (1964)
Gregory Berns (1964)
Michelle Obama (1964)
Robin Sharma (1964)
Peter Wohlleben (1964)

Christopher Penn (1965–2006)
Carmine Gallo (1965)
J.K. Rowling (1965)
Mark Pincus (1966)
Richard Wiseman (1966)
Li Lu (1966)
Grant Schreiber (1967)
Tom Butler-Bowdon (1967)
Abi Morgan (1968)
Dave Logan (1968)
John Dickerson (1968)
Anna Maria Chavez (1968)
Jennifer Lopez (1969)
Katie Salen (1969)
Sheryl Sandberg (1969)
Elizabeth Gilbert (1969)
Dave Willis (1970)
Rana Foroohar (1970)
Gonzalo Arzuaga (1971)
Elon Musk (1971)
John Chester (1971)
Ephrat Livni (1972)
Tony Hsieh (1973–2020)
Larry Page (1973)
Simon Sinek (1973)
Jeffrey Karp (1973)
Georgia Cates (1974)
Stephanie Storey (1975)
Brandon McMillan (1977)
Jonathan Safran Foer (1977)
Raina Kumra (1977)
Kobe Bryant (1978–2020)
Noah D. Oppenheim (1978)
Michael Smith (1979)
Scott Belsky (1980)
Neil Blumenthal (1980)
Venus Williams (1980)
Dylan Dreyer (1981)
David Tisch (1981)
Dr. Josh Axe (1981)
Fredrik Backman (1981)
Chloé Zhao (1982)
Jared Isaacman (1983)
Mark Zuckerberg (1984)
Alexa Clay (1984)
Marie Kondo (1984)
Farrah Gray (1984)
Colin O'Brady (1985)
Taylor Swift (1989)
Bethany C. Meyers (1990)
Amanda Nguyen (1991)
Saquon Barkley (1997)
Gitanjali Rao (2005)

WISDOM DEMOGRAPHICS

Countries represented in Consolidated Wisdom

Afghanistan
Albania
Algeria
Argentina
Armenia
Australia
Austria
Bangladesh
Belgium
Brazil
Canada
China
Columbia
Cuba
Czechoslovakia
Denmark
Egypt
England
France
Germany
Greece
Holland
Hungary
India
Ireland
Israel
Italy
Jamaica
Japan

Laos
Lebanon
Lithuania
Malaysia
Malta
Mexico
Mongolia
New Zealand
Pakistan
Persia (now Iran)
Peru
Philippines
Poland
Portugal
Prussia
Romania
Russia
Scotland
Serbia
South Africa
Spain
Sweden
Switzerland
Syria
Tibet
Turkey
Uganda
United States
Vietnam

RECOMMENDED READING & VIDEOGRAPHY

Diane Ackerman from *Deep Play*

Jay Abraham as quoted in *The Passion Test*

Robert U. Akeret from *Family Tales, Family Wisdom*

C. Alexander from *Simple Zen: A Guide to Living Moment to Moment*

Arapaho proverb from *Native American Wisdom: The Sacred in Everyday Life* by Cameron Fleet

Charles D. Aring MD from *JAMA* Volume 237, No. 12

Chris Attwood from *The Passion Test*

Marcus Aurelias from *Meditations*

Dr. Josh Axe from *Ancient Remedies*

Fredrik Backman from *Anxious People*

James Baldwin from *Nobody Knows My Name*

Julian Barbour from *The End of Time*

P.T. Barnum from *The Art of Money Getting*

John D. Barrow from *The Book of Nothing: Vacuums, Voids, and the Latest Ideas About the Origins of the Universe*

Mark Benioff as quoted in *The Innovation Secrets of Steve Jobs*

Warren Bennis from *On Becoming A Leader*

Bernard Berenson from *Forbes Magazine 12/26/05*

Gregory Berns from *Iconoclast*

Yogi Berra from the author being a New York Yankees fan, and *The Yogi Book*

Boethius from *The Consolation of Philosophy*

Angela Halvorsen Bogo from transformationalplay.net

Edward de Bono from *Lateral Thinking*

Tom Butler-Bowdon from *50 Prosperity Classics, 50 Philosophy Classics,* and *50 Success Classics*

Gregg Braden from *The Divine Matrix: Bridging Time, Space, Miracles and Belief*

Richard Branson from *Losing My Virginity: The Autobiography*

Claude M. Bristol from *The Magic of Belief*

Dan Brown *from The Lost Symbol*

Warren Buffett from *The Snowball: Warren Buffett & the Business of Life*

Joseph Campbell from *The Hero With a Thousand Faces...*
and *A Joseph Companion: Reflections on the Art of Living.*

Julia Cameron from *It's Never Too Late Too Begin Again: Discovering Creativity and Meaning at Midlife and Beyond*

Jack Canfield from *Chicken Soup for the Soul*

Curtis R. Carlson from *Innovation*

Richard Carlson from *Don't Sweat The Small Stuff*

Dale Carnegie from *How To Win Friends & Influence People*

Courtney Carver from bemorewithless.com

John Chester from documentary film *The Biggest Little Farm*

Joan D. Chittister from *Wisdom Distilled from The Daily: Living The Rule of St. Benedict Today*

Yvon Chouinard from *Let My People Go Surfing: The Education of a Reluctant Businessman*

Deepak Chopra from *The Seven Spiritual Laws of Success*

Tom Clavin from *The Heart of Everything That Is*

Alexa Clay from *The Misfit Economy*

Clayton Christensen from *The Innovator's DNA: Mastering the Five Skills of Disruptive Innovators.*

John Cleese from *On Becoming A Leader*

Paulo Coelho from *The Alchemist*
Herb Cohen from *You Can Negotiate Anything*
Herb Cohen & Richard Cohen from *The Adventures of Herbie Cohen: World's Greatest Negotiator*
Terah Kathryn Collins from *Feng Shui: Room By Room*
David A Cooper from *Silence, Simplicity and Solitude*
Stephen Covey from *The 7 Habits of Highly Effective People*
Mihaly Csikszentmihlayi from *Flow: The Psychology of Optimal Experience*
Ray Dalio from *Principles: Life and Work* and *Principles for Dealing with The Changing World Order*
Ram Dass from *Compassion in Action*
Clive Davis from his autobiography *The Soundtrack of My Life*
Dennis Deaton from *Quma Learning, Quma Inspirations*
Ceanne Derohan as quoted in *Vein of Gold* by *Julia Cameron*
Charles Dickens from *a Tale of Two Cities*
Dylan Dreyer on TV: *Journey S2E11: Climbing Mount Kilimanjaro*
Peter De Vries from *The Sun Magazine April 2006*
Jared Diamond from *Guns, Germs, and Steel: The Fates of Human Societies*
E.L. Doctorow from *Bill Moyers: A World of Ideas*
Alfred D'Souza as quoted in *Seven Choices*
Will Durant from *The Story of Philosophy*
William and Ariel Durant from *The Lessons of History*
Peter F. Drucker from *Innovation and Entrepreneurship*
Bob Drury from *The Heart of Everything That Is*
Dr. Wayne Dyer from *10 Secrets for Success and Inner Peace*
Jeff Dyer from *The Innovator's DNA: Mastering the Five Skills of Disruptive Innovators.*
T. Harv Eker from *Secrets of the Millionaire Mind: Mastering the Inner Game of Wealth*
T.S. Eliot from *Four Quartets* and *Little Gidding*
Black Elk from *Black Elk Speaks*
Clarissa Pinkola Estes from *Women Who Run with the Wolves*
Thomas Ashley-Farrand from *True Stories of Spiritual Power* and *Mantra Instruction Manual*
Feng Shui for the Home by Peter Pauper Press
Luc Ferry from *A Brief History of Thought: A Philosophical Guide to Living*
Richard Feynman from *What Do You Care What Other People Think?*
Rana Foroohar from *Time Magazine*
Mavis & Merle Fossum from *The More We Find in Each Other*
Matthew Fox from *Creation Spirituality*
Viktor Frankl from *Man's Search For Meaning*
Benjamin Franklin from *Poor Richard's Almanac*
Erich Fromm from *The Art of Loving and The Art of Being*
Robert Fulghum from Maybe (Maybe Not)
China Galland from *Sun Magazine April, 2012*
Carmine Gallo from *The Innovation Secrets of Steve Jobs*
Timothy Gallwey from *The Inner Game of Tennis*
Mohandas (Mahatma) Gandhi from *An Autobiography: The Story of My Experiments with Truth*
and *Wisdom: 365 Thoughts from Indian Masters*
Shakti Gawain from *Living in the Light*
Michael J. Gelb from *How To Think Like Leonardo da Vinci* and *Discover Your Genius: How to Think*
    Like History's Ten Most Revolutionary Minds, and *Mastering The Art of Public Speaking*
Kahlil Gibran from *The Prophet*
Rumer Godden from *A House with Four Rooms*
Jonathan Goldman from *The Seven Secrets of Sound Healing*
Mark Goodson from *Alex Trebek: The Answer Is...*
Doris Kearns Goodwin from *Leadership in Turbulent Times*
Arshile Gorky from *The Artist's Mentor*
Baltasar Gracian from *The Art of Worldly Wisdom* translated by Christopher Maurer
Hal Gregersen from *The Innovator's DNA* and *Questions Are the Answer*
Michael Grosso from *Soulmaker*
Albert Szent-Gyorgyi from *Breathe* by James Nestor
John Hagelin, PhD from *The Passion Test*

Graham Hancock from *Fingerprints of the Gods*
Rick Hanson from *Hardwiring Happiness: The New Science of Contentment, Calm, and Confidence.*
Thich Nhat Hanh from: *Touching Peace: Practicing the Art of Mindful Living*
    and *Be Still and Know: Reflections from Living Buddha, Living Christ*
David George Haskell from *The Song of Trees: Stories From Nature's Great Connectors*
Reed Hastings from *No Rules Rules: Netflix and the Culture of Reinvention*
David R. Hawkins MD from *Power vs. Force*
Harville Hendrix from *Getting the Love You Want*
Belinda Henwood from *Feng Shui: How to Create Harmony and Balance in Your Living*
    and Working Environment
Esther and Jerry Hicks from *Ask And It Is Given: Learning to Manifest Your Desires*
Napoleon Hill from *Think and Grow Rich*
Nancy Hillis from *The Artist's Journey: Bold Strokes to Spark Creativity*
Conrad Hilton from *Be My Guest*
Phoebe Hoban from *The Artist's Mentor*
Thomas Hobbes from *The Ethics of Hobbes*
Wim Hof from *The Wim Hof Method: Activate Your Full Human Potential*
Gary Holz from *Secrets of Aboriginal Healing*
Homer from *The Odyssey*
Hopi Elders courtesy of *Zacciah Blackburn*
Tony Hsieh from *Delivering Happiness: A Path to Profits, Passion and Purpose*
Christmas Humphreys from *Zen Wisdom*
Aldous Huxley from *Island*
Lee Iacocca from *Iacocca: An Autobiography*
Robert Iger from *The Ride of A Lifetime*
Robert Ingersoll from *Sun Magazine/May 2009*
Phil Jackson from *Eleven Rings*
Roger Jahnke from *The Healing Promise of Qi*
Rick Jarow from *The Ultimate Anti Career Guide*
Joseph Jaworski from *Synchronicity: The Inner Path of Leadership*
Franz Johansson from *The Medici Effect*
Michael Jordan from *For The Love of The Game: My Story* and *Driven From Within*
Carl Jung from *Memories, Dreams, Reflections*
Joe Karbo from *The Lazy Man's Way to Riches*
Eugene Kennedy from *On Being a Friend*
Theresa A. Kestly from *The International Neurobiology of Play*
Hazrat Inayat Khan from *The Mysticism of Sound and Music*
David S. Kidder from *Intellectual Devotional*
Billie Jean King from *Quma Inspirations Volume 3, #41 (Quma.net)*
John King from *Tribal Leadership*
Martin Luther King Jr. from *Stride Toward Freedom*
Viki King from *How To Write A Movie in 21 Days*
Henry Kissinger from *World Order*
Marie Kondo from *The Life-Changing Magic of Tidying Up: The Japanese Art of Decluttering*
Ray Kurzweil from *How To Create A Mind: The Secret of Human Thought Revealed*
Dalai Lama from *Beyond Religion: Ethics for a Whole World* and in *Beyond the Road Less Traveled*
Anne Lamott from *The Week* magazine 12/17/2021
Leonardo da Vinci from *Leonardo Da Vinci* by Walter Isaacson and
    How To Think Like Leonardo da Vinci by Michael J. Gelb
Art Linkletter from *How To Make The Rest of Your Life, The Best of Your Life*
John Locke from *Second Treatise of Government*
Dave Logan from *Tribal Leadership*
Vince Lombardi from *Bart Starr: When Leadership Mattered*
Nancy Lopez from *Winning: Great Coaches and Athletes Share Their Secrets of Success*
Clare Boothe Luce from *Stuffed Shirts*
Lee Lyon from *The 112 Meditations From the Book of Divine Wisdom*
Wangari Maathal from *The Week Magazine 3/24/17*

Niccolo Machiavelli from *The Prince*
John Madden from *Winning: Great Coaches and Athletes Share Their Secrets of Success*
Maimonides from *Ancient Wisdom*
Nelson Mandela from *Long Walk To Freedom*
Prince William Marshal from *Swordsmen, Saints, and Scholars* by James Weiss
Karl Marx from *The Communist Manifesto*
Abraham Maslow from *The Psychology of Science* and *The Farther Reaches of Human Nature*
Bryan Mattimore from *Idea Stormers*
Dr. Charles Mayo from *The Tao of Abundance*
Cormac McCarthy from *No Country For Old Men*
John McEnroe from *Winning: Great Coaches and Athletes Share Their Secrets of Success*
Marshall McLuhan from *The Medium is the Massage*
Gerald A. Michaelson from *Sun Tzu for Success*
Michael Michalko from *Cracking Creativity: The Secrets of Creative Genius*
Henry Miller from *Ions Noetic Sciences Review 9/2001*
Stephen M. Millett from *The Futurist* magazine September-October 2011
Dan Millman from *The Laws of Spirit: Simple Powerful Truths for Making Life Work,*
     The Hidden School, and *Peaceful Heart Peaceful Spirit: The True Story of My Spiritual Quest*
Maria Montessori from *Education and Peace*
Ajit Mookerjee from *The Tao of Abundance*
Thomas Moore from *Care of the Soul*
Marlo Morgan from *Mutant Message Down Under* and *Mutant Message From Forever*
Toni Morrison from *Paradise* and *God Help the Child*
Bill Moyers from *A World of Ideas*
Vik Muniz from the documentary film *Waste Land*
Stephen Nachmanovitch from his book *Free Play*
Friedrich Nietzsche from *Twilight of the Idols*
Kent Nerburn from *Letters to My Son* and *Neither Wolf Nor Dog*
Native American quotes from *Native American Wisdom* by Kristen Marie Cleary
C. Northcote Parkinson in *The Week Magazine 3/24/17*
Henri Nouwen from *The Way of the Heart: The Spirituality of the Desert Fathers and Mothers*
Mary Oliver from *The Summer Day* (a poem)
Jiro Ono and Yoshikazu Ono from *Jiro Dreams of Sushi*
William Ophuls from *Apologies To The Grandchildren: Reflections on our Ecological Predicament,*
     Its Deeper Causes and Its Political Consequences
Noah D. Oppenheim from *Intellectual Devotional*
George Orwell from *1984* and *War of the Worlds*
Alex F. Osborn from *Your creative Power: How To Use Imagination*
Arnold Palmer from *Winning: Great Coaches and Athletes Share Their Secrets of Success*
Randy Pausch from *The Last Lecture*
Luciano Pavarotti as quoted by *Madelyn Renee*
Peace Pilgrim from *in Sun Magazine April/2012*
M. Scott Peck from: *Abounding Grace* and *The Road Less Traveled*
Lawrence J. Peter from *The Peter Principle: Why Things Always Go Wrong*
Kyra Maya Phillips from *The Misfit Economy*
Guo Po from *The Book of Burial*
Teresa Polanco from *Feng Shui Journal: A Guided Workbook To Bring Harmony Into Your Life*
Neil Postman and Charles Weingartner from *Teaching As A Subversive Activity*
Colin Powell from *My American Journey*
Jean-Claude van Rijckeghem from *Ironhead or, Once a Young Lady*
Rick Rubin from his book *The Creative Act: A Way of Being*
Rumi from *Rumi's Little Book of Love* by Maryam Mafi & Azima Kolin
Christopher Ryan from *Civilized To Death: The Price of Progress*
Jean-Paul Sartre from *Existentialism is Humanism, The Devil and The Good Lord* and *Dirty Hands.*
Robin Sharma from *The Monk Who Sold His Ferrari*
Sharon Salzberg from *Lovingkindness*
Jamie Sams from *Dancing the Dream: The Seven Sacred Paths of Human Transformation*

Recommended Reading & Videography

Anne Wilson Schaef from *Native Wisdom for White Minds*
Howard Schultz from *Pour Your Heart Into It: How Starbucks Built a Company One Cup at a Time*
David J. Schwartz from *The Magic of Thinking Big*
Ben Shahn from *The Artist's Mentor*
Shantideva from *The Wisdom of the Tibetan Lamas* by Timothy Freke
George Bernard Shaw from *Man and Superman* and *Back To Methuselah*
Barbara Sher from *Wishcraft*
Marci Shimoff from *Happy For No Reason: 7 Steps to Being Happy from the Inside Out*
Dr. Bernie S. Siegel from *365 Prescriptions For The Soul*
Rosalind Simmons from *Feng Shui: The Art of Living*
Annellen Simpkins from *Simple Zen: A Guide to Living Moment to Moment*
Simon Sinek from *Find Your Why* and *Together Is Better: A Little Book of Inspiration*
Maxine Singer from *Bill Moyers: A World of Ideas*
David Sobel from *Healthy Pleasures*
Socrates from *Socrates Way: Seven Master Keys to Using Your Mind to the Utmost*
Takuan Sōhō from *The Unfettered Mind*
Robert C. Solomon from *A Passion for Justice*
Rebecca Solnit from *A Paradise Built in Hell: The Extraordinary Communities That Arise in Disaster*
John Steinbeck from *The Acts of King Arthur and His Noble Knights* and *Once There Was A War*
Elaine St. James from *Inner Simplicity*
Anthony Storr from *A Return To The Self*
William C. Sullivan from *Enemies: A History of the FBI*
Shunryu Suzuki-Roshi from *Zen Mind, Beginner's Mind*
Stephanie Storey from *Oil and Marble*
Rabindranath Tagore from *Wisdom: 365 Thoughts from Indian Masters*
Barb Krantz Taylor from Quma Inspirations Volume 3, #6 (quma.net)
Twyla Tharp from *The Creative Habit: Learn It and Use It for Life*
Alma Thomas from *The Artist's Mentor*
Robert B. Thomas from the *Old Farmer's Almanac*
Lillian Too from *Total Feng Shui: Bring Health, Wealth and Happiness Into Your Life*
    and *Chinese Wisdom: Spiritual Magic for Everyday Living*
Alex Trebek from *Alex Trebek: The Answer Is...Reflections on My Life*
Jim Tressel from *The Winners Manual For The Game of Life*
Lao Tzu from *Tao Te Ching* and *The Tao of Peace* and also quoted in *Human Tuning by John Beaulieu*
Sun Tzu from multiple translations of *The Art of War*
William Ury from *Getting Past No*
Virgil from *Eclogues*
Barbara Walters from *How to Talk With Practically Anybody About Practically Anything*
Wu Wei from *I Ching Wisdom Volumes I & II: More Guidance from the Book of Changes/Power Press*
Dr. Andrew Weil from *Breathing: The Master Key to Self-Healing*
Charles Weingartner and Neil Postman from *Teaching As A Subversive Activity*
Linda Weltner from *No Place Like Home*
John Welwood from *Ordinary Magic*
Edward Osborne (E.O.) Wilson as quoted in *The Week* magazine 8/6/2021
Dr. Charles Windridge from *Tong Song: The Chinese Book of Wisdom*
Richard Wiseman from *The Luck Factor*
John Wooden from *WOODEN: A Lifetime of Observations and Reflections On and Off the Court*
Halee Fischer-Wright from *Tribal Leadership*
Ronald Wright from *A Short History of Progress*
Richard Saul Wurman from *Information Anxiety 2.*
Paramahansa Yogananda from *The Laws of Success:*
    Using the Power of Spirit to Create Health, Prosperity and Happiness
Yuan-Wu from *Zen Wisdom: Daily Teachings from the Zen Masters* by *Timothy Freke*
Lin Yutang from *The Importance of Living*
Jon Kabat-Zinn from *Wherever You Go There You Are: Mindfulness Meditation in Everyday Life*
Lama Zopa Rinpoche from *Transforming Problems into Happiness*
Gary Zukav from *The Heart of the Soul*

ABOUT THE AUTHOR

As a nationally acclaimed game show host and creativity consultant, Gene S. Jones has dedicated his life to entertaining and inspiring others. In *Consolidated Wisdom,* Jones recounts more than fourteen hundred profound and potentially life-changing quotations acquired during his many years as a game show host, with the specific purpose of encouraging readers to live happier, more fulfilling lives.

From seminars on innovation to years of professional speech writing, the breadth of Jones's eclectic career in the world of entertainment spans five decades. During those years, Jones has enjoyed success as a producer, director, writer, professional juggler, fire-eater, radio personality, character actor, arts administrator, television sports commentator and sound healer. As a popular concert Master of Ceremonies in the 1970's, Jones appeared as MC for major concerts such as Tina Turner, Pink Floyd, Kiss, the Grateful Dead, Duke Ellington, James Taylor, the Ann Arbor Blues & Jazz Festival, B.B. King, and many others.

From 1986-1990, Jones served as Associate Editor of the *Guinness Book of World Records,* frequently appearing on network television as their official spokesperson and world record judge. During this time, Jones created the *GIMME A HINT! Trivia Game Show.* Touring nationwide, he has since performed this comedic theatrical game show more than 2500 times. In addition to hosting game shows, Jones teaches seminars on the *Art of Breakthrough Thinking* and the *Art of Presentation* while continuing to write customized speeches for his numerous corporate and private clients. Jones' writing career spans numerous genres including radio commercials, comedy sketches, magazine articles, murder mysteries and poetry. His previous book *Younger and Wiser* (Dreamquest Publishing, 2020) was penned over the course of his extensive career, often in exotic locations around the world. In a much more spiritual role as facilitator of sound healing workshops, Jones received the *Friendship Award* from the United Nations in 2005 for his series of concert performances with crystal bowls.

For more information about Gene S. Jones, visit his website
gimmeahint.com

Consolidated Wisdom is dedicated to the memory of Thomas Ashley-Farrand, my beloved spiritual teacher who initiated me into the profound world of Sanskrit mantras, most specifically, the very powerful *Gayatri Mantra*:

Om Bhu, Om Bhuvaha, Om Swaha, Om Maha, Om Janaha, Om Tapaha, Om Satyam, Om Tat Savitur Varenyam Bhargo Devasya Dhimahi Dhiyo Yonaha Prachodayat
(Please note: spellings and pronunciations of this mantra often vary slightly)

Thomas Ashley-Farrand describes the *Gayatri Mantra* as
"The mantra of the universe itself in all its upper spheres of spiritual light"

**In the spirit of love, this book is also dedicated
to my lovely wife Lisbeth Lloyd**

Made in United States
North Haven, CT
21 October 2024

59265425R00221